Midnight Confessions

TRUE STORIES OF ADULTERY

Also by Pat Gaudette

HOW TO SURVIVE YOUR HUSBAND'S MIDLIFE CRISIS:
STRATEGIES AND STORIES FROM THE MIDLIFE WIVES CLUB,
by Gay Courter and Pat Gaudette

ADVICE FOR AN IMPERFECT MARRIED WORLD

ADVICE FOR AN IMPERFECT SINGLE WORLD

Midnight Confessions

TRUE STORIES OF ADULTERY

PAT GAUDETTE

Home & Leisure Publishing, Inc.

Midnight Confessions:
True Stories of Adultery

Published by Home & Leisure Publishing, Inc.
P. O. Box 968
Lecanto, FL 34460-0968
USA

Published 2005

Printed in the United States of America.

ISBN 0-9761210-4-2 (Paperback)
ISBN 0-9761210-5-0 (e-book)

"Which is the greater sin? Taking a lover? Or putting your lover in the position that they need another?" — from the 1995 film "Nina Takes A Lover."

"CNN found that Hillary Clinton is the most admired woman in America. Women admire her because she's strong and successful. Men admire her because she allows her husband to cheat and get away with it." -- Jay Leno, NBC's *Tonight Show*

Contents

Introduction

When I began putting all the parts of this book together, I wasn't sure how everything would fit or even the course it would take as it was being written. There are a lot of books written about infidelity so the topic isn't new. I have written this book, in the manner in which you see it, because I think it might provide some insight into the "whys" of adulterous relationships.

The stories in this book were gathered in various methods through the Internet. In the majority of cases I have not met the people who shared their stories. Some stories were submitted anonymously through a questionnaire on my *Friends and Lovers* website (www.friendsandlovers.com). Some stories were submitted by freelance writers who were paid a nominal fee; each person verified their submission was their personal story and not a work of fiction. Other stories were submitted anonymously through yet another forum established for the sole purpose of collecting submissions for this book. And, other stories were emailed to me with permission to use them in this book.

All stories have been edited to protect each person's identity and the identities of their families, friends, work associates, etc. Names, dates, places, family composition and other identifying data have been changed to protect participants from discovery.

I hope you find this book as interesting to read as it was for me to write.

Pat Gaudette

Men Who Cheat

Most of the stories that follow are told by wives who were betrayed by their husbands. Their anger is real, their pain goes deep. Some marriages are still together as both partners work to repair the damage; some are over either because she could not forgive his betrayal or he chose to leave the marriage to be with the other woman.

A few of the stories are told from the betrayer's perspective, the husband who stepped outside of his marriage and either regretted doing so and is now paying the price, or who felt justified for cheating and has written to tell his side of the story.

I want to emphasize again that the people and stories in this book are real; names, places, and other identifying information have been changed as necessary in order to provide anonymity to the storytellers.

Cassandra:

Things had always seemed questionable, the relationship just never felt right. He acted as though I were the one true love of his life, but somewhere behind his bright blue eyes, I could see the devil. I tried to deny my thoughts that this man would ever do anything to hurt me. I loved him more than anything in the world and would give him anything he needed.

Unfortunately, my efforts would prove to be very useless, since he wanted me only for security, and his true ambition was to be a young stud ready to please his boss to get to the top. I never did like his boss, but never in a million years did I expect to learn about their relationship, a sexual relationship. I was appalled, but I knew what I had to do. I had to catch him red handed, and that's exactly what I did.

The beginning of our relationship, like all others, was very exciting. We were high school sweethearts, and voted the most popular couple in our senior yearbook. Everyone thought we were meant to be, and I thought so too. So after graduation we married and shortly afterward purchased our first home together. I went to work in the branch office of a large corporation and my husband went to work in a local company.

Things just seemed to fall together just fine. He seemed happy with our life and with his job, and I was very content with our quick transition to adult living. We enjoyed living together, throwing parties, and just having fun, until things started to change.

One night he came home with a proposal for a scheme to make a lot of money without doing a lot of work. He said his boss had made tons of money and she'd show us how. His work and my work seemed to complement each other perfectly, and it wasn't long before we started making some decent money. Money that came in and went out faster than you could count it because my husband was a spendthrift! He spent hundreds of dollars on clothes, underwear, trucks, cars, and anything that caught his eye.

Money was beginning to get tight when the company I worked for decided to close the branch office where I worked and offered me a job in their corporate office in an adjoining state. I had to do something to keep the money coming in.

My husband basically spent his income as soon as the money hit his hands, and all of our credit was in my name, since he had no credit and made less money than me. So, if I wanted to save my credit and keep the things we had, I had to make a tough decision. I had to take the job I had been offered.

My husband liked his job, and even though he wasn't making much money, he still very much enjoyed his work. I explained to him that I had to relocate out of state and he insisted we keep the house. He would stay there, and I could come home on the weekends. Since everything was going so good for us, and we really liked the house we had, I thought his idea was a good one, problem solved!

Okay, I should have known that leaving my husband home, while I was working out of town, would be a problem. What made me think he would be as true to me as I was to him? I swear I must have been blind. But, I was deeply in love and he loved me too, or so I thought, until I started picking up the clues.

The clues were so subtle at first, that I hardly noticed anything was different. I would come home on weekends and he would be there. We would talk about the week, and share a nice dinner. Everything seemed to be fine, as a matter of fact, too fine. I missed him so much during the week, it almost killed me to leave every Sunday, but yet when I got home, he wouldn't even touch me, he'd just talk and talk.

At night when we cuddled in bed he started pulling away and not wanting to have sex anymore. I found this to be very odd, but figured maybe he was aggravated with my job, and he just wanted me home, and so he was acting out. For a while I let myself believe that his distancing himself from me was my fault. Boy, was I stupid!

It got to the point where I would get home and he'd be on the phone, and he wouldn't even acknowledge my presence! Then he would either start talking much lower into the phone or hurry to hang up. Then, when the phone would ring, he would leap to get it. It wasn't long before he wouldn't even give me the chance to answer the phone. This is when I knew something was up, I didn't know what, but I was going to find out. So, I decided that when he went out for something, I would search the house for clues.

My goodness, it took a while to find my first clue, but oh what a clue it was! My husband said he had to go into work for a couple hours one Saturday morning. He said he had a meeting with a nice young couple about a special job, he also added that the couple reminded him of us, and then, he gave me a kiss! After that little get away excuse, with all the warm fuzzy toppings, which he had stopped using with me, I knew without a doubt that he was cheating!

As soon as the car left the driveway, I began the search. I went through every cupboard, every drawer, under beds, in the basement, basically I looked everywhere! Exhausted I flopped myself down on the bed, and would you guess that right before my eyes was the clue I was looking for, I could see something hanging from under our dresser.

I got up went over to the dresser and looked underneath, and was crushed to find that a tiny, lacy negligee, not one of mine, was taped there! I wasn't sure where to throw myself, should I take it out and confront him with it, or should I not say anything and gather more evidence so I can catch him in the act? I decided I was too upset for a confrontation, and now that I knew what was going on, it would be better to catch him in the act. By catching him red-handed, he could not deny it, or make up any stories.

When he came home that day, I hardly spoke a word to him. Not speaking didn't bother him too much, because he had become so distant anyway, so he had no idea I was even upset. Over dinner, I asked him about the young couple he met with earlier that day. He looked lost at first, but then said, "Oh, those kids, just like we were!" I continued the conversation by telling him that I missed those days, and I wanted to be like that young couple again. He just nodded.

I told him that I thought I should move back home and find something else to do so I could stay home. He suddenly became very talkative, and insisted that I keep my job. He said I wouldn't be able to find a job that would pay enough and that I was making great money and he really didn't mind my being away during the week, because he just worked all the time anyway.

Okay, now I had plenty of insight, I knew he was cheating and I knew he wanted me to keep bringing in the money, but not be there to enjoy it with him. Wow, what a blow to the self-esteem! I calmly agreed that he was right, and stopped talking for the rest of the night. All the while inside my head, I was struggling to make a plan to catch him, but how? Then it hit me... the hushed phone calls he would have... who was he talking to, and what were they talking about?

I remembered a girlfriend of mine who tapped into her phone line to listen to her husband's phone calls and as much as I thought she was foolish when she told me about doing such a thing it seemed like the perfect answer to my situation. I met her for coffee later that afternoon and told her what I was thinking of doing. She was more than delighted to loan me her phone- tapping device (she worked for the phone company) and give me instructions for its use. And, yes, I did know that what I was doing was illegal but at that point I was more intent on catching a cheater than on doing "what was legal."

It was snowing when I started my four hour drive right after work on Friday night like I had always done. My mind was racing about what I might hear when I tapped onto the line. I couldn't wait to find out.

When I reached the driveway, I shoved the device deep into my laundry bag and walked in like usual. Sure enough, he was on the phone, but he hung up right away. I told him I was beat from the drive and I needed to hit the sack, he said goodnight, and I went to bed.

The next morning I got up early and told him I was going to do my laundry, he nodded, and started to get up too. Our washer and dryer were in the basement, which was perfect because it was the best place to tap the line. I could hear my husband walking upstairs, and could tell he had made his way to the phone. I placed the pinchers of the device onto the phone line and sat quietly, listening.

He was talking to one of his buddies. Why was he whispering I wondered. Then I knew why... I heard this... "hey, you think she knows?" ... "No, she's never here!" ... "So, you guys getting together this week"…"well, yeah! She is so hot, I can't believe she's my boss"... "dude, you are so bad, I thought women slept their way to the top"... "hey, it's nice to be on top, and it's nice when she's on top"... "I hear that dog!" ... "I cannot wait till Monday man, we are going to rock the house"... "well dude I'm jealous..."

Okay, now I had enough! I was ready to kill him right then, but that would land me in jail and break my plans of catching him in the act. I stashed my handy device back into my laundry bag, and tried my best to go upstairs looking as though I knew nothing at all. Thankfully, he had stopped paying attention to me for quite some time, so I just grabbed my jacket and left for the day.

I went to my friend's house, returned her device, and when I let her in on what I'd heard she wanted to go kill him herself. I asked if I could stay over on Sunday night, because I was going to make it look like I was headed to work, like usual, but was going to stay in town to catch him Monday.

And so, I went home to the longest Saturday night of my life, and lay there thinking about what the next couple of days would hold. On Sunday morning I packed up my car, said goodbye to my husband, and went straight to my friend's house.

We hid my car in her backyard, so no one would know I was in town. Then we stayed in and talked all day and night about his sluttish boss, and how awful a person my husband was, and what I should do to make him pay.

That night I was so anxious I did not sleep at all. I just couldn't wait to surprise them both! Early Monday morning I had my friend drop me off down the street from my house. There I sat behind a snow bank, waiting for the tramp to show up. Sure enough, at nine a.m., she pulled into the driveway.

My heart started racing, my palms were sweating, and I couldn't believe this was really happening. I wanted to just sit there and cry all day, but that wasn't the plan. So, I waited a while to give them enough time to get cozy, and when I thought they were cozy, I made my way up the hill, to my house. Hands shaking, knees knocking, I quietly made my way up the stairs to the door, and like a spy, opened the door without a sound.

I could hear their voices coming from the bedroom upstairs, and knew they were definitely cozy. I made my way up the stairs as quietly as possible, and when I reached the top, I was frozen with fear. Could I handle seeing them going at it, my very own husband and his boss in MY bed?

With a deep breath I barged into the room, swinging the door open as I said, "What the hell is going on here?" Sure enough, they were going at it... they both stared at me open mouthed... pushing away from each other and trying to gain composure.

I ranted and raved calling them both every name in the book, and before the slut could grab her clothes, I took them and threw them out the window, and told her to get the hell out of my house now! Then I looked at my husband, started grabbing his things, and threw everything of his I could find, out the window.

The tramp of a boss did just what I said and ran out of the house with only a sheet, grabbed her clothes and left. My husband tried to talk to me; I couldn't hear a word he was saying over the fire burning in my soul. I turned to him and told him to get the hell out of my house, and my life. I told him he would get divorce papers as soon as humanly possible and then forced him down the stairs and out of the house.

He would never hit a woman so he was easily pushed where I wanted him to go... OUT! He stood on the porch and tried to say some crap to get his stuff and end things nicely, but I was too furious for such nonsense. I went outside, grabbed his shoulders and with all my might, I pushed him off the porch backwards; he was just lucky there was snow! With that done, he got into his car and left.

It took forever to complete the divorce. I got the house and everything else, including the maxed out credit cards and eventually, I had no choice but to go bankrupt as he had racked up over 200,000 dollars of debt in less than 8 months! He ruined my credit, he ruined my view of men, and he almost ruined my life.

But, you know, I didn't let him ruin my life. It took a long time before I ever committed to a man again, but four years after the divorce I met a great guy. I drove him crazy for a couple of years with insane jealousy, but he knew what had happened, and put up with all of the accusations and drama. He showed me that men are not all the same, and even though they all have a penis, they don't all feel the need to share it with everyone.

He was and still is the most faithful and loving man I've ever known, after being together for eight years, we finally married. We moved to a place with no winters, and we have rebuilt my credit, rebuilt my trust in men, and even enjoy our beautiful daughter. Since hindsight is 20/20, I think my first husband being a cheater was the best thing that ever happened to me, because had it not been for that, I wouldn't be as happy as I am right now!

Melanie:

I have been married for two years now. We have a beautiful one- year old baby girl. A few months ago we separated because the fighting had increased and it was not easy on either one of us. He swears up and down he thought it was over.

While separated my husband rarely called about his child. After we got back together he revealed that he had a relationship while we were separated. This relationship got serious and there was sex involved. Now he says he did not know what he was doing and that it did not mean anything to him! I find that hard to believe. My husband spent so much time with this girl that it is nearly impossible to believe that.

I am devastated and very hurt.

About a week ago we went to a club. He was intoxicated but he grabbed another girl's butt right in front of me. He says he does not remember but he does because he laughs in my face when the subject comes up.

I still have reason to believe he is seeing someone. I even found a pair of underwear in my drawer last week that did not belong to me. They were a size 12, I am a size 3. But of course he denied it. And until I catch him red-handed I can't prove it.

Sandra:

I have just ended a 10 year marriage due to an adulterous affair on my husband's part. We had a wonderful start. However, my husband had an affair two years after we married about the time he was going through some rough times with his family.

His father died at a young age and they had not been on the best of terms at the time. My husband was ill as a child and, as a result, his mother had always given him the most attention, he was the middle child. All of this played a very good part in the affair. However, I never was brave enough to confront him about the "whys" of the affair.

So our marriage went on until a very good friend of mine told me he was having an affair with the woman he works with. I confronted him with the information and he denied it, so I had to believe him but always kept my eyes open for signs.

Our sex life had deteriorated to almost nothing! Again, I was still afraid to confront him about anything. But, I had a feeling something was going on one night so after I was out with my girlfriend, I drove past his coworker's house. Lo and behold my husband's vehicle was there.

I was totally furious, and devastated even though I knew in my heart what was going on. I went home and called her house and she tried to deny that anything was going on and told me she was going back to bed and hung up. I called back and she finally put my husband on the phone.

I told him that it was now over! I typed up the divorce papers and we filed for divorce. Two months later he moved out of the house and moved in with her. Not even two months after that, she told him he had to find another place to live and he was forced again to move.

Even though he had been living with her, he and I have remained on a talking relationship and he has admitted many times that he really screwed up and was so sorry for hurting me.

I have been hurt badly, but I am not the vindictive type of person. My upbringing has taught me that people make mistakes, that is why we are called "human." It was much healthier for us to talk things out finally and not scream and yell which just makes a persons health suffer.

I have likened his situation to an alcoholic. Until the alcoholic hits "bottom" and chooses to change his lifestyle, there is not much anyone else can do. When I finally told him to leave, he realized his mistakes and is much more appreciative of what he had. I told him he could not move back in, and that he had to live on his own (something he has never had to do) to find out what it is like.

I have learned a lot through this. I learned that my biggest mistake was not communicating in the first place. Not by accusing, or blaming, but honestly admitting to my own mistakes and letting him know how I feel by the way he treated me.

Yvonne:

I have been married for seven years, high school sweethearts. Just recently my husband and I caught up with an old girlfriend of mine and we exchanged numbers and went out all together (a large group of friends) several times.

Suddenly the meetings stopped but she kept calling my husband. My husband has told me they have feelings for each other and want to take the next step but that she was hesitant and needed to hear from me permission for their relationship to move on.

I have since moved out of our home, and feel betrayed by an old friend and my spouse. He tells me the excitement is the conversation about old times.

I still love my husband and I worry that he is going to be brought down by this girl. She has a young child from another man she used and she has a running history of sleeping around with married men (she was with a married man when we met her at the bar).

I just don't understand how my husband can be so naive. If she is willing to be the cause for a marriage to break up and stab an old friend in the back, I just don't understand women like this and how my husband can enjoy the company of a woman with these obvious motivations.

This has all happened so fast, within 2 months. My husband still calls me and tells me he will not see her since it causes me so much pain. I can understand if he needs his space, but not to jump straight into a new relationship with a girl with a history of being a homewrecker.

The odd thing is my husband still talks to her, and now he lies about it, but he wants to always be friends forever. Yeah right! So I can continuously be hurt. I'm out of this drama. Thanks for letting me vent.

Linda:

About 3 years into our marriage my husband started getting really abusive to me. I was a homemaker who always cooked 3 meals a day for him. I always had his supper ready when he came home from work. Sometimes he would throw the food on the floor and call me a stupid bitch and say "I hate being with a fat, ugly woman like you. Why couldn't you be pretty like Jim's wife Jill?"

He would stay out all hours of the night saying he had to work overtime. One day a man from his job told me Jill was picking him up after work so the next day I hid in my car across the street from where he worked and saw him get into Jill's car. They had enough nerve to lay down in the front seat of the car on top of each other and all but have sex right in the parking lot.

When he came home that night he found me gone. In a note I told him I wanted a divorce and he was free to have the slut. He begged me not to divorce him, but I did anyway.

I am now in a relationship where my partner loves and adores me and is always willing to try to make me happy. Since getting rid of the bum my self-esteem is much higher and I have lost 120 pounds.

Girls if he cheats or treats you bad kick him to the curb. It never gets better just worse.

Carol:

I recently discovered that my husband had a one-night fling with my friend. She was a friend to my children, her kids played with mine and she was a friend to my parents.

My husband had a prior affair but I never dreamed that this would happen again. I feel as though everything that I believed in is now a joke, our love, my friendships. The two people that I thought I could trust have hurt me so deeply that I wonder if I can recover.

My kids are torn because she was a friend and they don't understand what is going on. I want my relationship to work yet at the same time feel like why bother fighting for something he was so willing to give up.

They both had no excuse or reasoning behind the affair other than both being too drunk to realize the hurt they would cause. He wants to get help both for the drinking and our relationship. I just wonder is it too late?

Nora:

My eyes are swollen and red, nose still running, heart broken, and my mind exhausted. I found out about my husband's affair when I was pregnant. He had an affair with a girl 10 years younger than I was.

I had given him everything. I can't begin to name all the countless sacrifices I had made for him and I resent each and every one of them now. I feel so pathetic.

I used to be such a strong person and now I feel shattered. I have never felt so worthless. All I keep saying to myself is "Why me? What did I do wrong?"

What makes all this worse is he still tries to say they were "just friends." He even admits the circumstances suggest they were more than just that. He has never told me anything, only lies unless caught red handed.

He tries here and there for a little bit but I think he is angry that I caught him. He is a perfectionist and used to put down this sort of thing. I hate him and her so much and have wished such horrible things to happen to them. I just can't seem to function. My life and my mind is in complete shambles.

Every time I try to straighten things out I end up falling down again. I don't know how I can ever get though this. To top it off I contracted a veneral disease while pregnant. That wasn't even enough for him to admit what he had done.

What is fucking wrong with me to stay with him?

Linda:

I wasn't the one fooling around! I was married for 15 years and thought my hubby was really in love but thought we were just doing the in and out of love thing! I was *wrong* to the fullest. He was having an affair with his best friend's wife!!

I had suspicions but every time I confronted him of course he would *deny* it and say I was nuts! Finally, after he walked out on me I realized how *dumb* and *stupid* I was.

20

It was terrible at first but I have dealt with it and since moved on with my life. If this helps anybody, *don't* believe what men say. I knew the answer but just closed my eyes wishing it would go away and it did just he went with it!!

I am now divorced and seeing a great man! I just hope my ex is as happy as I am now.

Donna:

I would like to share a life full of adultery of my husband. He had no honor. I can tell you that it had not one thing to do with me. It was him that had the problem. He did not like himself or know how to be happy with true love.

I can tell about our talks about his affair. I was never the reason for his affair. He never blamed me. He did it for one reason. He did not feel good about himself. So if he found someone of a lower class, he knew he was better than this person. This is in his mind. He said only low class persons would have an affair with a married man. He never lied about being married. He never took off his ring. He never said a bad thing about me.

There is a lot of stuff that we talked about. I was not hard on him about the affairs. I did try to understand. I have never left him before. I left him last year after an act of abuse on me. I called to tell him I was coming back to live in the house and he moved out the same day I came back. I do understand the man is sick. I care about him. Would I ever go back to him? No! I am happy with knowing I am safe.

I go to an abused women's group meeting. He has been in AA for many years and I have been in Al-Anon for even more years. We have been to marriage counseling many times but he would quit going because he did not like what they had to say to him.

I will not talk with him. I will not see him. I have to build a wall to keep me safe from the pain. I know he hurts more than I do. I will no longer help ease his pain. He will have to handle it himself.

Lois:

It makes no difference whether the cheater is a man or a woman. They cheat because they are selfish pigs who have no feelings for any one else. Most of the a-----es who cheat are men. Chauvanistic pigs are the most likely cheaters. They have such oversized male egos that they think the women (yes, plural) in their lives are too *stupid* to figure it out. The only stupid thing we do is to fall in love with the jerks in the first place.

It is so darn easy to see when someone is cheating. They are never where or when they say they will be. They reassure you that they are faithful, even when the subject has not come up!

As Shakespeare said in his play "Me thinks thou dost protest too much." In other words, if he/she is proclaiming his/her innocence before they are accused, you can bet your life they are cheating - making like bunnies with everything of the opposite sex.

If they bring a new person into the office, workplace, play place, etc. and tell you to stay out of that place, they are screwing that person.

If they are in a position of employer and you have been working for them and they hire someone new, tell you to stay out of the office, and pay that person 1 and 1/2 times your pay (when they pay you, which is rare) they are paying them for other "services rendered" and to keep their mouth shut.

It doesn't matter how much love they get at home, how good the sex is when there is sex, how much you love them. Once a cheating jerk always a cheating jerk. Look really carefully at their history, if the other person was always at fault, if they found reasons to cheat on the women/men in their past, they are and always will be a cheater!

I ought to know. Here I sit, broken hearted, trying hard to become departed, but stuff and houses and no savings alas, I live and breathe and put up with his sorry ass! I *will* get out.

Here is the lesson hard learned I shout, before you move in with a cheater, check them out and get the heck out of the relationship. Do not give them any spheres of control over your life. Most cheating a——es are also major control freaks. Lover beware!!

Jane:

I've chosen to tell my story in the form of a letter from the betrayed wife to her best friend (Sally) who had an adulterous affair with her (Jane's) husband. All names and places have been changed to protect both the innocent and the guilty...

Dear Sally,

Twenty-two years is a long time. Twenty-two years ago we were so young, and our children were just babies. You were a perky blonde, and my hair was going prematurely gray. Funny, now I'm the blonde and you're the graying grandma.

Jake and I moved to our new home all those many years ago, to a city where we knew no one. One day while I watched my daughters out on our front lawn, your oldest daughter came walking by. She looked like an all-American girl, blonde, well-dressed, scrubbed clean. After some small talk, and before she could get away, I asked her if she babysat. Much to my relief she said yes, and I immediately signed her up. It was always a challenge to find good, decent, and available babysitters.

For almost a year she was our regular sitter, putting up with stomachaches and general malaise that manifested themselves every time we went out.

When it was time for nursery school, as fate would have it, our daughters both enrolled in the same school and that is where we first met. I was taken with your outgoing personality, how friendly and warm you were. You were especially good with the kids, and I instantly liked you.

Since we lived only a couple of blocks from each other, I was soon included in the carpool, and our daughters became friends. At first our friendship developed through them spending time at each other's homes after school. In those days very few of our circle of friends worked full-time. We felt privileged that we were able to devote most of our time to raising our children. Soon Friday afternoons at your house became a highlight of the week.

You were always so generous and gracious... the more the merrier, plenty to eat, plenty to drink. First it was just we girls and the kids. Then the guys started joining us after work. Thus began our first of many traditions, Friday nights.

It became an unspoken understanding that Friday nights were reserved for you and me and our husbands. Often others joined us, but we were the core. There was no fuss, no bother. Your house or ours, it didn't matter, except in the summer, when we always hung out on your screened porch. There was no set time, there were no rules. Whoever got home earliest would make the call, "Want to do take-out?" Shorts, jeans, sweats, whatever felt good. Sometimes we just listened to music. Sometimes we rented a movie, and sometimes we even went out on the town. When we were in a quandary about what to do, we could always pull out the Trivial Pursuit game.

We watched our girls grow up. Their hearts were really into gymnastics then... they, in their leotards, doing those round-off back handsprings as though their little bodies were made of elastic.

By the time the kids reached adolescence, they had become pretty precious... the curled lips, the rolling eyes, the utter disdain for us. You and I supported each other through the roller coaster ride of their raging hormones and bad decisions. Despite, or because of, our anxieties and concerns, our friendship stayed intact.

After they reached high school, both of us had decided to return to the workforce full time and we each found our appropriate niche in the corporate world.

23

Next thing we knew we had become empty nesters and started spending more time with each other. We now had the time to take longer winter vacations, and we four visited some amazing places together.

Life and marriage hadn't always been perfect, but that fateful summer, thanks in a large part to you, I was at a very good place. You, on the other hand, were restless and disturbed. I tried to talk to you, but you withdrew.

Then it all made sense. You called to speak with my husband. Right then I knew something was wrong. Your husband had confronted you and you had admitted to having an affair, an affair not with just anyone, but an affair with my husband... your best friend, me, my husband. I was betrayed by the two people whom I trusted the most, but the hardest betrayal to understand was yours.

Words fail to express the pain I felt upon learning that for so many years you really hadn't been my friend. You had been manipulative, controlling and purposefully pursuing my husband, all the while professing your loyalty and love for me.

Our friendship died then, and I grieved as I'd never grieved before. I became a physical and emotional wreck. Thank God for my daughters, my family, my real friends, and counselors who helped me through the nightmare that my life had become.

You were the best friend I ever had. Part of the beauty of our friendship was that as different as we were, we complemented each other.

In her book A Year by the Sea, Joan Anderson wrote, "You must always retain some part of yourself which is nobody's business. The minute you let others in on your secrets, you've given away some of your strength." I gave, and you took, my secrets, my truths, my soul, and ultimately my strength.

Our history of memories that runs long and deep will always be tainted with a dirty, bitter taste. Forever forth, we, who were best friends, will be, as Tracy Chapman so succinctly put it, "less than strangers." I have regained most of my strength, and will trust again. And I will share my secrets, my truths, and yes, even my soul, but from now on there will always be a part of me I will keep for myself.

Tanya:

We met when we were in the ninth grade. For the first half of the year we were friends, but by spring we were an item. Things just seemed right. He was a football player, I was a cheerleader, Spring was here and love was in the air. We instantly fell in love and became high school sweethearts. It was the beginning of a perfect fairy tale.

We stayed together all through high school, the prom, the banquet. Sound like a movie? It felt like one. We both stayed home during college and went to universities close by.

During the first year of college, even though we had been going out for four years at this point, we finally "did the deed". He was my first, I was his first and it was awful! Yes, it was horrible. We had no idea what we were doing, but we continued to try and finally, we got it right.

The college years were fantastic. Things between us were better than ever. We had so much fun, felt so grown up and thought the world was ours. It was.

After graduation, we both worked hard to create fulfilling careers. We both made a promise that no matter how much money we made, we would never change. Our priorities would always stay straight and we'd always stay "down-to-earth." Three years after college, we were engaged.

During our engagement, we took classes with the church and during those classes we came to realize that we really were the perfect couple. We seemed to agree on everything. We were on the way to a wonderful life together. Our wedding was beautiful. Everything was perfect. Of course it was, that's how everything was when it came to us.

The first year we lived in a small apartment. Soon, we saved enough money to buy a house. It was so exciting! The perfect little house that we made into a perfect little home.

Two years later, we decided to try and make our perfect little family grow. We had the house, the dog, the cars, the boat and even the picket fence. Now it was time for children. We both agreed that we wanted our first child by 30. At the ripe age of 29, we were ready to get started. At least I thought so.

Over the next few months, he started to act very strange. He was very distant from me, never wanted to have sex, was coming home late and stopped talking to me the way he used too. I thought he was just stressed out from work. Never in a million years did I think it was me.

I finally had to ask him what was wrong. He broke down and told me he didn't want children. He said he actually never wanted any and he lied to me. He thought if he told me the truth, that I wouldn't have married him. He said he would have done anything to make me his wife, even lie about our future.

Needless to say, I was shocked. After thinking about it for a few days, I told him that being with him was more important to me than having children, so if he didn't want kids, we wouldn't have any. I was willing to give that up.

I was quite surprised at his reaction. He was mad. He got mad at me and told me to leave him alone. The next few days, he stopped coming straight home from work without telling me why. I'd have dinner ready and just wait until finally I'd call to see where he was. He'd tell me he was "out" and it was none of my business where he was or who he was with. He said I was treating him like a baby.

This continued to happen over the next few weeks. All through this time I tried everything I could to make things work, but it was completely one-sided. I asked if he wanted to go to counseling, talk to a priest, ask a family member for help. No, No, No. That became his answer to everything. I cried, I yelled, I begged, but nothing.

When he started sleeping in the extra bedroom, I decided that I had finally had enough. I did something I never thought I'd do; I checked his cell phone for messages. There it was, my worst fear. The message said, "Hi Hon, it's me, it's 3:00 and I just wanted to see what was going on for tonight." I almost passed out.

I'll never forget that message or the sound of her voice. The fact that she called him hon and that she said it's "me." She didn't even have to say her name, he already knew the sound of her voice.

I asked him who it was, but he wouldn't tell me. He said it was just a friend. After a few minutes of yelling at each other, I said something I never thought I'd say; I told him that if he was cheating on me, to get out. He left that day and he never came back, not for good at least.

The night he left, I called his cell phone and begged him to come home. I was sure that we could work things out and get through this together. I couldn't imagine my life without him. All those years together, growing up together, our fairy tale life. What happened to it? What would I do without it?

Over the next few months, he came home three times. Once he stayed for a week, once he stayed for two days and once I woke up in the morning after a night of incredible love making and he was gone.

All this time and I still questioned whether or not he had cheated on me. He was still telling me he never did. I was so confused, torn and depressed.

There was just no light at the end of the tunnel. I felt dead inside and I wanted to die. There were several times when I actually thought about committing suicide. Thank God for friends and family during those times.

I couldn't eat, I couldn't sleep, I couldn't stop crying. I lost 25 pounds, but looked horrible. I cried all day at work, came in late everyday, stayed late every night. I just didn't want to go home to an empty house.

I would continually picture him with another girl, would wonder what he was doing and if he was thinking of me. Finally, after six months of being separated, he told me he wanted a divorce. He finally admitted that he committed adultery.

How could I have not realized that when I heard her message. The not wanting children story was false. He thought that I'd never agree to not having children and that I'd leave him. This way, he wasn't the bad guy.

That's when I hit rock bottom. Instead of thinking about suicide, I actually tried it. I started taking sleeping pills when I came across a picture of my nieces. I realized what a horrible story they would have to live with and what a bad example I would set for them. I called one of my friends and she came over immediately.

I started therapy the very next day. It was so hard. Most of the time I just cried. I was so disappointed; in me, in him, in our not so happy ending to our fairy tale life together. My dreams of our future were shattered, my heart was broken, and I had no idea how I was going to make it without him.

I was scared to death to look into my future and see nothing. People would tell me to take it day by day and that things would work out for the best. That seemed nearly impossible, especially when all you could do is think about what's going to happen tomorrow, next week, a year from now. All I could see was loneliness.

My first step was to come to the realization that this wasn't my fault and there was nothing I could have done to stop it. The next step was to believe it. After months of therapy, talking and sharing my feelings with friends and family, and more crying, things started to look better for me.

I was on my way to happiness when I realized I had overcome my biggest fear: being alone. I was crying to a friend one day and told her that I was so afraid of being alone and she pointed out to me that I had been alone for eight months already and that I was okay. In that second, it was like the world had been lifted off my shoulders.

I'm okay. I'm actually okay. Financially, I'm okay, I'm surrounded by the greatest friends and family, I have my health and I'm going to be fine. What an accomplishment. I was actually proud of myself. I don't think I ever felt that way before.

I began to sleep at night, wake up early and wake up happy. I started eating healthy again, exercising and making my own life. I started to smile again and laugh. Really laugh.

One night, my girlfriends and I were out and we were laughing all night long. I looked over at one of them and she had tears in her eyes. She looked at me and said "welcome back honey, we missed you and we're so glad to have you back."

What a great feeling. To feel alive again and know you're worth it. To have the confidence to know that no matter what life throws my way, I can handle it, I can overcome it and I will always land on my feet. The light at the end of the tunnel may become dim at times, but I will always be able to see it.

A year and a half later, and I'm happier than I've ever been. I run my own business from home, which gives me lots of free time and the money to volunteer, spend time with family and friends, own my own home, spend quality time with my nieces and most importantly, have the time to spend on myself and treat myself to whatever I want. I absolutely deserve it!

Grace:

It had been some time since I had heard from my husband. Something was wrong. Though the calls had always been almost non-existent and the letters even more sparse despite my daily letters to him, I was worried at this lack of contact with the only man I had ever really loved. I began to doubt the wisdom in having chosen to accept a job across country for the summer.

Finally, I decided the distance was too great and that there was too much I was losing by not being at home with my husband. I knew my decision was not a good one professionally but regardless of the steps backward my decision would have, I decided to return home on the next available flight. I called the airlines, and arranged for a flight back to my hometown and then phoned my boss and explained the situation. It wasn't a good career move, but by this time I didn't care.

I attempted to call my husband several times to let him know I was coming home and to give him my flight information, but there was no answer. This worried me because he hadn't answered my calls for the past several days and I could only think the worst, that there had been an accident, maybe he had been hurt. Surely the authorities would have contacted me by now. These thoughts and others plagued me on the long flight home.

By the time the plane disembarked and I got my bags, I was irritable beyond belief and I pushed against a seemingly endless flood of people going the opposite direction as I made my way to the ground transportation outside the terminal. The cabbie's chatter on the way home didn't make my mood any better as I was too concerned about what may have happened to my husband.

At our condo complex, the taxi driver took my bags to my front door and I tipped him more than I normally would have. As I struggled to get the front door open I was terrified that I would find my husband's body on the floor, somewhere in the house, and dropping my bags just inside the door, I headed for our bedroom, which was empty, and then to the master bathroom, which was not.

My husband, my faithful husband, was in the shower with a woman. The sound of the running water apparently drowned out the sound of my entry and the two of them had no clue that I was just outside the shower enclosure while they were having noisy, wet sex. I felt the nausea rise and hurried out of our home.

Myra:

My husband became very secretive. I couldn't drive his car, nor could I open his mail. After twenty three years together, I could no longer open his mail and a big red flag went up. He even mentioned he was thinking of leaving me.

He was emotionally distant. It seemed as if he was living independently and I didn't exist. He made his decisions and didn't consider what I thought of them.

My husband knew the times I would be gone from the house and when I would return. His job is not the type of job where you work 9 to 5; somedays he gets off early and other days he gets off late. He was continually getting off work late, that is what he said at least. His paycheck stub comes in the mail because he has direct deposit and I looked at the hours worked and the time he came home and it was clear he was doing something else besides working.

I started receiving a number of telephone calls at home and on my cell phone with wrong numbers. I knew in my gut this had something to do with him. He mentioned the prostitutes he had seen on the way to work at 4:30 in the morning, and also the prostitutes at a store on his way home from work. There were also other sneaky situations occurring.

He started putting on lots of cologne before going to work and deleting his cell phone calls, both outgoing and incoming. He continually told lies which was something he'd never done before.

I accused him of an affair and instead of looking me in the eye and denying the affair, he got angry and left. I view his body language as deceptive. I can tell the days he has been with her. When he comes home, he will not look me in the eye.

His entire behavior is odd. Once he came home and started doing the laundry which is another first for him. Our sex life continued to go down hill and, currently, we have no sex life.

I'm tired of him and his lies. I'm thinking seriously about my future. Honesty is very important to me. It will too difficult to live the rest of my life with someone who doesn't respect me or I don't trust.

John:

This story, which is in no way fictitious, is in the "married man/married woman/emotional" classification. However, it has always had high potential for being sexual although physical contact has never gone that far.

My wife described a "look" the girl in this story often gives her with those "stormy blue eyes," so I'll refer to her as "Stormy." Personally I've seen only love, warmth, and concern, never hostility in those angelic eyes.

My adult daughter moved back into our home in early summer, along with Stormy, while my wife was away on business for a month on the other side of the country. Both girls were out of work, out of money, and needed a place to stay.

My daughter called to ask my permission. Knowing that I care about people and want to help even strangers if I can, she told me the details of Stormy's rather sad story just to be sure I'd say yes. She never lies to me, but she is an expert at manipulating my feelings. I immediately felt sorry for Stormy and told her to bring her home.

My daughter and I are so much alike that her choices of friends are the same as my choices would be (with a couple of notable exceptions), so I've usually hit it off with them. In fact my wife often criticizes me for spending more time with my daughter's friends than with her.

Her friends are one thing, but I was completely unprepared for Stormy. My first impression was that Stormy was a very nice girl, considerate, quiet, but not unfriendly. It sounds corny, but after a couple of days of apparent lack of interest in each other, our eyes met, and we both realized something powerful was happening.

As we shared our living space and our lives over the next few weeks we learned much about each other. Everything seemed to fan that initial fire and there was no way to stop it. We have a great deal in common and are much alike. Of course this learning process continued after my wife returned home.

What was happening was so spontaneous and natural that Stormy and I didn't think how it might look to anyone else. Inevitably my wife dragged me into our bedroom one day and demanded an explanation. I stammered around and tried to come up with some excuse to cover feelings I couldn't help.

My wife let me off the hook that time, and said only that she couldn't compete with candy. I wanted to say that Stormy isn't "candy," she's an entree in the finest restaurant in Paris. But by now, a couple of months later, I realize that I love and respect Stormy so deeply that I can't possibly think of her in those terms.

Although my wife has been and continues to be a somewhat unwelcome presence in my home (I was never in love with her), the situation is unusual in that she has been on medications for a number of years and, after she takes her meds in the early evening she zonks out for the night. So Stormy and I were still able to pursue our limited life together after dark.

Sometimes it was just the two of us. Other times it included my daughter and a couple of her friends. Unlike my wife, Stormy is not demanding when it comes to entertainment. Usually all she wants is to be with me. We talk, or watch movies, or listen to music.

We have an unwritten contract to follow our Catholic principles (at least to some extent) and not make love until our individual lives no longer interfere with our relationship with each other.

We have also chosen not to talk about our "significant others" while we are with each other. Stormy resents my wife as much as I resent her boyfriend who sits in a jail cell because of his own stupidity. We don't want anything to interfere with the incredible feelings we have when we are together, even though in the back of our minds we are always aware of our commitments.

One of her favorite movies is "Save the Last Dance." In the movie the love affair is interracial and therefore not acceptable to a significant portion of society. In our case our age difference puts us in an "unacceptable" category. But we are both free spirits and care nothing about social convention.

My daughter and Stormy are working now, and will move into their own place as soon as they can afford it. Stormy's boyfriend gets out of jail in a few months. To avoid my wife when I'm at the office, Stormy has been spending more time with one of her friends, a girl who chooses not to be part of our circle of friends. When Stormy is gone for even one night I miss her more than I can put into words.

If you want to write a happy ending for this story, please be my guest. I can't write any more.

Carol:

Finding out my husband had an affair was devastating. I cried every evening after work for months. I pleaded whatever chance I got for him to make things right. I wanted my husband back without the attachments he had made. It was not to be.

Looking back two years later, I am grateful to him for it and grateful that I found out. It woke me up to the fact that my marriage had gone sour. I had given up too much and I wasn't thriving as a person. It had been going on a long time. Yet I had been holding on through loyalty and a sense of responsibility. I held on for more than 25 years.

My point is, although the affair he had was painful and not the right way to end a marriage it was almost necessary to wake me up to the fact that my own needs were not being met. I deserved some attention too. At this point I am thankful for the affair. I still mourn the marriage but I am looking forward to getting reacquainted with myself.

Is this just rationalizing? Is this odd? If he had spent the time and energy on me instead of other women would our marriage have lasted longer? I really think there were a lot of reasons our marriage should not have happened in the first place. I was so idealistic that I thought love would conquer all. Problems that I didn't even see yet because we didn't know each other well.

We met during the summer. We lived a continent apart but we wrote letters and talked on the phone for five months. When we met again during the Christmas holiday we decided to get married. It was too fast and we didn't know each other well. I was 24 and he was 28. We weren't young. We were in love.

We are not really compatible. But I committed myself to him. He was a good friend to me. Our marriage was that plus sex. When the love faded I saw the problems but knew that I was in there and I was going to make it last. After all, a good friendship was the basis of a good marriage, right? That is what I thought then. I don't know about that one now. I think a good marriage needs a lot more than that. If he had not paid attention to the other women or paid it to me instead would that have been enough? No, not now that I see so many other weaknesses in our marriage, our relationship.

My husband and I used to jokingly say about our getting married fast, "...and they said it would never last." We did for over twenty years. Maybe that is lasting. Maybe we did make it but something changed, in me as well as in him. Changes in who we were, what we wanted and what we were willing to live with.

I agree about there being no formula to a good marriage from the outside. Many authors have tried to talk about it though. I know people in arranged marriages. They are still married but I wouldn't necessarily say that means their marriage is "working." In at least one case one of them is "enduring" and I want more than that in my marriage.

Sybil:

My husband and I have been married for over eight years. Last Saturday, he admitted to having an affair with the neighbor for the past eight months, and as recent as two weeks ago. He gave me all the gory details, when, where, and even visuals that I didn't care to picture.

My husband says he fell in love with her deeper than he has ever been in love before, but after she left, he felt used because she didn't say goodbye. She called him days before and told him not to call anymore, because I told her husband to watch the phone bills and keep the cell phone on him.

After she left, we decided to see if we could work on us by starting to date again. We have been talking about what happened and how we felt about it over the past few days. We even said "I love you" many times during each of our phone calls.

In a book I was reading, it said one of the first steps to recovery in infidelity was to get checked for STD's, so I asked my husband to do it. He said he would, but was offended. Now he says he won't touch me, sleep next to me, or even kiss me until the results come back. Even if they come back negative he may just still leave.

Anyway today, the other woman calls him. He says he missed the call, but do I believe him? She was hiding the call from her husband. After she called, he couldn't tell me that he loved me.

I am so scared that I will lose him because some bored housewife cannot stop playing with his mind. I know it takes two to tangle, but just when it seems things are calming down, she gets involved. Why can't she stay with her own husband?

Ellen:

He held my heart and behind my back held her attention. We had been married for five years and then in four days he just left and moved in with her. He fed me a line that he was "living with some friends" and that he merely "needed some space" and that "things would be alright."

I did some digging and found out he was living with another woman. He wouldn't admit it, but I knew. He became very irritated at that point because had I not found this out and forced him to divorce me and let me go I believe he would still be bouncing from me to her, whatever his convenience deemed necessary.

My advice to anyone who is in this type of situation is to cut ties. If he is lying to you, then odds are he is lying to his wife. Don't let a man, especially one that lies, put you into this type of triangle. Don't allow a man to have power over you. Don't allow a man to lie to you and still expect love. If he is lying now, he will only lie more in the future.

Mary:

My husband is married to the woman he ran off with. He needed her financially because on his own, after child support, he would not have had the money to afford a vehicle or home. They swear all is "just perfect" but I know different. Within one year he was months behind on support and when the state cracked down on him he called and wanted to sign his rights over. He no longer has any connection with my children.

His new wife thinks she has a man, but she merely has "her turn" with this man. Men like him (and yours) do not change. Once they learn they can have more than one doting lover they will continue to thrive on that desire.

Brenda:

My ex-husband may have his new love, her new car, and her new home. Heck, now that they don't have child support they even have a timeshare somewhere, but he doesn't have his kids. Sometimes a man truly is only worth the skin he is in and sometimes he is even found lacking of that price.

If your lover is married, learn to make it on your own. Don't let him lie to you. If he loved you so much, where is he on the nights he is not with you? Making love to his naive wife (whom I am sure would not be happy about this either). If he can make love to her and then double dip with you where does it end?

Do you really want to be another notch on his bedpost? Find someone who believes in love and all its virtues. Find someone who believes in being a family and can portray a family man. Don't find someone who will leave you in despair again!

I was crushed for quite a while, but have dug myself back into the real world. I no longer miss him. Heck, I'm glad I found out, otherwise what would he have eventually taught my children?

Lizbeth:

I found some makeup on the collar of my husband's shirt after he returned from a business trip. The first thought that entered my mind was that my husband would not cheat on me. As time went on, I intuitively felt an emotional distance from him. I asked if there was someone else. At first he denied it, and later confessed that there was someone else.

I had a sinking feeling in the pit of my stomach. I wanted to know everything about the other woman and who she was. He was extremely protective of this woman. It's too bad he was not as protective of our children and me.

I wanted to go to counseling to save our marriage. He had this arrogant attitude about going to counseling. He did not show any remorse about the hurt that he caused me or our kids. He decided that he wanted to get a divorce, without trying to work out our problems, and served me with divorce papers. He ended up moving away from us, and marrying the other woman three months after our divorce, with our children present.

I am still hurt and angry today, and the divorce has really affected my daughter in particular. She has confided to me that she sometimes cries before she goes to sleep at night because her father is not a regular part of her life. I still to this day can not believe that a man that I loved and trusted for so many years could do this to all of us.

Britney:

My ex and I were married for over five years. We had two beautiful children. I went to visit my parents for four days and when I came back he had not even been in our home, he had stayed with her. He said he wanted a "separation" and he needed "time" but he was sure "things would work out."

He took the kids one weekend and my son came back talking about "this woman." I got the address and actually went there. The apartment manager was more than helpful as I could have had child protective services do a thorough investigation of the building due to the "terms" that my husband was there on.

I found out that he had moved in with another woman who had just become divorced herself. I was devastated and angry! How dare he take the kids there! What was he thinking! What was he trying to show them! What in the world did she think she was doing with my kids! I gave him a chance to do counseling, thinking perhaps he would acknowledge this massive screw up. He wouldn't take it.

I expressed how divorced life would be. I told him with his money blunders he would not be able to make child support and support his own life. He didn't believe me and said I was just trying to scare him. He didn't pay his child support regularly. I had to get aid through the state for child care, which meant the child support went to the state, not me. They finally went after him.

When he got in a bind he decided to sign over his rights. The day we met at the lawyer's I was wearing my work clothes, nice, but plain. He walked in with frosted hair, new clothes, squeaky leather shoes, and expensive sunglasses and of course she followed closely behind in "coordinating colors." I was flabbergasted. If they had wanted to pay the child support, they certainly could have, judging from their attire, they just didn't want to. I paid for the entire legal process.

I also made the hard decision that a man like that is not needed in the lives of my children. They now have an adoptive father and no contact with their biological father. I gave them a chance to contest the adoption, even had a lawyer write them. They wrote back that they "do not wish to contest the adoption" so at least my kids won't believe her when she says I "stole" them.

I am desperately afraid that when my kids come of age they will hunt him down and if she is still there she will tell them a distorted version of the truth, but I have to take that chance. Right now I do not believe either of them deserve these children, with their past actions being what they are.

I don't understand how a woman who has never known me can despise me and lie about me so much, but it is there and happens almost on a daily basis. Further more, I don't see how my ex can look at her, when what they did together has cost him so much.

If you've had this happen to you, just have faith that payback will be coming around. Try to move on and build a life you're proud of. Don't ever compromise yourself or your opinion of things. Your kids will know right from wrong in their hearts. Perhaps they will learn a valuable lesson from this.

Pamela:
This is the short version of my story. Married 20 years no children, both professional. One year ago I had a "gut" feeling backed up by cell phone numbers on his bill to not one but two

different women. My husband convinced me they were only phone calls nothing else. After talking about separating, divorcing, etc., we decided instead to seek counseling. A condition I had was no further contact with either of these women. My husband agreed.

We went to counseling throughout the summer until it became apparent to our therapist that this wasn't just husband/wife problems but that my husband was deeply distrubed. We stopped marriage therapy and he began (and is still in) psychotheapy.

I discovered earlier this year that not only did the contact with the other women not stop but that he had affairs with both at the same time. On top of everything he confessed that he also had an affair with another woman that lasted several years.

I am not a stupid woman but I truly did not have a clue to my husband's "secret life." All affairs are now ended (this I am fairly certain of as I know passwords for all voice mail, email, etc.) and I am trying my best to see my way through this hell I find myself in.

Why am I still here? It's complicated, but I believe my husband had a slow melt down and wound up in a cesspool of his own making. He wants our marriage to continue.

Anna:

My husband cheated with my friend who is also my boss. Right now I have so many emotions, anger, hurt, you name it, I got it. Their relationship didn't last long but it doesn't matter. My husband says he's sorry and I think I believe him but the "friend" is acting like nothing happened, talking to me like she always has.

I confronted them the same day, husband then friend. What makes this worse is that it happened in my house while I was working for her. I want to move or burn the house down.

It's hard for me to understand how they could look me in the face knowing what was going on. I should have listened to my gut feeling because I knew, but that stupid part of me said he wouldn't, she couldn't. I was wrong.

There are a bunch of reasons that can be given for the cheating but I don't want to hear them because I have a response for them all — husband saying he was lonely; well, the answer is, so was I, but I didn't look elsewhere. None of them matter. I feel my husband not only betrayed me but he also betrayed our children.

I am the mother of two wonderful kids so I also have to think of them. I am not sure if I can get over this, the hurt is very deep. I haven't gone to work this week because she is making me so angry by her actions since I confronted her, like it's no big deal.

I have to figure out if I want to try to work things out with my husband. And what about my job? I have big time trust issues and I guess I will have to work through my feelings and see where that leads me.

Brad:

Adultery is bad. I mean bad news! I did it and regret it every day of my life. The reason is not just my wife but doing something like that in the sight of God's eyes. Read the Bible, King David did it although he loved God and he suffered the consequences! Read 2 Samuel 11 and 12 chapter. So the same will happen to all those practicing adultery including me.

I don't do this anymore, I have come to respect God and my wife more. God never intended for such things to happen; we live in Satan's world and he has designed this system of things to be against everything God is for.

What really changed me was when I read 1 Corithians 6:9: "Do not be mislead. Neither fornicators, nor idolaters, nor adulterers, nor men kept from unatural purposes, nor men who lie with men, nor greedy persons, nor drunkards, nor revilers, nor extortioners will inherit God's Kingdom." I believe God will change this world and get rid of Satan the devil and adultery will go along with it. So I have stopped this.

I want to apologize not only to my wife but also to every human on earth for committing this crime that has brought so much human suffering to humanity. Thanks to Jehovah God that forgives in a large way as long as we repent and return to him. And repenting means to make a complete turnaround and that means not thinking that God is a fool and go repeating serious sins over and over again. 1 John 1:9-10

Carly:

My husband of 10 years cheated on me. Now if you had asked me what I would do about it before it happened I'd of said "See you later" no second chance. Funny when the shoe's on your foot, you can suprise yourself with the actions you take especially when there is a lot at stake.

Things had reached a no turning back point. We no longer kissed each other goodbyes; really had choresome sex, when we did have it; and had lost that respect you should have with your partner. We were heading downhill fast.

I decided to have a weekend away with the kids. He stayed home and said he'd be having a few friends over. Sounded fine with me and like a great idea for some time apart. The people he invited were all just good work friends but having a few drinks turned into a few too many drinks.

Everyone but the person I will call "C", went home after far too many drinks. That, of course, set it all up, "C" being young, with no commitments, and very free-spirited about sex.

My husband said he let lust control him and not his brains. He felt he didn't take control of his actions, which in looking back he should have and if he had it wouldn't have continuted.

This affair continuted for weeks until one of the other friends who had been at the party that night came to me and told me that my husband was having a sexual relationship with "C."

When I confronted my husband I didn't know where to begin. I let him do the talking. He spoke to her immediately after our talk and told her it was over and there would be no more contact between them. She said it was a pity they couldn't still be friends.

Believe me it wasn't that simple. They still run into each other at work, but no conversation takes place. Lucky for our relationship she didn't try to keep in touch with him, so we didn't have to deal with a third party interferring with what we have had to work very hard to keep.

We had counseling and he did have times of uncertainty about what he felt for her and for me. We had, and still have, long conversations about our feelings. It has been a hard 12 months for us. I am probably the person with the uncertainty now as I have to work hard at trying to regain the trust he is trying to prove to me.

One thing we have learned is that our communication was as bad as it could be. We had fallen out of love. Communication is extremely important and we have improved 90%. We're looking at it as a second chance. We know we will still have some ups and downs, but feel at this stage we can make it work.

After what we have experienced I feel it can work with a second chance, as long as you learn the reason behind why it happened, how you allowed it to happen. If it does happen again, you haven't learned.

···►··►··►

Women Who Cheat

I was surprised at the number of men who wrote about their wives' infidelity. I expected to receive stories from women willing to "lay it all out" about their husbands' betrayal and even regarding their own infidelity, but I was somewhat fearful that this book wouldn't have the male viewpoint to add balance.

I wasn't sure that my collection methods -- the adultery questionnaire and forums -- would be found by men. Even if they were, would men be willing to write about their wives cheating on them? As you'll see from the stories that follow, I needn't have worried since men and women were anxious to share their stories, as betrayers and as those betrayed.

Again, the people and stories are real; names, places, and other identifying data have been changed to provide anonymity.

Daniel:

My wife is involved with a married man. We all work at the same place and I'm here to tell you that it is really hard on me. My wife and I been married for six years now and I am going to divorce her. The hurt and betrayal she inflicted in my life is so painful and I don't think I can trust anyone again with my heart like that.

My wife would look me right in my eyes and be lying though her teeth about everything she said. I would go on her lunch break and we would sit and eat, talk and she would say how much she loves me every day. We used to do so many things together then all of a sudden she wants to do things on her own. She needs space.

I loved my wife with all my heart and how could she do such a thing to me? She would go out and wouldn't even call to see if I'm okay or if I called she would ask me what I want. I started to have some gut feelings about her behavior. I know that I was an honest and faithful husband to my wife and she knows that. So I started to investigate and came across everything I needed to stop this woman from lying to me.

I became sick from all this lying and deceit and this woman broke all my trust. We are not together now, she left, and is still seeing this married man. *Yes I am angry and hurt* but I will let her go on with her *adultrous life*.

Stephen:

I married at the tender age of 21 years of age to a girl of 19 years. I had a good job and I thought I would be able to be a good

40

husband in a loving relationship. I was so naive that I couldn't even think that this girl, whom I knew for several years, would have married me not for love but for my money.

I worked while she went to college. I dutifully paid the tuition and the bills. However, within a few months of our wedding, the lovemaking became less frequent, tenderness became non-existant, and she became downright belligerent any time I tried to talk about our deteriorating situation. I tried to get her to agree to marriage counseling. I went to the counseling to discuss my plight, having no family to go to.

My suspicions began to grow when she started coming home very late at night. This suspicion became more intense as she arranged her schedule so as not to see me when I was awake. I took to cruising the school and our neighborhood to find her car. I found it one evening at a bar in the next town. Sure enough, she was sitting with a man I didn't know. When I confronted her, she became violent and I left to avoid legal entanglements.

Armed with the knowledge that she was probably unfaithful, I found a good lawyer and began divorce proceedings. She dragged me into family court and civil court to force me to pay for her tuition. My legal costs skyrocketed, but the divorce became final two years after we were wed. It was the best money I ever invested.

I married again four years afterward to a wonderful woman. Twenty years later, I feel like I'm still on my honeymoon. My early marital experiences taught me to talk openly with my lady, to share my feelings, and to always ensure that in everything, she comes first.

I strongly suggest to all those I know who are engaged to make it a point to begin discussing expectations, desires, and expected duties prior to saying "I do." Although I didn't use one, pre-nuptial agreements can provide a base for future understanding.

Thomas:

My wife cheated on me after fifteen years of marriage. She started going out with her girlfriends on Friday nights and like the good stupid husband that I was I thought a night out with the girls would do her some good. She was drinking too much and staying out too late. I knew something had to be going on.

Then one night she told me that she had been with other guys. First just kissing and sharing stories of marriage woes. Then the kissing went too far with one guy. They ended up in the front seat of my car my wife getting felt up. She told me he had his pants down and she touched him. Then stopped thinking of her family. I don't know if I should believe her. But I am hurt none the less.

Please, if you are thinking about cheating on your spouse. Think of the family before yourself. The hurt that indiscretion caused is unbearable. Love your spouse and respect yourself. If you must leave your relationship, leave it. Don't cheat. You'll feel better about yourself, and you won't add extra hurt.

Carlos:

I discovered my wife's affair six years ago, and I think I haven't recovered from it yet. The affair happened years before that and I have reasons to believe that it went on for a very long time. Upon discovery I forgave her almost immediately and tried to resume our normal life.

But she ignored my grief and loss of self-esteem and I felt that she was taking it as my weakness. I tried to get her to talk about it from time to time to help me recover, but we always ended in big fights reinforcing the pain.

She just couldn't relate to what was going on inside me. She didn't want to take it seriously. All I wanted was for her to say sorry remorsefully, humbly and sincerely. But it never came. She developed a big fat ego and I have a feeling that she had been under severe depression for a very long time because of the guilt, that it had rendered her the inability to extend and receive forgiveness.

But I must admit that our marriage had not been smooth all the way right from the very start and probably led her to the affair. I have a feeling my children are affected by it all emotionally. We are now separated and I don't think I would come back to her unless she apologized the way I wanted willingly.

I am using the separation to reflect and ponder on the issue. I have a feeling she is doing the same. My problem is that I love her dearly although I have not been able to express it the right way.

Richard:

I am in the military, so that should let you know right away that my marriage was in trouble. That is strike number one. We have been married for ten years now, I am 29 and she is 27, strike number two.

We had been stationed overseas and things were ok, but never great. When I was deployed, I didn't want to leave her, but what choice did I have?

We missed each other at first but it didn't last long, she found a friend or two to keep her company. I didn't see her again for six months but I heard stories, it's funny how news travels. When I returned, she was pregnant with some other man's child. I wanted to kill her. Here I was defending my country, taking care of her and our child, living under harsh life-threating conditions and she was fooling around! It tore me apart inside.

When I did get back I moved out. Eventually she had the kid and of course she wanted to get back together since the guy took off and didn't want anything to do with her. Maybe I just felt sorry for her, but we got back together and man do I love that boy, it's not his fault.

I would be better off without her, just me and the boys, but it costs too much to divorce her and the military would screw me hard. So we just live our lives together but separate.

Ben:

My wife and I had a great marriage, or so I thought. Just recently, in the past month, she said she needed time to think and clear her mind. Time to find out what happened to the love she had for me. You see, last year she met a friend, as she called him.

I was very skeptical of this as would most husbands. But we had moved away from the only friend she had ever had and, I thought it was good for her to have someone to talk to. So, being the good husband I was, I allowed her friendship until I noticed it was getting too close. By that time things had changed for the worse as she had started to have feelings for this man. Little did I know it was more than feelings.

She told me she had sent me a letter and that I really needed to read it because it explains a lot. I have not received this letter yet, but I know what it is about. She has been sleeping with him for several months now and I, being the trusting, faithful, unexpecting husband, did not want to accept the truth as I knew it, until she was ready to admit it to me.

Actually I am a little relieved and feel a little better knowing that I know what was going on; because I don't have to guess any more. Of course the whole time I was questioning her about this she denied everything, until she got away and realized that she had to tell me the truth just so she could move on.

I don't know what will come of all of this but I know in my heart I can forgive her and if she were willing to try I would be able to see past all of it in time. If you are still writing this book when I have a conclusion to this story I will submit it to you. As far as I am concerned I can only be there for our children until she can forgive herself and is willing to try.

Russell:

My wife cheated on me short of having sex with this person and I have forgiven her. She ended it before I found out. I know all the details as she tells me and I wish I would have never asked.

She had been sending me messages for two years that she was lonely and I ignored them. Sometimes I think that I should just leave and try and get on with my life but we have a child and it makes leaving hard.

I am just so confused that I don't know what to do. Sometimes I have had opportunities to cheat but I never did because I loved her and I didn't want to hurt her. She was going through some rough times with her family and became depressed and I wasn't there for her but this doesn't give her an excuse.

Kevin:

One of the first things that attracted to me to my wife was her ambition and independence. It didn't hurt that she was extremely attractive, but there was more to her than just physical beauty. She was determined to get through college and reach a variety of goals through her own hard work, and I found her determined spirit adorable.

We worked at the same company, in different departments, and we dated for several years. In the time we dated, we only broke up once, and this because she was eager to get married and I wasn't prepared to yet. After three months apart, we got back together and decided to make the ultimate commitment. I was certain that we were going to be together forever.

We were married just short of three years, and I thought everything was perfect. We didn't start having problems until she began working with a divorcee who spent most of her evenings picking up men in bars and taking them home with her. This woman became her newest confidant and role model, and soon, they were hitting all the bars after work and she wasn't making it home until at least four a.m.

I confronted her, and things got back to normal for a while, but eventually, she was back to the bar scene, and I was at home worried about her.

We had one session of marriage counseling, but she stormed out after fifteen minutes because our counselor got confrontational with her about her behavior. We had ups and downs, and during a peaceful period, I came home from work to the announcement that she wanted a divorce.

We were still working out the details and trying to decide if we would stay together or just get separated, so I moved out and continued to pay her bills.

Once, I came back to our old house to pick up some of my things and found her under a blanket, "watching a movie" with a guy that she has known since high school. A few weeks later, one of my co-workers called to tell me that he was in a bar and could see my wife in a booth with some strange guy all over her.

Within a few weeks, she was calling again to see if I wanted to get back together. She even held out until the day our divorce became official and called me to see if I'd reconsider our decision. A week after the divorce, the guy from high school moved in with her and lasted six months before she kicked him out to marry her best friend's ex-husband.

Today, I am remarried to a wonderful woman. At first, I was hesitant to trust someone again, but we have a lot more in common than I ever did with my first wife, and my devotion does not go unreciprocated.

Being angry or bitter wouldn't serve any real purpose in my life. I'm happy now, and I'm glad I was lucky enough to move on.

Greg:

I was so happily married. Just going on five years, and so many exciting times and places already behind us. Our new business was struggling, but the customers loved us, and the daily cash register receipts increased steadily.

My wife was so beautiful, so smart and so lovely. Her smile lit the room, and the fire in my heart for her. I believed in my heart that the feelings of love, respect and honor were mutual.

I was so wrong. So wrong. I knew I was wrong when I saw her pose for a seemingly innocent picture with another man, one of our employees. I watched the way she gave him a kiss on the cheek -- her eyes were half-lidded, her body pressed against his, and a look of complete happiness and love on her face. In that instant of the shutter-click, I realized that she was giving him more attention that she had been giving to me. I felt weak, drawn and scared in that shutter-click instant.

Things fell to pieces after that, for sure. I asked my wife about the physical contact paid to him and not me, and she laughed it off -- but I saw in her eyes that she was caught. A couple of nights later, I came out of my office to find the both of them drunk. The store was closed, and they had been into the liquor inventory for awhile.

I fired him on the spot, and much to my open-jawed dismay, she ran after him -- slamming the door on our marriage.

I saw her two days later, and she said our marriage was over and that she was moving in with him. I didn't know where or who she was anymore, and I was in a sad, sad state of affairs. I couldn't concentrate on the business at all -- it was all I could do to keep from just walking away. Just keep walking and walking and walking until I died of heartbreak. I didn't care about anything anymore.

I shut the business down and took incredible financial losses. Did the money and business matter anymore? No. I wasn't in the game anymore. I was a broken man. All the love and all the laughter was a lie.

She was so cold and efficient in those last few days of our marriage. No remorse, no apologies -- just a matter-of-fact methodology. This is the way it is, and that's that. How painful and confusing for me -- it was all a blur of wretched memories and venomous emotions.

Finally, I decided to leave town, so I bought a van, loaded it with some stuff and drove it two-thousand miles before I came to a stop. Life is rich, and God plays hard with those that he loves.

Harrison:

Yes, my wife has cheated with her old lover, my stepdaughter's father. It hurts but you know there was a reason we have been together all these years and he is always trying to get back in. This time she said he really has changed so I told her go on back; she has done this three times since we have been together and his true colors always come out but this time I am finished.

How will this will work again? And can somebody keep going back expecting things to work? Is this insanity or what? Should I just let her go because I control my destiny and I am content with or without her because I love myself and I am true to myself. I am not selfish or self-centered just an easygoing guy who has learned a lot the hard way.

Cassie:

For 11 years I have been married to a man I do not love. When I met my husband I was a single mother to two young children. He seemed safe and dependable, something that my children's father did not offer. We moved in together a year after we met. It looked good on paper. We had the same taste in music and the same core values. Soon after I moved in I found that my husband cheated on me. He did this a couple of times.

I forgave him due to the fact that I wanted the children to have stability. After all, I knew it could be worse. I felt my needs were secondary to providing my children with a good life. I was blind to my husband's distance and put up with lies for the sake of stability. We had our ups and downs. I had health and career concerns all without my husband's interest. He turned a blind eye.

My former brother-in-law and I had always been good friends. I cared for and respected him. He just brought me comfort with his words and presence. I tried for years not to think of him in a sexual sense due to obvious complications.

I knew him as a friend years before I met my ex-husband, his brother. He was a friend through my first divorce. We were just best friends. The attraction grew stronger over the years. He listened in the bad times and shared the good. We had seen each other at our worst and at our best.

I knew my feelings for him were growing as each year went by but tried to deny them until the day came that I had enough of my husband's distance. I admit I made a mistake. I remember trying to talk to him again and once again he turned away. I turned to him and said that I was so done.

I picked up the phone and made a call. It was to my ex-brother-in-law. He was moving and had some things that he wanted to give to the children. I told him I would come to where he lived and help. I knew at that time what I had planned.

I remember walking into his house as I often did and everything being the same. We talked for a while. He went to his bedroom and began going through his things. I walked in and smiled. I sat on his bed and chatted as I often did. He sat down beside me. I started to spill my heart out and talked and cried. Then we began to hold each other and found ourselves making love.

It was amazing. I really feel it was the first time I actually made love to another person. We shared our bodies and our souls. From that moment on I visited often.

We tried to stop. We swore this could not go on. We even ended it for a few months. We tried to carry on as before but knew our feelings were more intense.

It all started up again the day before he left. I stopped in to pick up some things for my children. He went to give me a hug goodbye and somehow we found ourselves taking comfort in each other's arms. I knew I loved him and hoped with time apart it would fade. A couple of months later he came home and we have spent every possible free weekend together.

I separated from my husband and we still go back and forth about leaving the relationship. We think how something like this will affect the children. We both love them so much. He has been their major male role model for years.

Neither of us ever wanted this to happen, but we now find ourselves truly in love and do not know how to walk away from that. I wish I had never started it in some ways, but am glad that if I end this for the children that I have known love and connection like this. I just feel that I gave up a good friendship for complications and heartache for others. We can never be the same again.

Lily:

I have decided to share my story here because I need to vent. I have no one else to talk to about this because I have lost my family as a result of my affair.

This morning I received a hate mail from my daughter; I couldn't even bear to read it entirely so I deleted it after reading the first paragraph. Last week I wrote to her and once again tried to explain my position, but to no avail. My family has found me guilty as charged, and I have received a life sentence of alienation.

This story begins way, way back. From birth I would say. I was born very shy. On top of that my parents became alcoholics, were divorced, and had poor parenting skills to say the least. I was also sexually abused for several years. All in all I experienced not so good a childhood, like about 25% of the population.

I hated school, just couldn't stand being in groups of people, so most of the time I didn't go and I was eventually asked not to return because of my truancy.

A high school friend introduced me to my husband. He had just broken off with a girl because she was pregnant. I believe the parents put an end to it. Anyway he made quite an impression on me and I fell in love. He wanted sex right away but I put him off until he told me he would end the relationship if I wouldn't have sex. He said he needed it. I was sixteen. I gave in because I didn't want to lose him. Then I spent the next 30 years giving in because I didn't want to lose him. But the thing is, I never had him.

He had sex with others just before we were married, and for the many years after. I have no idea how often, but I found out about several of them and did nothing.

After so many years I was pretty numb. Between my parents and my husband I felt pretty unimportant. I put on my best face at work. I didn't want anyone to know what was going on inside.

Then I became good friends with a male co-worker. The friendship led to an affair. After nearly 30 years of being completely faithful I decided that if it was okay for my husband to do, then it was okay for me to do. That was three years ago.

The other man was younger than me so when my husband found out it hit him hard. I had not only cheated on him, but I did so with a younger man. We went back and forth for a while, trying to save our marriage. But it didn't work because he became abusive, and I couldn't live with that.

I was also seeing him in a different light. I saw how manipulative he was at winning people over so that they would believe him when he was lying. He was like an actor. That is why he had me convinced for so many years that his cheating was my fault.

The marriage is over now and we are divorced. He has the house, the furniture, and mental custody of our adult children. He has the children convinced that I am crazy, a whore, no good white trash. I tried to carry on a relationship with them, but I have now given up.

I am going to try to move on and start over. I wish my life had been different, but you can't change the past. We make the best decisions we can we the information and experience we have. Unfortunately I just didn't have enough.

My message to other women is that if you have a man who cheats, get out of the relationship immediately. Because if he cheats, then he also lies and steals. He will do all of those things to you, if he has to, in order to fulfill his own needs, wants, and desires . These kinds of people do not need a relationship; they just want a person, any person, for self-fulfillment.

Camellia:

By the age of 25, no one expects to be looking at a second failed marriage. But, that's exactly the scenario I was facing. Three years into my second marriage, the words "I don't want to be married anymore" were flowing from my then-husband's lips.

This phrase haunted me as I searched for ways to salvage the young marriage, but he wasn't budging. He was back in his old stomping grounds, where his old classmates were still single and partying, and he wanted to be part of that action.

Money was the thing keeping us together at that point. Neither he nor I could really afford to move out quickly, not with the cost of living being so high in the city. So, for months, I lived under the same roof as the man I'd married, hoping for some happiness to return into "our" lives. It didn't. Just more emotional abuse, until at last, I was so beaten down that all it took was a friendly gesture from a member of the opposite sex to lift me up. That gesture came from one of his friends visiting from another city.

When my husband introduced me to "Steve," there was instant chemistry – we couldn't deny it or each other. He was warm, thoughtful and listened without interruption. Steve was just as my husband had once been, and I had been longing for the return of that person I fell in love with in vain. Yet with the entrance of Steve, I felt hope again and alive again.

It didn't take long before Steve and I began talking on the phone secretly, and eventually, we met privately. I was petrified and excited at the same time, drinking to keep my nerves in check. Several drinks later, I was ready to cross the line from borderline affair to full-fledge adultery. That night, Steve and I made love for the first time. Afterward, I spent an hour crying and throwing up in the bathroom as Steve tried his best to soothe me and assure me his feelings of love toward me were genuine.

Over the following weeks, I made excuses to see a girlfriend of mine who lived in the same city as Steve just so he and I could be together. My husband never suspected a thing. After all, his interest wasn't in me, it was in getting a divorce and being single again like his friends. And before long, I found a place that I could afford and moved out. He was glad to see me go, and with the recent reemergence of positive emotions, it didn't devastate me as much as I thought it would.

As they say, "absence makes the heart grow fonder," and it applied with my husband's feelings toward me after I moved out. Within weeks of my moving out, he was making efforts to get me back. But time had changed things. Now, it was me who was no longer sure if I wanted to be married.

Steve and I were getting along famously, and he'd even asked if I would move to the city to be with him. I said I still needed time. He was so supportive and understanding as I battled my conscience and my fears of being divorced again. He didn't push, but gave me time to decide what course I should travel.

It turned out that time really wasn't on my side. Another one of my husband's friends found out about Steve and me, and couldn't wait to let him in on the news.

After hearing of my relations with Steve, my husband drove over to my place and stormed inside. He called me every name in the book, and then some. I cried and cried, and begged for his forgiveness but to no avail. He couldn't bear the idea of his wife being with another man. I couldn't stand to see him in seemingly so much pain, so I called off my relationship with Steve. He didn't take that well at all.

We tried to reconcile, but his pride got the better of him, and us. And over time, he began to twist events, saying it was my affair that ruined our marriage. I tried and tried, begged and pleaded for him to understand that my relationship with Steve wasn't the catalyst for our split.

He wouldn't listen, even though I was the one who fought for our marriage when we lived together. Eventually, after enough abuse, and coming to the realization that there are times when a person doesn't fall into the arms of someone other than their spouse, they're pushed, I said "enough."

The revelation of my affair didn't end the marriage. It was already dead before then; I just didn't know it until too late. The lesson learned from my affair I carry with me to this day: Learn to recognize the beginning of the end before the end is upon you.

Marla:

I married a man who was simply not into sex. He would tell me I turned him on, he could be a great kisser when he wanted to be, yet when it came down to our getting into bed, he was a wet rag. Unfortunately, wet rags do not make sufficient boners. He was well intentioned and that was it as far as our romantic, sexual life went. I considered sex a pretty sacred affair, something I didn't want to live without. So I looked elsewhere.

I wasn't purposely looking for a guy, but when one made himself available where I worked, I didn't pass up the opportunity. His appearance turned me on. His eyes were sparkling, he had a great smile and I liked the deep sound of his confident laugh.

When he asked me if I wanted to go home with him after a few drinks after work one night I just looked at him kind of funny and said, sure. Somehow I knew he'd be a good lover and he didn't disappoint me.

When I went back home, my husband suspected something, yet he didn't say a word. I think he realized he could not satisfy me in that arena and didn't even want to attempt to. The funny thing was, I think in the long run I may have been hurting more; not only did I hurt myself, by my betrayal, I hurt my husband and weakened his trust in me.

When I began actually having conversations with my lover, I realized we had almost nothing in common, and I noticed that his organ wasn't getting hard when we were together, either. One evening as we sat together on his couch, I actually, for the first time, saw how fat he was and heard how all he could talk about was his ex-wife. Shortly afterward, I wished him good luck and walked out the door.

I went home to my husband, we never talked about it, and as disappointed as I was in our lovemaking, I was more disappointed in my former lover and mostly disappointed in myself.

Like most great things, my sneaking out of the house had to end. The next day I armed myself, determined to turn our relationship around: with a negligee, a book on lovemaking for dummies, various sex toys and for me only, "the world's most incredible dildo" that I snuck into my bedside drawer. It was my new secret lover. I decided that we had at the least, a good friendship thing going. And that was sacred in itself.

Tilly:
I was an adulteress in my marriage. I wish I could go back and change it. We've divorced since then, and yes, what I did was a factor, but perhaps not the way you might expect.

He was more than willing to work towards forgiveness, I couldn't though. I knew, in my heart and my soul that I had destroyed the sanctity of our marriage. The trust, the sacred union, it was gone forever, and I still can't forgive myself.

My choice to do what I did destroyed our lives together, and robbed my children of a life in a home with two parents. I don't want to whine and snivel about WHY I did it, because, regardless of the reasons I may find to justify it, the fact is, I made the choice to do it and I did it.

I look at our kids now, and the troubles they've faced, and I wonder if those troubles would not have existed if they had been raised in a home with Mom and Dad.

Deandra:
Married for 13 years and four children later, I found myself becoming very attracted to my family therapist. I often spoke to him about the children and the inconsistant parenting styles my spouse and I shared. I explained the frustrations I had with living in a lifestyle which moved us around alot.

I discussed my lack of sexuality and attraction to my spouse and the marriage counselling which we had already been through. I discussed my fantasies and sexual needs. It was something which I had never spoken to anyone about, not even my girlfriends.

Each meeting I became more and more excited and looked forward to making my therapist squirm. Despite the age difference between us, I had a strong desire to seduce him. My days were lost with the thoughts of how I would do it, he was in my mind.

He was a great conversationalist, he had common interests, he was fit, unmarried, attractive, had a nice voice with a pair of lips which drove me wild when they moved. I found myself teasing him with tantalizing tidbits of happenings of my girlfriends and I out on the town.

I often squirmed in my seat and blushed when talking. I was always the good girl with all the morals and everyone had trust and faith in everything I was. I was doing the biggest no no and it was exciting.

My last appointment, I planned to arrive and ask for the appointments to end that day. I then felt it was necessary to tell him in all fairness exactly why. The hour seemed to drag on forever. The blood surged through my veins. My breathing was rapid and I was horny. It was a thrill to be this excited again, and so turned on by my out-of-character behavior.

I sat quietly in the waiting room, pretending to read the morning paper. I couldn't eat breakfast because of the level of nervousness and fear for the actions I contemplated. My name was called from around the corner.

I followed him into his office. He sat, I sat, we chatted about the weather and how the day was looking and then I stated my reasons for the day's appointment. I explained my reasons to cancel any other appointments I had scheduled for the following weeks. I then asked him if I could be frank with him and tell him I was feeling attracted to him and fantasized about us together.

I told him explicit details and told him I was masturbating nightly thinking about him touching me and him deep inside me. He was shocked... and flattered. I asked if I could give him a kiss before leaving... he hesitated... and I leaned forward grabbing him by his tie... pressing my lips hard and long onto his.

I was hot and wet for this guy. I told him I had to follow through on what it would be like to kiss my fantasy. He was dumbfounded. He asked me if I wanted to talk about this. I told him all I want to do right now is RUN!

I left... and he watched me all the way out the door to my vehicle. I calmly drove away out of sight. I then screamed "Oh my God!" What have I done? Then I began to realize I did it! I was proud! I was thrilled.

Weeks passed and I was high, as high as the day I stole the kiss! Three or so weeks had passed when I received a call from him asking if I was okay. I told him better now than I have been in a long time. He asked if I felt there was anything I would like to talk to him about. There was. I met him in a coffee shop.

We spoke of the passing weeks... and I discussed my increased passions for him and my desire to be with him. He told me he too was attracted to me and was impressed with my tactful way of ending the sessions.

I then told him I wanted to be with him and wanted him deep inside of me. I expressed my insane feelings of desire to be with him. We planned to meet. We did. For two weeks straight we were intimate... we shared an intense beautiful lovemaking. I had experienced an awesome growth in my life. It was amazing! I would never take any of it back.

I ended it with tears after our last night together. It was sad but I knew it had to end. The sadness was terrible. It was necessary to have it end.

We speak today as if we are old friends. We talk today about the times three years ago. We save them for our conversations only. It's a wonderful memory!

P.S.: I told my husband I had an affair. I didn't tell him with whom. I was hoping it was something that would end our marriage. It didn't. I believe I will stay until the youngest is on his own. It's a sacrifice I am willing to make. I do not have the courage to end my marriage.

Valerie:

At the time I met and dated my lover, my husband and I had already been dating for two years and because I was only 20, I wanted to be sure that I was ready for a serious relationship and if so I wanted to be sure that it would be with him so I told him we needed a break.

After our breakup I didn't date many guys, but a few months into the breakup I met this one in particular and I liked him a lot. The catch with him was he had a girlfriend and I came to the conclusion that everybody generally has somebody and I appreciated his honesty but I had to be careful not to get too emotionally attached to him as I wasn't sure if he was just a dog looking for a bone or whether he really was having some problems in his relationship like he said and was looking for an outlet.

As much as I wanted to, I was afraid that if I had sex with him, that he wouldn't take me seriously and even if he and his girlfriend did break up, he wouldn't respect me and more than likely would eventually do me the same way. I made certain not to have sex with him until I knew him better and felt the time was right.

He wasn't sure that I was being totally honest with him in regards to my whereabouts and was not sure if he could completely trust me because of my age and because he couldn't believe an unattached, young, attractive, woman like myself would be tied down to just one person who she wasn't even seriously involved with. So, due to some issues we were having communicating we stopped seeing each other. I really felt bad about it and I wanted to call but my pride wouldn't let me.

About 2 weeks after our "thing" ended my boyfriend at the time and I got back together. However I always thought about this guy and what could've been and often times I wished that I could talk to him and start over. He called me a few times months later, but because I was pregnant I had to accept the fact that we could never be. We had cordial conversation but I pretty much let him know that I was going on with my life and that it wouldn't be a good idea for us to keep in touch. That still did not take away my could've should've and would'ves.

I still thought of him a lot and hoped our paths would somehow cross again. It happened when I was out with a girlfriend and she linked up with a guy who actually worked with this other guy. There was an exchange of telephone numbers and when he called me, we talked for hours.

He had gotten married and he caught me up on some things that had been going on with him and vice versa. Later that afternoon we met for drinks. We both confided in each other that our relationship ended prematurely and that we often thought of each other and cared a great deal for one another in such a short period of time.

When it was time to go, I didn't want to let him go. I asked him if he would like to get a room so that we could finish some unsettled business. Shocked, he did. And I made love to him like I had with no other man. Not even my husband. I let him do everything to me that he could think of. Even though he was older, I was more sexually experienced and he said I was the best woman that he had ever been with.

I have developed strong feelings for him and I feel those feelings are reciprocated. I know that we could probably never be. The odds are against us and I have to think this way so that I don't build false hopes of us leaving our spouses to live happily ever after with each other only to have them shattered because there is so much much more to that scenario than one would imagine.

We have great sex. Uninhibited, passionately erotic sex. True, it has taken away the desire for me to want to be with my husband but I manage to perform my duties consistent enough so that he will be satisfied. As for my lover, he and his wife don't have a sex life but he has all he needs in me.

We've done a good job so far, keeping it a secret... the key is not going outside of the normal routine. No coming home late from work. If I need to be with him, I make certain it's between normal business hours even if this means I have to take the day off making certain that he knows I have to attend an off-site training class or if I schedule to leave early for work then he knows I have a few late afternoon meetings. We have planned a few weekend getaways for the summer and are now plotting and planning months ahead so that we may prepare our spouses way ahead of time so not to give way to suspicion.

I don't know what's going to happen and I don't know how long it will continue to go on, but I do know that I don't have any intentions on ending this affair anytime soon.

Kathy:

The phone rang. Once again, I heard Bob's voice and started to feel the excitement. He worked in the media and had a deep, powerful tone that was not only his bread and butter, but extremely sexy. Over the next three months, as I waited for a job offer, he and I had intense phone sex and conversations. He knew my marriage was falling apart. I knew it, too, but had trouble admitting it, even as I was committing a milder form of adultery each time I spoke to Bob on the phone.

Then the call came that would change my life. A job interview that would mean I'd be seeing Bob again. We both were probably aware deep down what we knew we were going to do. I was on the verge of asking my husband for a divorce, but needed something or someone to push me over the edge.

Jump ahead a few weeks and after a day of interviewing, I met up with Bob and his buddies at a martini bar. As we drank, we get looser and looser. After months of intimate phone contact and feeling alone in my marriage for the past two years, I decided to just take the plunge. I told Bob I wanted to make love. He didn't protest. Minutes later we were in a cab and headed to his tiny apartment.

We not only made love, we made love all night—I distinctly remember hearing birds chirp as I fell asleep in his arms. It was the first time in two years I felt peaceful inside and felt love for a man again. I knew I was going to have to get a divorce.

I got back on the airplane, headed home and waited for a job offer which came in short order. What I didn't expect was four weeks later—a skipped period and subsequent pregnancy from our one-night encounter. We made the decision to terminate the pregnancy, what with a divorce on the brink, a forbidden love affair, adultery and me moving and starting a new job. Even worse, my husband believed the child was his (strange, since we hadn't made love in a year!)

Our love has held strong since this all happened—my husband and I divorced and now I'm married to Bob! Happy endings are possible, even in the face of betrayal prompted by loneliness. I think falling in love with Bob accelerated the rate at which I was finally willing to recognize that my marriage wasn't working. We were in marriage counseling for months fighting to save it but after getting together with Bob, that was the end of our marriage.

As for my ex, he later admitted to me he realized he was gay. I had suspected it when I caught him in a gay Internet chat room but he had admantly denied it at the time, saying that he was there out of curiosity only.

Diane:

My ex-husband and I were divorced this year. I still feel tremendous loss and sorrow. We were married almost 25 years and have three teenaged kids. I feel sadness about how this has affected them and feel responsible for creating the beginning of the end.

My husband was emotionally distant. He abused alcohol and pot and was abusive to me too. He was a workaholic and had little time left for me. I put up with a lot because he provided financial security and I didn't want to disrupt the family. He may have been emotionally abusive but he didn't go out on me. He always held it over my head that he was faithful. We had sexual closeness and I have some memories of romance but they didn't translate into our daily life. Most of the time I felt alone and disconnected.

I became the betrayer and I met many people who were more than willing to satisfy my loneliness for a night or two. I thought I could survive if I had some outlet where I felt sexually attractive and listened to. It wasn't as much about the sex. Actually the sex was secondary to the feeling I craved of feeling connected. Even to a stranger.

I met a man who had an open relationship with his wife. I had known him serveral years and fell in love with him but accepted he was married and we were in different states. I would see him off and on during the early part of my marriage.

More than 10 years ago my husband read my journal. I had written about my secret love and it devastated him. He never was able to forgive me. It was constantly being brought up and thrown in my face. Trust was gone forever. His ego was damaged beyond repair. We were in therapy for awhile because I really wanted things to work out for us. It held us together for a few months.

After counseling I never communciated with the ex-lover again. It didn't really matter. My life became a series of doubts and accusations. I could never win back my husband's trust and his controlling abusive behavior continued.

A year ago, I had checked out emotionally and I had another affair. Brief and so destructive, I wrote about it in my journal. I knew if he saw my journal it would be incriminating but, but I didn't care. I didn't want to suppress my journaling even though I knew he would snoop. He did, which was a violation. But, he confronted me and I told him I wanted a change.

I wanted him to deal with his anger and his addictive behavior. I wanted emotional closeness. I wanted to feel love and demonstrate that love to our children. I wanted to feel healthy and show them what a healthy relationship looks like. I wanted our kids to see me happy and not stressed all the time.

Since that time, my affair was the whole topic of discussion. That was why we were divorced. He has made it a convenient reason that no one could argue with. It took away from all the reasons I had for wanting change. He filed for divorce and hasn't stopped paying me back since. I feel sorrow and regret. I feel loss and I know the kids (who live with him) see me as the enemy. The whole divorce has been my burden.

I believe I made a huge mistake by turning to other people to satisfy my needs. My emotional needs were important and I felt such a distance in our marriage. I wanted to feel secure and loved and turned to strangers to make me feel better. I don't believe in infidelity. I think loss of trust was a death blow to our marriage. I did it though, because I didn't want to give up what I had.

I didn't want to ask for a divorce years ago. I kept thinking maybe something would change but it didn't. The further along I got, the harder it was to live a lie. I felt confusion about what was love. I grew up in a chaotic dysfunctional home and now I was reliving my own sad childhood. I was becoming the poor role model I said I didn't want to be. I wanted to be real and present and happy.

My ex has made it a point to take his new girlfriends to exotic places. I feel as if he is courting women in ways that he couldn't court me. If pay back is hell... I get it. I mention certain aspects of how this hurts me, but he will hang up on me or in a gloating way tell me how he has moved on. He has, too.

So, I was afraid to ask for what I wanted. I went out on him to get even or find solace but he has used it against me. This has taken the focus off him needing to change and places the blame on me... the adulteress.

I regret what I did. I'm sorry for going against what I believe in. Truth, honesty, respect, communication... it caused me to lose myself and head down a self destructive path.

I would hope that in my future relationships, I can learn how to be true to myself and treat others with respect instead of contempt. I will chose people who are safe to communicate with and won't get angry. I think about how I want my children to see me and what I wish for them. I wouldn't want them to stay in a bad relationship and I wouldn't want them to betray their partner.

I would like to convey that dishonesty cost me years of anguish. How I ended this relationship feels incomplete. I guess the love feelings I have for my ex-husband would be less intense if I had done things in a more compassionate way. I could have maintained my integrity because I became someone I didn't know. Lying and cheating don't go well with trying to find truth and love.

When I was in the midst of my affairs I would justify my actions and find temporary pleasure. It didn't last long. I like having one partner and feeling connected.

Anyone I talk to about affairs, I assure them that affairs are destructive if you don't have an open marriage. I hope I can help someone else. I wanted to tell my story.

Rachel:

My husband and I had the most perfect relationship. We worked hard as a young couple and started a business. It became very successful and we were very blessed. Our business took a lot from our personal life and things began to change.

I changed. I met this married guy when we started our business and I thought he was very good looking. Everyone joked about him being "my boyfriend." It started out as only a joke.

One day the opportunity came to me to call him. I began to call him on a daily basis. We talked more than my husband and I.

Eventually we slept together. I was not proud, so I called it to a halt. Weeks later I called him back because I missed talking to him. We met again. Three years later, this was out of control.

I never stopped loving my husband, nor my child or life. Somehow, I felt that I was already guilty and was "too far in" to stop. My husband traced my cell phone bill and caught us! I could not imagine my life creating such turmoil in so many other peoples' lives. We are in a living hell at this time.

It has been four months after the truth has been revealed. My husband can say that he still loves me and can't ask enough questions. I'm not sure that we'll ever understand or ever have the answers. It hurts more than the betrayal was worth.

Please, if you have not had an affair, and may be thinking about it, think again. Don't do it. Leave your spouse before you hurt them as I have hurt my husband.

Communication is so important in a lasting marriage. There should be nothing that you can't talk to your spouse about. Grab him and shake him if he doesn't want to listen. Take it from me, please!! It hurts like nothing else. I have learned a great deal from this infidelity.

Find yourself and form a relationship with God. If you think you need anyone else other than your spouse, then you probably need to go to church. Love one another and be honest to yourself.

Stephanie:
It's been just about two years now. I was married two months before anything happened. We went out for a few drinks. His eyes drew me in. He is a very handsome man. The first night we were out for drinks I knew there was something special. We stopped at his house so I could use the bathroom and we had a few beers there. We talked and then he kissed me. I told him I had to go home and that was the end of that night.

Over and over we have gone out. We have learned everything about each other. His lives with his ex-wife although they live as if they are still married. He is still in love with his ex-girlfriend who broke up their marriage and then there is me. I have meet the wife and I also know the ex-girlfriend. They both are very jealous of me.

My husband and I have hung out with this man and his (ex) wife. We are so good about not showing our feelings. We say we are very good friends, but we make love, go out to lunch, sometimes have sex at lunch, and hang out after work. When we are together we can hardly look at each other in the eyes because when we do it's like something hits us and we become so attracted to each other.

Our relationship (sexually) was on hold while I was pregnant (with my husband's child). A month or so after the baby was born we were lovers again. Friendship was there the whole time I was pregnant.

We get upset when another (new) person lays eyes on the other. Every detail going back to our childhood we know about each other, like we have known each other our whole lives. Sometimes we joke and say maybe we are from the same womb. I don't know if we are in love or just very good friends but neither of us is about to let the other go.

Angelica:

I was married at 18 years of age with very little sexual experience and no real sex education. Six months after my marriage my husband enlisted in the military. Six months later he was sent overseas. I got a job as a waitress in a truck stop so we could have money when my husband returned home.

I mostly worked the late night shift. I often had a coffee break with the service bay's employees, one of whom was an older black man who was very friendly and I felt I could confide to him my loneliness and my missing having sex.

One evening after we got off our shift he asked me if I would like to go park on a site overlooking the city and see the beautiful city lights. We parked and we had a conversation about me being lonely and he made an advance to me I didn't resist.

Soon we were what some call making out. I was still on birth control but I didn't want to take a chance so I told him no sex without a condom. He said that was no problim as he had some in the glovebox. We had sex twice that night in the back seat of his car.

The affair continued the entire time my husband was overseas. It happened several times after my husband was home and out with his friends. I have cheated on my husband many times but always with black men. So far I have gotten away with it.

Andrea:

I have been with my husband 17 years, I moved in with him when I was 15. I have now been with him more than half my life. I love him more than anything, and he is my soul mate.

But, something is missing although I'm not sure what. I have cheated on him several times and I once left him for a guy who promised me greener grass on the other side. Trust me people... the grass isn't always greener on the other side!

I was lucky enough for my husband to take me back after two years! We are happily together raising our boys, but that something is still missing. So I still cheat!

I feel you can love your partner even if you cheat! I know a lot of you have and do. You know computers have a refresh button, why can't we? Just practice the safe sex law!

Rhonda:

I am a mother of two kids. My husband takes good care of me. The only problem is he loves me, but is not demonstrative about it on a day to day basis. Whenever I get pregnant, we avoid sex for fear of harming the baby within. At this time my husband never communicates with me. I need some love and attention on a day to day basis and more so when I am pregnant.

My husband's brother has lived with us since we got married. First he and I were only friends. But several years back, when I was pregnant, he had a long distance relationship that left him physically and emotionally hungry. We had an affair.

From my part what was important was he cared for me, was interested in me as a woman. But both of us quite understood that he was getting married to that girl and I was not going to leave my family due to this affair. He never promised me anything, so I did not feel cheated. Then he e got a job in another state and left.

He has been married for several years now and recently my husband, myself and our kids were at his place for vacation. We did not get time together.

I had forgiven and forgotten him and myself and did not want any extra marital relationship again. I felt used, because he never once said he loved me, but always said we had special feelings for each other. During the vacation, we got only one hour together. He confessed that he still had a special place for me in his heart. He wanted to have a physical relationship with me if we ever got a chance. I refused downright.

Now he is on chat -- Instant Messenger -- every day. Sometimes he tells me that he fantasizes about me at night, sometimes we have quite normal conversations, about what I did today, where I went yesterday, etc.

I do not really mind the friendship, as I am still a bit in love with him, but I don't want to cheat on my husband. If this is exposed, then, he might not forgive me, I might not have a good relationship with my parents, in-laws, common friends, etc. My own kids will not respect me.

Darlene:

My relationship with "Tim" seemed to have a destiny of its own. We were in our mid-twenties, both enlisted in the service, and far from our respective home states. We never talked about it, but in hindsight, we were lonely for a sense of family, for emotional nurturance.

After only nine months of dating, we both professed love for each other, although my feelings for Tim waxed and waned. We married in a judge's chambers to save money. Relatively soon afterwards, Tim started calling me "stupid" and "worthless," making references to divorce during heated arguments, and he started drinking regularly.

At the time, I didn't understand what had triggered these behaviors, but I tried to play the counselor and listened to him, convincing him each time that he owed it to us to stay committed to our relationship. During his more somber moments, he sought reassurance from me that I would never leave him.

Then he started hitting me; a slap on the face, a choke-hold around my neck, a closed fist suspended in the air with a verbal threat to launch an attack. I was far too independent to want to tolerate much abuse, as I'd received enough in my own childhood with my parents.

I loved him and wanted to help him but every time he hit me, I grew angrier and more emotionally withdrawn. I started thinking that if he really loved me, he would have better control of his temper; he wouldn't tell me how stupid he thought I was.

As was typical, he blamed me for the loss of his temper. If I would just treat him like a king then he wouldn't have to hit me, he used to say. Soon, our love-making decreased and when we did engage in sex, it was rather mechanical: fast, rough, and speechless.

Five months after our marriage, he received orders to a new unit overseas while my term in service was completed. We packed up, breezed through his home town where I met his mother and we continued on to my home town.

During that month before he was to report to his new unit, I talked to him often about his need for counseling. I knew it wasn't my fault that he couldn't control his anger, but he seemed to be in denial. He headed overseas where he lived in the barracks until he'd secured a base home for us. After two months of separation, I booked an international flight and met my husband at the airport. He seemed happy to see me. He gave me a tour of the base that first week and showed me off to his military comrades.

During the second week, he left the country with his unit on an extended military exercise. While I missed him after he was gone, I felt an unburdening in my soul. I wouldn't have to live in fear of his next attack, of his attempts to damage my self-worth. In the furthest recesses of my mind, I had predicted that our marriage would end within five years, and with that prognosis, I no longer wanted to be his intimate lover; just a caring friend.

It felt as if he didn't care how his behavior was affecting the health of our relationship so I made a conscious decision to stop caring as well. I was the only one who would protect my heart.

Two months had passed since the time he left for his military exercise and I received only one letter from him as mail traveled slowly between bases. During that time, I met "Cindy," a married woman my age who liked to have fun and listen to music.

Neither of us had children so we often got together and talked, listened to music and discovered that we shared similar expectations for our relationships. I noticed that Cindy had a wild streak; she liked to smoke, drink and flirt with men. I found myself drawn to that behavior.

It had been months since I had been able to enjoy myself with Tim. I longed to experience again the heightened sensations of romance, seduction, and arousal. I was hungry even for the more subtle emotions of feeling wanted and cherished. Soon, we were flirting with the single men on the military base. It was not difficult for us to find an attentive male audience.

One evening, Cindy invited two of the base guards to join us for dinner. I was excited by the prospect of flirting and laughing with them and that evening we entertained them in my apartment with drinks and conversation. Although Cindy and I did not overtly express any romantic interest in either of the guys, there was heavy sexual tension in the air.

We were all full of expectations that none of us dared to act on because they knew that we were married. A couple of evenings later, we invited the men to my apartment for dinner. Again, we talked and laughed and the sexual tension was tangible. When one of the men started flirting heavily with Cindy and she responded positively, the other came on to me. When Cindy and her guy moved to the sofa to talk and kiss, I invited the other guy to my bedroom to give Cindy some privacy.

In my bedroom, I was already drunk with the desire to kiss this man, to taste forbidden fruit. Outwardly, I remained calm and talkative. Inside, I was anxious to feel him on top of me, inside me.

The knowledge of my desire scared me. Was I ready to cross the line into adultery?

Guilt surfaced as I questioned my motives for having a man in my bedroom. The thought of my husband finding out shook me back to reality. Then a new wave of desire replaced the fear and the guilt. Suddenly, he kissed me. My breathing escalated instantly and all my thoughts and fears were suspended. All I wanted was his warm mouth, his beautiful smile, the lust in his eyes. He removed my clothes and as he did, another wave of guilt surfaced.

Part of me felt ashamed and was screaming, "You can't do this to Tim." But I couldn't embarrass him by stopping things at that point. I couldn't humiliate him after his clothes were off. There was no turning back. I resigned myself then to enjoy the moment.

After the men left my apartment, Cindy and I said goodnight. I knew we both were feeling guilty and it was awkward. For the first time in her marriage, she had slept with another man as well.

We didn't see each other for a couple of days and when we got together, we talked about it and laughed nervously and hysterically about what we'd done. We got together with the two men again. This time however, we were alone in our respective apartments. My lover and I had sex for several hours and he left before the morning. After that night, we never saw each other again.

A few days later, Tim phoned for the first time and as we spoke, he started to behave suspiciously. He asked me why I sounded different, like something had changed between us. He asked me if I was sleeping with someone and I immediately denied it. He asked me if I still loved him and I lied because I no longer felt anything for him. In fact, I had decided that I would stay in our loveless marriage for the sake of financial security.

After the phone call, I became afraid that he would find out that I had had an affair. I took a non-prescription pregnancy test and vowed to live a pure life for the remainder of our separation. I wanted to be innocent again.

Within a week or two, I was on the hunt for a boost to my waning ego. On top of feeling poor self-worth, I was also feeling heavy guilt from my sexual acts with a relative stranger. I needed a panacea and I found it in another man I met on the military base who was also married. His wife was on assignment in another country and he had no children.

Unlike my first encounter, this affair progressed into a steady relationship. I was soon feeling in love and fantasized about leaving Tim for him. But it was impractical and I knew that at some point, this relationship would end. I only hoped it would end before my husband returned.

I didn't have the courage to leave Tim. After listening to him tell me that I would never survive without him, I was afraid to go it alone. I had been on my own before I'd met him, but being far from home lent credence to his argument that I would end up in poverty if I left him.

Four months into my affair, I received word that my husband's unit was returning. Without hesitation, I terminated my affair. When Tim came home, he was more than suspicious. He held me hostage in our apartment and interrogated me for several hours demanding to know who I had slept with. I was unwavering as I pleaded innocence.

Then my fear of him beating me senseless or wanting a divorce dissipated in those exhausting hours and almost surrealistically, I confessed the affair. In my attempt to win back his trust, I told all the details of my relationship that he wanted to know.

The only information that I withheld was my first affair. I couldn't let him think that I'd been a whore while he was gone. I would be nothing but tainted goods then. If my husband had any old-fashioned values, it was that his wife would be as close to virginal as he could get. He had always refused to hear about my relationships before him, even when we were dating.

His demand for the truth and my confession only did more damage to our fractured relationship. Surprisingly, he never raised a hand to me that evening. Instead, he threw books and cans of beer across the room. Then he raped me in an attempt to humiliate me. He called me a whore and as he had intercourse with me, he kept asking me if that's the way whores like it. Later, he cried most of the night and wouldn't touch me.

The next day we talked and he said that he wanted to stay married. Out of compassion and pity, I told him that I loved him and wanted to make our marriage work. I felt sorry for hurting him as I had. In my heart, I had justified my affairs with his abuse toward me. Now I felt that what I had done was far worse than his emotional and physical attacks.

We remained married for several more difficult years that were fraught with fights, threats of divorce and physical assaults where the police were involved. He now had a great weapon to use against me, that I'd cheated on him. The frequency of abuse increased and physical affection diminished.

One morning after an especially brutal night, he told me he wanted a divorce because he felt that he would kill me if we remained together. At first, out of fear and a twisted sense of commitment, I tried to persuade him to remain committed to our marriage. He was adamant about the divorce this time. After a brief attempt to dissuade him, I agreed to divorce him. Within a week, we had consulted a lawyer, signed papers and were granted a no-fault divorce. He moved out of the apartment shortly afterward.

Three weeks later, he came over to get the remainder of his belongings. I knew then that he was dating someone so I found it strange when he started begging me to take him back. He wanted to get marriage counseling and mend our relationship. I was also dating a man steadily and after painful thought, I agreed to get back together with him.

We received marriage counseling once a week for three weeks and in that time, I broke off our relationship and was talked back into it on three occasions. After our fourth counseling session, I said I needed time alone because I felt like the bond between us had been irreparably severed when he had demanded a divorce.

I was never one to go back and it had been a painful three weeks of counseling. After each session, I felt only great anger, depression, and a sense that things were beyond repair. It seemed like too much work to mend all the wrongs, especially when I felt no love for him.

After the fourth counseling session, as we sat in his apartment, I told him that I needed several months to think things over by myself. He said if I walked out the door, I was never to return. I never did.

Lana:

I have been involved with a married man for two years. When we met, I was also married. We started out as friends, consoling each other on our bad marriages. We talked a lot about our respective relationships and we found we had a lot of other things in common.

I remember the first time I actually looked him in the eye and knew that I wanted him. It came over me in a wave and has been with me ever since. I had this incredible urge to kiss him but we were in a situation where that wasn't possible. For me it was a moment in time, and I remember it still. I don't remember what he was wearing or what I was wearing, but I can remember looking into his eyes and feeling like I was seeing into his soul. I felt a connection at that moment.

Our relationship began as a purely sexual one. We agreed that we only wanted one thing from each other and that it would never become anything else. We were already friends and agreed that the friendship would continue, but we also agreed that anything else between us was simply physical. It stayed that way for a year.

I found myself slowly getting feelings for this man, but I pushed them aside because of our agreement. I eventually divorced my husband for reasons outside of the relationship I had with this man (my husband never knew about the relationship). Times have not been easy for me, but I have made it through and feel like I am a better person now that I am on my own.

Now I am stuck. Our relationship seems to have progressed somewhat. He talks more and more often of leaving his wife. Not for me, but because he is miserable in his marriage. He spoke of us living together but has backed off of that for now. I have told him that I have feelings for him but have really gotten no response.

I know that he will never divorce his wife. I know that for a fact. But I love this man now and cannot seem to extricate myself from the relationship. So I go on with everything pretty much the same as it was two years ago.

I don't know how to get out of this position that I am in. I have two choices: stay with things the way they are or stop seeing this man. I cannot stop seeing him. I have tried. Not only do I love this man, he is truly my best friend. To lose him would be like losing part of myself. If my life is dark now, it would be absolutely starless without him in it. Yet I know that this relationship is going nowhere. He will never leave his wife and he doesn't love me, he only wants a physical relationship with me. So I am stuck.

Gayle:

The other man and I knew each other from work. We didn't work in the same department, but we knew who each other was. We started talking to each other and there was a chemistry there that I haven't felt with anyone ever in my life.

My husband is a good man, loving father, devoted to me entirely. He had always worshiped the ground I walk on. The kind of devotion that I hope my children find some day. But there was just something missing and I found what was missing with this other man. Chemistry and lots of it.

We started talking, mostly in e-mails and they got progressively more steamy until we decided to make our fantasy a reality. And this was an actual decision, not a heat of the moment type thing, but a real decision to mess around.

We started out with just great passionate sex and lots of it whenever we could. It moved on to be a great friendship. He is married and I am married, both of us happy in our relationships with our spouses but missing the passion that we crave.

He and I have put an end to our affair many times. But we can't stay away from each other for very long. There is no guilt and no regrets, just friends with benefits. We are not "in love" and do not plan to ever leave our spouses for each other.

I can tell him anything and not be judged and he tells me everything without judgment from me. We e-mail daily what is going on in our lives like friends do, and are there for each other.

This affair in no way diminishes the love I have for my husband and does not affect my marriage. My husband does not know and will never know of my transgression with the other man. I am happy with my marriage and even sex with my husband is wonderful. But the other man fulfills a desire I have for passion. And the chemistry between us is something that I can not ignore.

Brenda:

I recently started a job in which I am working closely with a friend from high school. We have always had a tension between us but we went our separate ways and we are both married now.

Now that we are working togther, the tension is back. I thought that it was only me, but he admitted, in a casual conversation, that he regretted not asking me out. I was floored when he said this! I admitted that I had always wish he had.

Things are like they used to be. Well, for me at least. My marriage is suffering. A lot of the problems are both mine and my husband's fault. I still love him very much. But when I go to work, it has become very weird.

Nothing has happened. But I feel terrible for feeling this way. I don't know what to do. Should I talk to him, or to my husband?

Darlene:

I am at present nine months into a relationship with a married man. He has kids and I am also married with teenage sons. I love my husband, that is what I do not understand. I want so much for someone to shake me and stop me. I start each day intending to end it, I have ended it so many times but I always go back.

The man that I am involved with is very high up in his career, he is quiet yet so gentle and caring, we talk and talk for hours. He is 15 years older than me. I feel he fills a gap that my alcoholic, abusive father never did. I feel like I have lived my whole life with this empty space within me. When I read the accounts of wives that have been cheated on, I know how selfish I am being. I feel so trapped by my own feelings and inadequacies, I want so much to be strong enough to not need this relationship.

I have told no one of this relationship, and I feel like I will pop, it is becoming such a big secret. I have a very religious upbringing and that makes me feel even worse. I really wish someone could help me to help myself.

Lenora:

I've been seeing someone else for almost two years and sleeping with him for a year now. I've been married for over 20 years, my first and only love. He works in a high stress job, long hours and not much time for me. When he is home and not working he's drinking.

I have two almost grown kids; he is unmarried. I just can't get enough of him, but have constant feelings of wrongdoing. Tried also breaking off the relationship several times. I love this man and my husband in different ways.

My lover wants to marry me and I've been considering a life with him but have been with my husband for so long it's hard to just walk away from that. I constantly feel like I am going to explode and that I can't keep going this way but I can't bear to stop either.

Sheila:

My husband has cheated on me so many times I can't count and will not get into that and I don't care. I also have had off and on affairs, but this time it's different, I have fallen head over heels in love with my friend.

We have constantly kept in touch since we were in our teens. He's married also. Before, we would usually meet about once every two years and hit and run but this time it has been going on for a year straight. We talk every day and make plans to see each other whenever possible.

I really want to leave my husband and be with my friend. It hurts so much when we have to leave each other. Both our spouses know but they can't put their eyes or hands on us, because we are just friends. I know it's wrong, he knows it's wrong but it has been going on for so long.

Did I mention back when we were young, he was my first? He is so easy to talk to and so understanding. Fate has just dealt us both a bad hand. I know what you think and I'm sorry but I love him and besides I knew him *first*.

Debbie:

I am a married woman having an affair with a married man. We both have kids and happy families and neither one of us want to end our marriages.

We have had an ongoing affair for almost three years and meet occasionally. Mostly we feel our relationship is friends with benefits. He is the one person I can share everything with and he never judges me. And I am there for him also.

It seems to both of us our friendship is more important than the sex. But could our relationship endure as only a friendship? Yes, I think it could.

We both know each other's spouse and have been known to all hang out together sometimes. In public and around each other's spouses everything is normal, it is just when we are alone do the sparks happen. We e-mail daily and try to stay in touch as much as possible.

I love my husband with all of my heart and soul and if I were to lose him it would kill me. But this is different, the other man feels the same way about his wife.

We are both discreet and hide our feelings for each other well when around other people. Maybe he does give me something that I am not getting from home. I don't know and I have not thought that much about it. He is my friend first and my lover second.

Rita:

It all started out pretty innocently, so in the beginning of the relationship with the other man, when the emotional attachment was forming, I did not feel I was really doing anything that wrong. Just a little flirting. When I was in the thick of it, I was able to "separate" my feelings for the other man from my husband and family. This was pretty easy because I really felt that my actions had nothing to do with my husband.

What I mean is, I knew I was not acting out because of some way he treated me. I did not "blame" him for my affair. After the affair escalated, I would feel so awful for the first day after an encounter, but then the desire to see the other man again would be so strong that it would outweigh the bad feelings I had.

Then there was no guilt because all I was concerned about was when I could see him again. That part blows me away. The obsession was so intense there was really no guilt anymore. I have talked with others who say they felt the same way and are so surprised. We all thought we were pretty good people. How can you not have guilt and cheat and still be a good person?

71

So, here comes the next phase... must blame the affair on the marriage and the spouse. Something's got to justify it. And the marriage and family is what is holding me back from being with the other man. The detachment starts. Just want to be with the other man (just want my drug).

When I did feel guilt I felt so bad. I can remember one day after I had just been with the other man, I was at the grocery store. I was there all alone and in such a fog. I looked at each person in the store and thought, look at them, they are all honest people doing the right thing.

I thought, I am not honest anymore, I am deceitful. I felt so yucky. That night, I went home did the family stuff, went to bed and could not sleep. Got up at midnight and wrote a note to the other man explaining how much I did care for him but I could not do this to my family. I did not want to be this person.

If I couldn't have self-esteem, how could I be a good mother? How could I have self-esteem and do what I was doing? It was a long letter and it was painful to write, but I did feel good about it. I gave it to him the next day. This was the beginning of our on and offness. Three days later I was back with him.

Eventually, I detached so much from my family and I was such a butthead to my husband that I created an atmosphere that made me quit feeling guilty about seeking love outside the home.

I don't understand how spouses can just walk away from their kids although I can see how they don't think they want to be married. I can see how they can forget how much they really loved their spouse, but I cannot see how anyone can blow off their kids. If anything, you would think because they are doing something that is so hurtful to the family, that they would try extra hard to make it up to the children. I don't get it.

When I was contemplating divorce and I was concerned about hurting my kids, my one comforting thought was "I will always be my kids' mom, no matter what happens."

I imagine the fog is pretty thick in their heads and they are not doing the soul searching to see why they are conducting themselves so. They are going through life reacting to their situation without much thought of others. Or perhaps, they feel like they are such a bad example to their kids, the kids are better off without them.

···✦·✦·✦···

Other Women and Other Men

Who is the other woman? Is she a predatory female who prefers to "steal" another woman's husband? Is she too trusting to believe that someone who would be kind to her could also be drawing her into an adulterous relationship? Is she a betrayed wife validating her desirability by seducing another woman's husband? Is she the neighbor next door or the woman at the next desk?

Who is the other man? Does he prefer involvement with a married woman so that he won't have to "commit" to a long term relationship and the responsibilities such a relationship would bring? Or is he drawn in by a sad story and locked down by passion or the need to play rescuer?

In many of the stories that follow, the people involved are not in a threesome but rather a foursome as they are both married to other people. Some of these relationships have been going on for years, others are just starting or just ending.

Like the stories in the preceding sections, the people are real, their stories are real, but all names, places, etc., have been changed to provide anonymity.

Kristal:

Well, here is my story. I met my soul mate about a year ago. I was taking night classes and he was there, looking great not only physically but it was like looking at somebody to whom I belong. Time went by and we never said anything.

I knew he was married because he had a ring but other than that I didn't know anything about him, and it wasn't until seven months later that we talked and that is how everything started.

We looked into each other's eyes and we knew that we were supposed to be with each other for the rest of our lives. It was like looking at a stranger and asking him "Where have you been all my life?" I was waiting for him since forever but like I said, he was married.

When he met his wife she had a kid already, a little boy of three and he has taken care of him since so he is his father and I am sure he will always be because he is an excellent father. They had another kid that is now five. He lives for his kids and I admire that.

How exactly did I get involved with him? I love him very much and I know that this must sound very familiar but it is happening to me and only me. I am the one in love with him and he loves me too but my question is why there are so many people in this world so lost when it comes to love and finding a way out.

In his case the kids are the excuse, the fact that she can take the kids away from him. I know how much he loves his kids and I am sure that she does too but sometimes people can be very selfish and they become possessive and they don't want to see reality and then love becomes hate and blindness becomes the passion that one time gave them faith.

At this point I don't know what to do. I don't want to give up and I hope that he can find a way out of this whole situation and I hope that at the end it will be good for everybody. Happiness is what we all want but at what cost?

For how long do we have to wait and how much are we willing to sacrifice for somebody? Our responsibilities sometimes are heavier than our own lives; we can't carry all the weight. I just pray for guidance and I pray so I can see the truth.

Men and women can lie easily and to trust somebody you need to take a risk. I am taking the risk because I saw the truth in his eyes and I want to believe that all his story is the truth. Only time will tell if the one I believe is my soul mate will be free to be happy or if I was a fool to believe that happiness was real.

Janice:

I met this guy last year before the opening of our class. At first, I was so afraid of him because he was too old for me. He's 32 years old while I'm almost 18. He showed much respect on me that day and I was so glad because of that attitude. He asked me if he could get in touch with me and I immediately said yes. So, we've been seeing each other for three months and spent an hour or more with each other in different hotels.

I'm in love with him and I strongly believe that he feels the same way too by the way he looks into my eyes and whenever we're together, he is so sweet and all. It's just that between me and his family, I really have to take the backseat. But that's okay with me because I'm just another girl and I don't have the right to demand for his time and affection. The problem is, I'm very much in love with him but he can never be mine unless they separate.

DeeDee:

Cheating, ha! I cheated on a partner once and I am with that other person now. I am totally afraid constantly that this guy is, thinks about, or is contemplating cheating on me. I don't know where this insecurity comes from. I watched my mom be a paranoid woman

74

for years and vowed not to be like that. Here I am today acting in the same ways my mother has. Where does trust come from? How do you shut off that inner voice that says you are not good enough to have and keep a faithful man?

Instead of responding with sympathy for my problem, he becomes defensive and argumentative. He doesn't understand how scary it really is to go day to day feeling this way and knowing that it is ruining the relationship. What is a girl to do?

Delilah:

One evening when I was at home waiting to have my dinner with my family an old family friend turned up and introduced himself to us. Since he had been away for almost ten years, at first we didn't recognize him.

Surprisingly, he remembered me very well, it was at that time when our triangle relationship began. He was very good looking and he portrayed himself very well to me. I was only 22 years old, and I was yearning for love from my family and he filled in the love for me.

I knew he was married and I don't know what the attraction was that his relationship with my family become a blind spot. I have been meeting him secretly without his wife's knowledge and I have been with him for more than twenty years.

The relationship in the beginning was sweet and loving but as the years passed it changed because he wanted to maintain his first wife with him. He had three children from her and he had an operation so that he can't produce any more sperms.

Carole:

I have been the "other woman" for nearly six years. In the beginning, our attraction was so strong I assumed he would leave his wife for me. Gradually, it became clear that he was afraid to upset the balance of his moderately happy domestic life.

He has a child and adores her, which is probably the primary reason for his marital inertia. He loves his wife, but he also loves me. I am not a "home-wrecker" or a horrible person; just someone who is deeply in love with a man who doesn't seem to have quite the backbone that he should.

I no longer harbor much hope that he and I will ever walk off into the sunset together, but we still love each other very much.

In the past year or so, however, I have been struck by the lies that surround this relationship. He lies to his wife about all things concerning me (where he's going, who he'll be with, who gave him this or that item that is now in their home). I often imagine myself in her position (I was once married) and wonder how much she knows intuitively about our relationship.

When I was a wife, I had zero tolerance for cheating and my husband and I swore that if one or the other wanted to sleep with someone else, we would end the marraige.

I know that many women would prefer to turn a blind eye and hope that it passes, secure (or at least hopeful) in the knowledge that their husbands will continue to funciton outwardly as husbands (financial support, parenting duties, etc.). After six years, I have to assume that his wife is one of these women.

My heart reaches out to her and I wish I could talk with her, get to know her, figure out why she tolerates her husband's infidelity. I see how much easier it becomes for him to lie to her and I realize how little effort it would take for him to lie to me, too, whether it be now or later.

We have tried to disengage from each other several times but we cannot seem to stay away from each other. I don't like being in this position — I would love to have someone to love without reservation and who could do the same for me.

For women who suspect or know that their husbands are cheating on them, please do not focus your anger or hatred on the "other woman." She is usually the biggest loser in the deal.

Marilyn:

I was looking forward to going to my high school reunion because I wanted to catch up on old friends I hadn't seen in a lot of years. What floored me was seeing my first boyfriend after so many years! We were sitting at separate tables, and we kept looking at each other across the room and smiling. He was my first, and I was his first. We danced at the reunion to "our song."

I talked with his wife for a while, and I really liked her. She mentioned that he talks about me quite a bit, and that she had been worried prior to the reunion. I gave her the whole story about my husband and his affair, and that I look down on people who would break up marriages. I told her she had nothing to worry about, which I have to make true, and I will.

Afterward, I walked with them out to the parking lot and talked some more. They both hugged and kissed me goodbye. When his wife walked off to the car, he stayed behind and hugged me tightly, kissed me again, and said, "I love you, I always have and I always will." I'm sorry to say that in my drunken state of mind, I replied, "Me, too."

I couldn't stop thinking about him after I got home but I'm not going there, no bleeping way!! I could not do to his wife what I went through with my own husband's affair. But it still doesn't stop the thoughts of "What would have happened if I had married him and not the jerk I did marry?"

Is this how potential affairs start? I refuse to be placed in the position of "potential other woman" or "other woman" so if his wife contacts me, I don't think I will reply. It would not be fair to her. I realize that what he and I had was special, but not special enough that I would want to try again with him, not with his wife and family at sake.

This is probably how affairs start... thank God that I won't go there, no matter how my feelings might start to overwhelm me.

Angelina:

My experience began three years ago, when a mutual friend introduced me to "Steven," a married man where I work. At first, I thought nothing of him although he was a very kind man and one of the nicest people I have ever met. I would find myself going up to his desk to start conversations because he was a pleasure to talk with, and would always offer a friendly smile and conversation.

One night at a bar a bunch of us from the office met up for some drinks and dancing. Before we knew it, Steven and I were off on our own, dancing closely, laughing and having a fantastic time. Our friends noticed the attraction between us and monitored our behavior.

I clearly remember the puzzled looks in my girlfriends' faces when they saw us together. But because he never spoke of his wife, I chose to forget that this handsome new man in my life was already taken. Over the next few months we would find ourselves making plans together for lunch, and even dinner. We simply enjoyed each other's company.

Slowly, I tried to get more information from Steven regarding the status of his relationship at home. He confessed that he and his wife were having problems and that he wasn't happy. I guess I took this information and used it to my advantage.

I liked Steven. I could tell he was a great guy. I wanted him for myself and I was willing to wait for him. He was my ideal man right from the start.

It was innocent in the beginning, until one night after one of our dinners, he pulled into a parking lot on our way home. We slowly got more and more intimate as we saw more of each other. I know it killed him inside to do this to his wife. I could tell he was struggling with the fact that he was committing a sin.

It was just a matter of time before he confessed he loved me. He was still legally married at the time. I remember being completely shocked by these words as we sat at a restaurant over dinner. I did not know what to say. I did not love him because I had not let him into my heart due to the circumstances. I had not let my guard down and was skeptical of his words. He was in fact, still married and how could I trust his words.

My friends warned me against the relationship, told me I was "playing with fire... and that I would get burned." I told them it was a risk I needed to take. And so far everything was happening in my favor.

I hoped that we would be together but Steven continued to live with his wife. He moved into the basement of their home. One night he called me from his house and his wife picked up the phone and heard us speaking. She started asking questions.

A few weeks later she went through his wallet and found my license and I.D. that I had given to him to hold the night before at a bar because I didn't have a purse. It was at that moment we had a serious discussion of what he was to do. He spoke with his wife and told her that their relationship was over.

I was pleased in the sense that this proved I was right all along about Steven. It proved to my skeptical friends that I was right. He chose me in the end.

After two painful years Steven and his wife got a divorce. It ate me up inside having to wait so long for the final arrangements. I often wondered if it really was going to happen after all.

Today, Steven and I are together. We bought a house and are optimistic about our future. He is still the same kind, loving man I met three years ago. Oddly enough, Steven still has maintained contact with his ex up to this day. She has forgiven him for his adulterous acts and the two of them have remained friends.

Sheree:
I am the other woman. We are both married, both have kids, both unhappy in our current relationships. People say you shouldn't stay for the kids but that is easier said than done. We are enjoying each other and taking things one day at a time.

He is as different from my husband as I am from his wife. Right now he is the only thing keeping me sane, has been there for me when things got rough, has worried about me, has listened to me--even when I ramble--and has not condemned my opinions or found them stupid. I know this relationship cannot last forever because we are both too chicken to leave our spouses, for now, but someday, who knows.

He may not be Mr Right but he is certainly Mr Right Now. And no, I don't feel any guilt when I'm with him. We meet when it won't disturb anyone's schedule (kids, husband, wife, etc.), we Hotmail each other every weekday and also talk on the phone. Weekends are hard, especially long weekends, but, that's part of the package.

Naomi:

The year I turned 30, I took a job at a prestigious university for the summer. I had been accepted to graduate school and the summer job was one in which I could have fun and very little responsibility for the summer before I had to buckle down to my graduate studies.

I would be doing some relatively mindless tasks and still have time for social activities during the summer. However, I was quite unprepared for the type of challenges the summer job would provide. It was connected to a senior management training program and executives from all over the world were invited to attend to work, study, and socialize for a total of nine weeks. The participants in the program were all men and all but three were married but their marital status stopped none of them from flirting.

The second week before the conference ended, I had dinner with one of the men and one thing led to another and I was having an affair. He was twelve years older than I was, had been married most of his adult life and had two children.

This was totally against my moral code, but somehow it happened. At the end of the session he returned to his wife and family and I packed and headed off for graduate school. After he left, he called every morning (this was before email).

Once I was settled in at the university, he flew in to see me. When he returned home, he moved out of his house and got a small apartment. The affair was going on mostly by telephone although we did meet for my birthday.

When he got back home, we began to make arrangements for me to move to be with him. He even bought my airline ticket. Two days before I was meet him, he called and told me not to come, he couldn't go through with a divorce, he couldn't change at his age and he knew that I would grow tired of him and his small town.

I was dumbfounded and shocked, but financially this was all on him as I was now living as a graduate student. I wanted to fly to him anyway. Maybe he would have changed his mind, maybe he would see me and remember how great we were together, but I didn't go. I returned the ticket and continued with my life.

Probably I knew that some of his objections were real. We had come from very different places and we were at very different places in our lives. The sex was utterly amazing from the beginning. It was spiritual/tantric.

I regret not only not having him, for I found him wise and comforting, but also still grieve the intensity of our emotional and physical relationship.

Pearl:

I met the love of my life three years ago. We sang karaoke at the same bar and he asked me if I wanted to do a duet with him sometime. We ended up doing a lot more than singing together. He made no secret of the fact that he was married and had two small children. I had been in several bad relationships and thought that I could handle a purely sexual, "no strings attached" kind of relationship. It didn't take long though, until we were completely in love with one another.

He was not a bad man. He wasn't out on the prowl looking for someone on the side. It just wasn't like that. He was in a bad marriage. He and his wife had no communication and no love left in their marriage. He never said a bad word about her, but I heard plenty of bad words about her from other people who knew her.

She didn't love him; she had even admitted that to his best friend. She said she loved him as a friend. Now is that the way you should talk about your husband and the father of your children? But she wasn't about to go anywhere because she had it made. He did all the cleaning, most of the cooking, and was the primary caregiver to their two sons. She worked, but paid no bills. He did it all. What woman would leave that?

Once he and I started seeing each other and fell in love, he said he was going to leave her. We were together every chance we got and were constantly making plans and professing our love to one another. We took trips together. Most of his friends knew about me even if they hadn't actually met me. And most of his wife's family knew about me, if you can believe that.

Everyone that knew about us swore we were the perfect couple. We complimented each other so well. When the time finally came that he was going to leave, he decided that he couldn't do it. He said he just couldn't live without seeing his boys each and every day. As much as that hurt, I couldn't turn away from him. I decided to keep seeing him and hope he would some day change his mind.

We had been dating for a year and a half when I found out I was pregnant. I had very mixed feelings. Part of me was devastated. I thought, "How could I have let this happen?" But part of me was optimistic and thought that maybe this was what it would take to finally get him to leave his wife and be with me.

When I told him that I was carrying his child, his reaction was one of shock and disbelief. We talked about what we were going to do. I told him I wanted to have the child. He said he couldn't leave his wife. He finally came out and said that he thought it would be best if I had an abortion. I fought him on this at first, but finally gave in to his wishes.

I was scared. I had two children from a previous marriage and their father was a "dead beat dad" who was behind in child support payments. I was barely making enough to support me and my two children, and here I was pregnant with another. I was afraid that if I kept the baby (against his wishes) that he would leave me forever and I would be forced not only to support another child by myself, but to explain to all my family and friends who the father was and why he was no longer in the picture. The situation seemed hopeless.

I agreed to go through with the abortion and we went out of town so that we wouldn't risk running into anyone we knew. That was the single most horrible day of my life. I remember crying all the way to the clinic and all the way back. I can still hear the sounds and smell the smells of that place. They will forever be branded into my memory.

Afterward he took me home, and I told him to get out, and that I didn't want to ever see him again. I almost had a nervous breakdown. I was a complete basket case. I regretted the loss of our child so much, and yet I still loved him with everything I had in me.

In a little over a week, we were back seeing each other. I hated him for what he had put me through, yet I loved him so much that I just couldn't stay away from him. Three weeks after I had the abortion I started seeing someone else. I thought I could never completely get away from my lover without having someone else to hold on to.

Well, all the things that your friends warn you about with rebound relationships are true. I got in too deep, too fast, and convinced myself that I loved this man that I had known only about a month, and when he asked me to marry him, I said yes. We lived together for over a year only to call off the wedding a month before the scheduled date, and go our separate ways.

In this period of time, I never completely broke contact with the married man. To this day, I haven't completely broken contact with him. I still love him just as much today as I ever did. He has apologized many, many times for what he put me through. And he has finally owned up to the fact that, even though he loves me and I love him, it isn't right for us to see each other while he is still married to his wife. He knows he will never have the courage to leave her.

He is trying very hard (as am I) to live a Christian life and do the right thing. But although I know he is right, and that it is the right thing to do, my heart still breaks every time I think of him and how much I wish we could be together. I have given so much to this man, and he has taken even more than that.

I don't know that I will ever be able to completely give myself to another man. I am ashamed of the fact that I was once someone's mistress, and I am very untrusting of men in general. I have asked God to forgive me, but I don't think I have completely forgiven myself. I still feel used and betrayed, but I also still hold on to some small shred of hope that maybe one day he will come back to me. I just can't help myself.

I am gradually trying to get back out there and would even like to have someone in my life. But it seems almost pointless, because I feel there is no one that will ever fill the void that this man has left in my heart and in my life.

I never really knew what love was until I met him. He was so good to me. He made me feel complete. He made me feel special. He made me feel beautiful. I still love him, but I also still harbor a lot of resentment and guilt over our relationship. Time has done nothing to heal those wounds.

I would take him back today if he would have me; that is the sad thing. I have no control over myself around this man. But as much as I still love him, I wish I had never met him.

Whoever said that it is better to have loved and lost, than never to have loved at all, had obviously never loved and lost. And they certainly had never loved a married man.

Brittany:

This is my story: I'm 19 years old and I have been involved, and sort of still am, with a 33-year old married man. We are currently apart because I moved to another state to study. It started when I had been working in an office for about six months before going to college. Everyone that worked in my department were older men. They all saw me as the "baby" of the office. They thought I was cute, but they would have never thought of anything else.

There was one certain co-worker that I thought to be extremely attractive, but I would have never thought anything of it other than a passing crush. When he would come in the office to turn in his work we would talk and joke around just as friends.

One day he calls me to go to lunch just him and me and I accepted thinking this is okay we're just co-workers going to lunch everyone does it. So we go to lunch, unluckily I was all dressed down in jeans and a t-shirt which didn't help much since I had a little crush on him and I wanted to look grown up to impress him.

Then he starts to call me at the office more often than usual, and he asks me to lunch, just him and I. At first I didn't want to talk to him because I wasn't really interested in anything. I was hung up over my ex so I was still hoping for something with him. He would come to the office a lot more often, just to see me.

Then one day I was in my office working and he came up behind me to turn in his paper work, but he didn't say anything. He just stood there until I tilted my head back to see who it was, and he kissed me. I was very shocked because we were in an office where people were walking around, in and out of places.

I knew I wasn't really willing to do this because when he would ask me to lunch most of the time I would make up an excuse not to go. I guess this sparked his interest even more, and he continued to pursue me.

One day there was a meeting and he suggested that we have lunch after the meeting, and that I ride to the meeting with someone from the office and then he would take me back to the office after we had lunch. I agreed, and after the meeting I left with him and the whole way back we were making out every opportunity we had. We were talking, laughing, and of course making out some more.

We got to the place where we were going to have lunch, and we started talking about personal things that we had never discussed before. I told him about my future plans and he told me about his marriage and how it wasn't working out too well. I felt compassion for him because it seemed somewhat difficult to deal with.

Then the subject of sex came up and I told him very clearly that I was a virgin, and that I would never have sex with him. He was very surprised to hear this, and seemed okay with the idea that I wouldn't have sex with him so that made me feel comfortable, no pressure, it was just a friendly thing.

After this we began going out a lot more often, and then we started going out at night after work. We had great conversation, and it was all really good. I still didn't have any feelings for him other than as friends, although, we did make out and things would get pretty hot, but I always left him wanting more, and never giving more. This went on for about a month, then one day he suggested we rent a hotel and just chill. Of course he was looking for more than that, but I told him once again no sex and he said that was fine, so I agreed to go. When we got there we watched some TV, cuddled, then started kissing and fooling around.

Then clothes started to come off and I thought to myself "I can handle this, I'm not going to do anything I don't want to do." The problem was that I wanted to, but at the same time I didn't. After a while I told him that I didn't want to keep going so we stopped for a while, but it started up again until finally we started to have intercourse, but something in my head started screaming, "NO! NO! I can't do this."

I stopped him abruptly, got up and began putting all my clothes on. He asked me if I was okay and I said "Yes, let's just get out of here!" He got up and put on his clothes. I started ranting on how I didn't want to do this because I didn't even love him, and I was in love with someone else. He just looked at me and said "You don't love me?!" I said not really in that way. I told him that I cared about him, but that's it. He said that he loved me and he was sorry about this, and that it wouldn't happen again. He took me home and that was that.

The next day he called to see how I was doing, and to tell me he was very sorry about last night. I said it was okay, and told him I had to go. The next day I was thinking about him all day, and I thought, "what the hell I'm 18 and still a virgin, I'm just going to call him and tell him I want to see him tonight." I called him and asked him if I could see him that night. He said yes, and agreed to call me later on to see where we could meet up and at what time. I waited for him to call until finally I got a call from him that he had to babysit his kids because his wife wanted to go out. I was like "that's what I get for fooling around with married men, dammit!"

Monday came, I'm at work and he called. I told him that I wanted to see him the next day and he was surprised in a pleasant way. So the next day we met up after work and I told him "let's go to a hotel" and again he was pleasantly surprised.

Of course he knew that if I wanted to go to a hotel it was for one reason. So we spent a wonderful five hours together. At this point I began to have feelings for him in another way other than friends. We talked every night, and went out almost every night. I really started falling for him. He would come to the office and I would write him little naughty notes and put them on his paperwork for his eyes only. We would go to the back room and make out.

It was very risky because if anyone in the office found out we would both get fired. These kinds of risks made it even more attractive because it gave this kind of rush of excitement. We had the most amazing sex and then we would talk for hours, it was just wonderful.

After two months I was really falling for this guy. All I wanted was to be with him. He would give me chocolates, and sometimes he would drive an hour just to bring me lunch, and then drive back down an hour to go back to work.

Time went by so quickly and I started to change my mind about leaving, I just didn't want to leave when everything was going so great. I knew that I shouldn't just change my plans for him, especially because he was married.

I told him I didn't want him to leave his wife for me and because he has children and I don't want to be the cause for him splitting up, it wouldn't be right. I told him I loved him very much, but I was only 18 and I had a lot that I wanted to do before I settled down. He said he understood, and we agreed to enjoy the time we had left, and leave the rest to fate.

When it was time for me to leave, we had our last lunch together and we tried to make the most of it. My eyes got teary and he looked away and told me that he couldn't stand to see a woman cry. I told him that I wasn't crying, it's the light in my eyes and I blinked away the tears that were about to spill. I could see his eyes were looking teary, too.

We finished our lunch and he was quiet the whole way back to my office. On the way he gave me a gift bag and I gave him a gift, one of those calendars that you rip off the pages daily, that I wrote a quote or a memory of ours in every day of the year so that he could think of me every day, and I gave him a gold pocket watch so that he could look at it, and remember that with every passing second it would be closer to the time we would meet again.

We both thought it would be best if we didn't talk to each other much, so it wouldn't be that hard on us, but it didn't work out that way. He calls me or I call him, and we talk every day. He tells me that I'm his only stress reliever and that when he talks to me he's in a different world and that I make him laugh, and that's what he needs at the end of the day. It makes me feel good to know that I relieve his stress even when I'm so far away; all it takes is a little laughing.

I'd been gone for about a month and a half, and instead of calling him I decided to text message him. I don't know why since I'd never done it before, but that night I decided to. I sent him a naughty message, and told him that I missed him a lot.

A couple of hours later around midnight I got a call, it was him and he said "She saw the message, everything's really fucked up, and she's leaving" and then he hung up. I could not sleep the whole night; I was so worried. I called him in the morning to see what was going on.

He told me that she was yelling at him, calling him all sorts of things, and then she made him play the messages that were on his phone. Unfortunately, he told me that he keeps my messages and listens to them so the messages on there were from me and she heard a part of one and she went crazy. She took the kids, and left.

I told him to go talk to her, and see if she could forgive him, and to tell her that if not for her do it for their children. So he did, and she forgave him and told him that she'd do it for the children.

We still kept talking, but more like friends, I didn't want him to ruin his marriage over a long distance "relationship."

At spring break I called him and told him I wanted to see him. I know that it would be better if we just cut it off, but I had to see him if only one more time. I know that he was trying to be good and keep away from me, but I told him that I needed to see him one more time for closure. And so we did. I've spoken to him twice since I got back. I think he's trying to put me behind, I hope so because it's probably for the best, who knows what could happen later on. I wish I could put him behind easily, but it's not that simple.

He tells me he thinks of me often, but tries not to, and sometimes he even calls people my name by mistake. I think of him often, but I don't try not to, which I know I should. I shouldn't dwell on the past, I should look towards the future, but sometimes I can't help but smile when I think of those memories. I hope I see him in the summer even if it's just for lunch. I suppose I love to torture myself... what can I say.

Georgia:

I have been with the man I consider my "partner" for 15 months. After 12 months together I discovered he was married. I confronted him and he told me his marriage was virtually non-existant, and that they were going to separate, were merely living together for convenience. Yes, I heard all the old lines about separate beds, etc! And I guess I loved him so much I chose to believe him. Hell, I still believe him!

He encouraged me to move to another state with my children (I am divorced) to be closer to him, and here I am. Last week something must have happened, and he suddenly was telling me he might turn up on my doorstep with his belongings as the tension was too much at "home."

With welcoming arms and bucket loads of support I let him move in. He was depressed and I was there offering an ear to his troubles. I cooked and cleaned for him, even helped him with his business as he was so depressed. Then, a week later he went to work and rang me afterward from the home he shared with his wife. I thought he had told her he had moved out, but apparently not.

She has now found his credit card bill, and he said she was most upset about the jewelry purchases and other things he had bought me. He has asked me to pay him the money he spent on these gifts to alleviate her tension, and that he had to move back there for a little while until things settle a bit. (He is trying to avoid a nasty property settlement?!) He told me he wants to be with me, and we will be together when he can "fix" things at home, but in the meantime he can't contact me as much for she is keeping watch.

I know I should tell him to take a flying leap out of my life, but I love him, and I don't know what to believe anymore. I'm not a vicious, wanton woman, I'm just madly in love, and he told me too late he was married. By the time he told me I was hooked on him.

I have been trying so hard to get out, but he clings to me so tightly, says he needs me. I now know I can't go on like this, his wife has left him after "finding out" about us, yet I still "feel" her there when we are together. He doesn't seem to understand my feelings.

I love him so much, yet I know I need to leave. I am trying to find the courage, and have decided my only option is to remove myself from this city. I'm going back to my home state, and it's breaking my heart. But it's the only way I know to "get out." I haven't told him, I am just going to leave and hopefully not ever look back.

···✦··✦··✦

Virtual Love, Virtual Lies...

Modern technology has provided the adulterous mate a whole new playground to play in with literally no boundaries. Going online brings a smorgasbord of ready and willing, single and married, men and women looking for sex and love. Unsolicited email invites men and women to discover online sex beyond their wildest fantasies.

Millions of junk emails with provocative subject lines are sent randomly to email addresses in the hopes that a small percentage will be read by people seeking sex without commitment. A suspicious spouse might mistake these "spam" emails as legitimate exchanges between their spouse and a lover.

There's nothing subtle about the majority of the emails as you'll see from the ones included here. If you'd rather not read the type of filth that is sent out by adult websites you'll want to skip this chapter.

The following is an unsolicited email sent with the subject of *"Divorced and Lonely"*:

Hey there sweetie!

How are you? I'm having a great time searching for men of all sizes, shapes, and colors! I see you're interested, and I'd like to let you know a little more about me......

I'm 48, very very sexy, I love to have a good time, and I'm not interested in a serious relationship, unless of course we seem to hit it off right away. All I'm really interested in is a fun date with a good guy who will give me a little respect, and then get nasty with me in the bedroom.

Is that too much to ask? I surely don't think so. If you think you might be interested, feel free to check out my site. These are my personal pictures, you won't find them anywhere else. My personal e-mail and contact info is also there.

There's a lot more info about me there, some great pictures, and this is also the best way to get ahold of me. So check me out and see what you think, hopefully you'll be interested! I'LL MAKE IT WORTH YOUR TIME!

Have a great day, Sharon

Here is another, with the innocent subject line of: *"re: your e-mail"* that makes it appear this email is in response to an email from the recipient. The email is actually another version of the previous email from "Sharon" and it links to the same website in "her" email:

Hey what's up?

My buddies and I wanted to build a website dedicated to M.I.LF's. You know what MILF's are, right? Mothers I'd Like to Fuck! We're talking sexy, older babes that you'd give your left nut to fuck. We're just average guys but we had an idea, a little cash and a camera.

We went on a search of sexy M.I.L.F.'s that needed cock. You know, the type that are neglected by their husbands. We hit the supermarkets, shopping malls, playgrounds, beach, anywhere we could find some sexy mom's that we could talk into having sex with us on camera.

You know what? It was a HUGE success! I couldn't believe what these sexy mom's were willing to do. It didn't even take cash, they just needed to be sweet talked and told how hot they were. They were almost begging for our cocks! These ladies are all married and have kids but they still are hotties! We couldn't believe our success.

After seducing more M.I.L.F.'s than I can count we started building our website dedicated to sexy moms everywhere. Here normal guys like you and I could worship these beauties and watch their hardcore exploits. Come and check out our work. We have countless M.I.L.F.'s in every pose imagineable. Each M.I.L.F. has a complete photo gallery plus hardcore fuck videos. Watch them suck our cocks, take it in the ass and get fucked silly. This site was so much fun to build we want to share it with you!

Don't believe me? Come and check it out and watch our FREE movie samples. That's right, watch us seduce these M.I.L.F.'s for free. You will be as addicted as we are.

You won't be disappointed. We are updating constantly, now all of our friends are on the hunt for even more M.I.L.F.'s to put on tape!

You'll love it!

-Tommy

Yet another that leads to the same site, with this misleading subject line: *"re: Dawn's personal ad"* and this potentially incriminating message that appears to be in response to email from the recipient:

Hello darling,

It's me Dawn! Sorry it took me so long to get back to you, as you can imagine I was swamped with e-mail! I am glad you are interested in me, let me tell you more about myself. I am 43 and divorced. My ex-husband was a real jerk and treated me like dirt. I am very glad to be rid of him although I do get very lonely.

I have long dark hair and a slender figure. I keep myself in shape by going to the gym several times a week. I'm not searching for a serious relationship just someone to spend time with and have fun with.

I have my personal photos and more information on my website. I'm not real skilled with computers so it's not the best looking page. But it's all me! My real pictures and e-mail address plus a little more about me.

Visit my site and learn more about me. If you are still interested then let's get together and see if we click!

xoxoxo, Dawn

The following email appears to be in response to email from the recipient with this subject line: *"are you online?"* How many suspicious wives might think this was an actual reply to an email their husband sent in response to a personals ad?

My name is Tammy, I'm glad that you e-mailed me. I'm looking forward to getting together and having some fun. I am 34 and single. I am a secretary at a mid-size law firm. My measurements are 36-24-34. Guys seem attracted to my D cup breasts. But there is more to me than my boobs!

I have a personal website with more info about me. It is free, and gives you a chance to get to know me better. I have many of my photos online so you can see what I look like before you decide if you want to meet me. These are my personal pictures, you won't find them anywhere else. My personal e-mail and contact info is also there.

There's a lot more info about me there, some great pictures, and this is also the best way to get ahold of me. So check me out and see what you think, hopefully you'll be interested! I'LL MAKE IT WORTH YOUR TIME!

Have a great day, Tammy

Some of the most prolific and obnoxious unsolicited email attempts to draw men and women to sites specifically established for cheating. Here's one example:

*Married But Lonely (A Service provided by MarriedButLonely.org) For the men: *Currently, there are 82,736 married women in the U.S. who are lonley and looking for some fun. For the women: *Currently, there are 98,085 married men in the U.S. who are lonley and looking for some fun.*

I visited the Web site and found this introduction on the home page of the site: *"A worldwide non-profit organization founded and managed exclusively by women featuring only REAL attached women in search of REAL sex on the side nationwide and in 20 countries. Based in Los Angeles, California: The World Capital for Sex On The Side. FACT: Over 27 Million visitors in less than 2 years without any commercial advertising means. 'The word spreads fast'."*

The site guarantees a "hook-up" within minutes.

I left that site and went to another one targeting married cheaters, marriedandflirting.net, which advertises "chat and personals for those who are married but curious, bored or both."

I click on the "Chat Room" icon and the sign-in page comes up. I need to put in my Username to get in, and if I want to give details about myself there's an Optional Profile box so that others in chat can see why I'm there. I give myself a non gender-specific user name but the chat room doesn't open so I click on "Free Personals" instead. While there is no charge to search the personals, there's no search until I "join for free." I click on a couple of the "sample" ads featuring swinging couples with full frontal nudity. Just a few steps into this site and I've seen enough. I leave.

My next stop is at marriedpersonals.com: *"Seeking passion? Sex? Excitement? Relationships without hassles? Married Match Where you never have to say 'Yes, I'm married, but....'"* I click on the link for "Women Seeking Men" but the message comes up that I can view the ads only after I fill out a profile (which is free to post) and pay $6.95 for a one-week trial (which I can instantly put on my credit card). I click out of the site.

I find *"The Discreet America Network Community Club"* at outsidelove.com – *"Free cellular accessible discreet email for up to the minute member interaction. Suburban American seeking love, discreet romance, extramarital, fantasy fulfillment, and more."* I click for more information and the next page gives all the details of this site geared toward paying male membership:

"Women of The Discreet American Network (D.A.N Community) have registered free and are a mixture of single and married women of all ages seeking love, extramarital, or other discreet romantic activity in a moderated community of safe and friendly men and women."

** As a male member of our community, you are placed on common ground with an abundance of available women nationwide who are seeking a secret romance, activity mate, extramarital, and more.

The next site I visit is hotmatch.com where I do a free search for males seeking females for a discreet relationship. Up comes a list of men in various part of the country, each listing accompanied by a photo – virtually all of naked men with erect penises.

The listings are by age, location and title:

"55 – West Palm Beach, Florida – sex toy f2or3females"; 60 – Why postpone joy…do it";

"51 – Looking to satisfy all of our needs…"

I move on to the listings for "Women Seeking" and see female body parts along with ages, locations and short titles:

"48 – Love it fat, black and hard!!!";
"51 – Enjoy giving you that needed relief";
"19 – College Sweethearts for Older Men";
"32 – Bi white couple seeking same, bi female/bi male."
I've seen more than enough and leave the site.

My research explorations will have a snowball effect over the next few weeks because literally every site I have visited has been able to get my email address from my computer (by the use of "cookies" on the site) and thousands of adult-oriented emails flood my email program until I am able to filter them out.

The onslaught of pornographic emails and those promoting adultery sites does not bother me as much as the fact that many of the adult sites I visited had no controls in place to keep children from entering and viewing the extremely pornographic materials.

If there was anything positive to be said about any of the adult sites, it is that the ones which required registration and credit card information before revealing their sexual content at least provided some type of barrier to underage visitors.

After my visit through the seamier side of the Web, I ask the men and women on my adultery forum whether they think the Internet increases the chances for a spouse to cheat -- a spouse who might be looking for "something extra" who didn't want to get caught with a co-worker, neighbor, or pick up someone in a bar.

Here are highlights of the exchange that occurred:

Anne:

Well, it certainly would serve to facilitate matters if one were so inclined, wouldn't it? Couple of glitches, though. I don't believe, for the most part, that most men or women would look first to the web for affair possibilities, unless they were (a) computer literate enough to know where and how to look, or (b) trapped at home to the extent that would be their only resource.

Most people, I believe, look to their work place, or friends, or friends of friends, when they get restless and start looking around for a little different menu. I think it's probably a passing thing. Something new. And I think something that could be just a little dangerous. But I tend to be a bit old-fashioned anyway.

Nina:

How about an ex-boyfriend contacting me in the guise of wanting to know how I was and what's been going on with me? I don't know if this topic pertains to me, but it is the Internet! A guy I dated in high school looked me up and emailed me out of the blue

20 years later. We chatted for a few weeks, caught up on the last 20 years. He was engaged to be married to a woman he lived with. She was aware of me, and we met in person not too long afterward. After meeting her, I was still chatting with him. During one of our conversations he mentioned that he visited a Website two to three times a day, and invited me to check it out. He said we could have a private chat room.

I can't remember the name of the site, but it was a site devoted to video voyeurism, with video and audio capability. Lots of women and men posing nude, and chatting with each other. I took one look, and ran like hell. I changed all my email addresses, and blocked his address out. Never talked to him again. I was totally pissed off that he was doing that to his fiancee (who I really liked) and trying to draw me in.

There were lots of chatrooms with "Lonely Married Woman Seeking Love." and similar. How sad. I'm fairly computer literate, although not a computer whiz by any stretch of the imagination. Neither am I trapped at home. The computer is my communication center. I probably use it as often as some people use their phone. I chat with family and friends, I send and receive tons of email, and do a lot of things most people probably do by phone.

However, I draw the line at seeking companionship, thrills, or whatever over the Internet. For that, I prefer warm-blooded, living people. I find plenty of those where I work, where I shop, anywhere out there in the real world I go.

Maybe the difference in WHO would use the Internet is the same as who would have an affair in real life. While not every person who has cybersex may have cheated with a "flesh and blood" person, they just may not have had the opportunity to do so although they probably would leap at the chance if it presented itself.

Some people have a personal code that doesn't allow cheating regardless of the circumstances. But, does the anonymity offered by the Web allow "closet cheaters" the chance to come out of their "virtual closet" to cheat?

Karen:

My ex put an ad on Platinum Personals, paid for it while unemployed. He thought so highly of himself that he wanted a "bi-sexual female that he could master."

He got several responses and was stupid enough not to log out of his email. Well, I read a few, the women seemed interested, that I don't understand, sight unseen, how could you subject yourself to that.

When I moved and hooked up the computer his edit page for Platinum Personals came up, and I just had to change a few things. I wonder if he ever thought anything about all the men responding to his ad?

Barbara:
Internet relationships. Whew. I think that for some people sexual relationships on the Net are a form of role playing. I know kids who play role playing games on the Net. They take on the persona of characters and then act them out in battles or romance. Who's to know if they are being themselves or someone made up and what really is the difference?

Other people on the Net are lonely and looking for more of a relationship. The Internet most definitely does give you more anonymity in terms of having a relationship.

The Internet also encourages intense feelings. I had one friend tell me that it increases the same feeling you would have in real life by three times. The Internet has and continues to change the nature of dating in the world.

I think women are less likely to use it for social/sexual relationships but not by a large margin. My experience tells me that if a man has a computer and a chat program then somewhere in the back of his mind are the sexual possibilities therein.

Women are more likely to be looking for a close friend. But that isn't to say that they would turn down a sexual relationship. It just isn't the woman's first drive.

I think the Internet does make infidelity easier. However, I am not sure that adultery is the goal of most people who pair up on the Net. They aren't looking for affairs. They are having innocent conversations and as feelings are touched they snowball into a more intimate kind of relationship.

It is still new and we haven't learned how to relate to the feelings it invokes in us. It is easy to get in very deep very fast.

Meeting someone face to face there is no way to make them any different than they appear. The Web connection can become the "fantasy soul mate" by just the right combination of words.

Just as some movies can't match the intensity of the books from which they are adapted, the Web lover might not always turn out to be as wonderful in real life. Although, the intensity of the fantasy relationship may be strong enough that if a meeting does occur one or both of the people involved may overlook those things that they wouldn't have accepted had they met in person before the emotional Web relationship developed. Or, as has been said many times: "the mind is the most powerful sex organ."

Karen:

It's not only that they can be the fantasy perfect person when you don't know them in person. It is that you are not distracted by the material things of looks and sound.

Naomi:

During the period of my chat sessions with my former boyfriend, I must admit that I was getting some kind of "vicarious thrill." It was a good feeling to be contacted out of the blue like that (made me feel as if I was "memorable" after so many years).

I was still thinking of him as a 19-year old, with all the attendant strong feelings that come with the hormonal teenage emotions. Feelings I had not had in years for anyone other than my husband, but feelings I knew I had control over.

It was a fantasy perpetuated by the fact that he only showed me what he wanted me to see, and that he was role-playing. I was content at the time (I'm pretty sure), that was as far as I wanted to go. I enjoyed the feeling of being "the focus" of his attention, and yes, the feeling of getting some kind of "illicit thrill" out of the whole thing.

I was a little uncomfortable with the fact he was engaged, but that soon disappeared when I met his fiancee and got along well with her. I was looking at this as a "renewal" of an old friendship, with the hopes of building up a new one (looking at them as a couple). So when his "ulterior motive" came into light, I felt very betrayed — not for myself, but for his fiancee.

I do have a personal code of conduct that prevents me from crossing any boundaries, and I would assume the same of the other person.

Helena:

Trust me ... you do not have to be all that computer literate to find this site. I came across it last year doing a simple search. I thought it was a site with a message board for support. I entered the site. It was quite different from anything I expected. There was a bulletin board all right, with a lot of nude photos of "members."

At that time, in order to gain membership, you had to give them a reason why you wanted to join. If the reason was good enough (in their eyes), then they let you in. Their chat rooms were, well, let's say "chatty" in a sexually explicit kind of way. My overall feeling was that this site was very conducive to "virtual cheating."

Yes, I believe the internet makes it very easy to cheat. Emotional bonds form very quickly ... too quickly, if you ask me. By the time the virtual participants meet in real time, there is already a shared bond. This bond makes it easy to overlook imperfections, of whatever nature, that would have raised an immediate red flag if the relationship was trying to be pursued in real time.

Crystal:

Interesting. This was the topic of a conversation with four of my gal pals Saturday night. There's no question as to the availability over the Internet or phone chat lines if you want to role play and live out a fantasy. But how many "connections" are made by people in the same location, or even close?

One friend admitted to actually having "cybersex." The "other party" (said he was a man, but who knows?) was 3000 miles away (maybe). No real personal information was exchanged (thank goodness). And, there was no cost. They used Yahoo's Messenger to "cyber" after they met playing a game on Yahoo.

Then another friend said, "But what about your husband?" She responded, "What about him? It was no different than masturbating while you're thinking about George Clooney." Another added, "What if he were here in town? Would you have met him at some later time?" She actually had to think about it! And, never really answered the question. She just kept dwelling on the fantasy and how cool he was.

So, based on that conversation alone, I would have to say yes. I have a quote by Goya that I think is fitting: "Fantasy, abandoned by reason, produces impossible monsters."

Jason:

I would have to say that yes, there is no doubt that the internet makes it easier to cheat. All of the instant message programs. You hide behind your computer just like the other person is hiding behind their computer. It is very easy to get personal very fast. The other person doesn't know you and a lot of the ones that are on the instant messages are lonely people in one way or another.

Another way that it is so easy is all of the adult personals sites. You can go into just about any personals site and find someone from the opposite sex, married or not, that is willing to have some sexual fun.

···▶··▶··▶

Finally, here are three true stories of virtual infidelity, the first from a man who found "love" after responding to e-mail he received by mistake, the second from a wife whose husband betrayed their marriage vows with someone he met online, and the third from the "other" woman in an online affair.

Darryl:

I am a married man 14 years into my third marriage. I have always been a lonely person inside and in search of attention from the opposite sex. I tend to fall in love with any female who shows me affection. I know that I am flawed badly, but the world is full of restless people.

I just don't exactly know why I feel that it is my goal in life to spread excitement and happiness to the females who show me affection. I guess I am just Male with animal instincts.

My latest experience was over a year ago when I received an e-mail by mistake, one that was intended for someone else and this person accidentally copied the e-mail address wrong. I, being the investigative person that I am, answered the e-mail and acquired a penpal, so to speak. The conversations continued until we both found out we had almost everything in our lives in common with the other.

What I liked, she liked. Things I did not like, she did not like. The main two things that we both did not like was that, one we were separated by a thousand miles and we were both married. Both of our marriages were not satisfying and we were looking for a way out, and a way that we could meet face to face.

I could not get away to go to her and she could not get away to come to me. This was a plaguing circumstance that required some careful planning. We finally found a way that I could meet her for one night near where I live.

She had a conference which brought her there and she was alone. I went to her and we spent one night in dreams that seldom all come true for any couple in one night. No honeymoon could ever cover the wonderful aspects of love between two people that we enjoyed that night.

This romance is a continuing thing with the e-mails and an occasional telephone conversation. We both want more out of the relationship than we are getting. I don't know how, but we both feel that there are more of the heavenly feelings somewhere that need to be experienced.

We are both locked into marriages because of finances only. All the children are grown and on their own.

Does someone have a sure way to win the lottery quickly? We don't want any more time to pass before we can be together on that beautiful island of love and happiness.

Paula:

I sat down at the computer to check in with my favorite housekeeping site, and to grab a few minutes of peace after a long night with the kids.

My husband had left for a quick trip to the grocery store and the computer was still on. An e-card popped up on the screen and curious, I opened it, not realizing that in a few seconds, my life as I knew it would end.

"I love you and miss you tremendously! - Jill" Dumbfounded, I stared at the screen. My heart stopped beating as slowly the realization of what I was seeing crept into my mind. No! It can't be. The pain coursed through my body. Anger? No, that came later. Hurt? Yes, it was hurt, but the degree of which I had never experienced before.

This was my husband, my love, my white knight. In a life that had been full of betrayal, it was not possible that he would cast me aside, betray me as so many had before.

I was shaking as I realized that there was more. Quickly, I opened e-mail after e-mail. Time seemed to stand still. Details began to spill out. Tiny glimpses into a life that was not mine, yet, seemed to be inextricably linked with my own.

Stories of children, a husband, of whom I did not know. And then, the words that seared into my brain. A woman, telling of her love, her longing. Responses to questions that had been put before her. And slowly my numbed brain began to accept that my husband, the man I surely had loved since the beginning of time, had been professing his love for someone else.

As if from a great distance I heard someone calling my name. I looked up from the computer and as my heart silently broke in two, spilling its contents upon the office floor, he saw my stricken face and knew -- not only had I discovered the truth, but so had he... I loved him and he had lost me.

It has been many months since I discovered my husband's infidelity. During that time, we have made great progress, both in understanding why the affair happened and how to prevent it in the future.

I am changed and so is he. Sometimes, I wonder if it had to happen, to release him, to allow him to truly see himself and to truly accept that I loved him, that he was worth loving.

But in spite of that, I hope anyone reading my story and contemplating an affair, if not already involved in one, would stop and picture yourself taking a knife and cutting out your spouse's heart, for truly, that is what he did to me, that is how it feels.

And there is no cure for this injury. It may heal, the pain may lessen, but the scars will remain throughout my lifetime, throughout our marriage, until the end of my days.

AnnaJo:

My lover and I started off as innocent internet friends. We only chatted occasionally. He seemed so loyal to his wife. He never crossed the line of propriety with me with sexual inuendos or requests. After about nine months of occasional chats I requested a picture of him. He sent me one of him with his family.

Since I had concerns about women my husband contacted on the net I asked him if his wife had concerns about him writing on the net. He said that she didn't like it but tolerated it because she was doing some things he didn't like too. I was so impressed with the courtesy, detachment and yet friendship and support he had offered me that I even offered to tell his wife how innocent his internet posts with me were.

At one point this man requested if he could e-mail me. My e-mail address was public. He could easily have done it without asking. That was another sign to me that his intentions were honorable. After one e-mail I knew I liked having him as a friend. His letters were deep, perceptive and meaningful. We started corresponding with more regularity, more involvement and yep, more excitement.

So, yes, I knew he was married. I felt the relationship changing. I was getting something out of the friendship and so was he. He did not use home evening or weekend time to talk to me. He used short moments at the beginning and end of work. I thought we were close friends and it didn't interfere with his marriage.

Our relationship online did get more intense and he admitted that it was affair status. He did not declare that since it was internet it was not an affair. He seemed honest.

We did meet several times eventually. I did it with open eyes and knowledge. Why? Selfishly I wanted him. Not as a permanent relationship but as an affair. I loved him and wanted to consummate that love.

He told me many things about his marriage that made me wonder. Things I believe, even now, although he is still with his wife and not with me. Most of it had to do with physical affection, sexual interactions and their overall personal relationship.

They had raised kids and forgot to look after their own relationship. Now they were alienating each other. The kids, though grown up, and the small community and extended family hold them together. I know he should have separated himself from his wife before we had an intimate relationship but there seemed to be too many obstacles.

I think now that he has gone back to the security of his family and the knowledge and desire to be a good provider.

···+·+··→

Why Do Lovers Cheat?

When I asked the question "Why do lovers cheat?" on my Friends and Lovers website several years ago responses came from around the globe, from men and women of varied ages, educational backgrounds, and social status. The question was not meant to provide a definitive study of cheating but the responses provided more insight than I expected.

Some cheaters felt justified in cheating, others were just sorry they were caught. Some people who were betrayed ended up cheating in retaliation. Some people gloated about putting something over on an unresponsive spouse while others wept over the dreams they lost.

The responses that follow have been edited to remove personal information and as needed for grammar, spelling, and to add punctuation for ease of reading. Otherwise, they are as they were originally submitted.

So, why do lovers cheat? Here's what betrayers, the betrayed, and the other men or women had to say.

····→

People cheat for a variety of reasons. There is nothing you can do to prevent it. And the school of thought that claims that people cheat because they are not being fulfilled at home is just plain stupid.

A person rarely cheats because they are not getting something from the person they are "supposed" to be in a relationship with. That's just an excuse.

A person usually cheats because either they feel they can get away with it without the person ending the relationship, or the bond of the relationship is not strong enough to merit fidelity, so they care less about the end result if they are found out to be dogs.

Instead of the person who has been cheated on feeling like they must have not been good enough, (which is pretty lame, everyone is worthy of commitment) I think they need to ask themselves a series of questions. For instance if a man or woman dogged you out with their cheating ways, you should wonder what type of signals you are sending out to have even attracted that type of person.

If you have low self-esteem; are a pleaser (a person who is constantly trying to please your mate without expecting he treat you the same way); carry yourself in a respectful manner; (for women) make him work to get you (ie. spending LOTS of time together, doing special things together, talking, etc.); respond to booty calls; cheated with him to take him or her away from their previous mate; never talked enough to solidify the basis of your relationship (is it a casual relationship, exclusive, talking about what your expectations are); or just settle for anyone; all these factors contribute to attracting the wrong types of men or women.

Infidelity is a sexual thing. If he or she is cheating on you they are just treating you as a sexual outlet. There is no deeper meaning to your "relationship."

Many times women have the expectation that if a sexual relationship begins, that means that the man and woman are exclusive and never verbalize before sex what they want and expect. Women just assume that that's the case. That's a woman's nature.

Men on the other hand think completely different. It is about can they get it and how can they get it and how often. After 3-4 times they are gone or you are a booty call.

I hope this information is helpful.

····➔

I think people cheat when they get bored with a relationship. I also feel that people cheat out of spite. People who cheat really hurt their lovers and should be punished severely. I should know, I cheated because I thought that my lover was cheating on me.

Distrust will ruin a relationship and can tear people apart emotionally. I just wish people weren't afraid to be honest in a relationship and break it off instead of cheating. It's best that way, trust me.

····➔

Women cheat when they think their man doesn't listen or try to understand them, and men cheat when their women lower the priority of their physical relationship (i. e. reluctance to perform oral sex, not keeping themselves physically fit, etc.).

This is not true in all cases, of course, but these are the biggest contributing factors to cheating.

····➔

My gay lover cheated on me once, and I'll never forget how hurt I was. I was on a business trip when my flight was cancelled due to to weather. My bed wasn't even cold before he had another man on my side of the comforter.

I don't really blame my lover, he'd been sending me clues that something was wrong. He wasn't as "giving" as he usually was. He wasn't letting go the way he used to. Things changed.

We stopped seeing each other shortly after; he got the cat and I got the shaft. What can I do? Stop dating?

···→

I have not cheated on my mate, he has cheated on me, but payback just isn't my style. However, ever since the incident happened, no matter how hard I try, I am not attracted to him sexually anymore. I have tried to let go of the past, but I was hurt so badly, and my mate wouldn't acknowledge how badly he had hurt, in fact, he didn't believe that I should have been hurt at all.

I am very unhappy in a loveless relationship and the only reason that I haven't left by now, is that I became pregnant and had a wonderful baby boy, and that was enough to keep my mind off of the fact that I was desperately unhappy.

Now that my son is in Daycare full time, I realize that nothing had changed, I still didn't feel anything for my mate, but I had something else to take my mind off of the situation for a while.

I would like to end this painful, lonely relationship now, but I feel that I shouldn't deprive my little son of his father. His father loves him and the baby loves his father, so it seems that again I have to sacrifice myself for the good of my child. I have done this before when my other children were little.

My life is so empty, if I didn't have my children, I would have nothing in this life that would bring me any enjoyment. I would like to have another relationship with someone new, but it is so hazardous in the world today, and I have been out of circulation for so long, I wouldn't know where to begin.

I know about loyalty and commitment, I just need to meet someone who deserves someone like me. It is always best for both parties involved to make a clean break and try to get on to a new life when at all possible.

···→

The concept of "cheating" is part and parcel of the sickness which pervades American culture. TV, religion, and most forms of entertainment (except for small children's entertainment) is full of this concept of cheating.

Turn on your TV and you will see jealousy, possessiveness, paranoia, shrinking boundaries, a turning away from the richness of life, ridiculous temper tantrums, and a bizarre overemphasis placed on the sexual act as the sole defining element of a loving adult relationship.

It is not. There is a lot more to a relationship than bumping bodies. A brief and fleeting sexual or sensual encounter should be seen only as an erotic experience not as an earthshattering betrayal -- unless of course the partners are not honest with each other and sneak around.

** Note: I said "brief, fleeting encounter" not an ongoing secondary relationship. There are too few days in the week for two lovers at once.

Why does this culture glorify jealousy? Why is the concept of "love" limited to exclusive genital sexual expression? If you love someone, set them free and if they love you truly they will stay. If not, what have you lost?

The concept of cheating and sexual fidelity are based on the idea that the woman is a possession to be controlled and dominated. Under this philosophy, the woman must also be jealous and try to enforce sexual exclusivity because otherwise she could lose her owner/man.

This is outmoded since women do not need a man to survive (although men are lovely people when they want to be and make life fun), and if a man is concerned about whether his children are "his" (note the proprietery term indicating that he owns children) or not he can get blood/DNA tests done if he finds it impossible to love them if they don't spring from his seed.

This is my philosophy, and I refuse to wallow in the muck of possessiveness and jealousy and guilt endemic in North America.

....➔

I think that people have affairs because of what is lacking in themselves. We search outside of ourselves for what we lack and when the partner can't be all and give all to us, we seek another to try and fill the void.

Hopefully we learn how to take care of our own needs and look inside and to the care of God and also supporting friends and relatives instead of affairs.

Affairs can also be an escape route for many women who are afraid to be without a man. So they go out and find a new one before they get rid of the one they've got.

My ex-husband had affairs. He was on the road all the time working and was lonely, drank too much, and got into picking up women. The more he drank and chased the worse he felt and we ended in divorce. It was too bad because basically he was a very good man. But it all became addictive to him, the excitement, I guess.

....➔

I think that people cheat for different reasons so it's very important to know your significant other. Some cheat because we forget to pay attention to them in our efforts to just live life, raise kids and pay the bills.

The person he cheats with deals with none of this reality basically just the good times they have (worry free) with each other. I say let her have him for a while and see how quickly she boots him back to you.

···→

All I've ever done is cheat on the person I'm with. It's not like I'm addicted to sex or anything, it's just that I can't stop cheating. I just lost my second husband not because I cheated on him, which I did and he forgave me, but because he lost his feelings for me. Cheating is bad and my whole life is screwed up because of it.

···→

I was the wife that got cheated on for years. Not once did he ever want to leave me for the other woman. Most of the time that doesn't happen, simply because he still loves his wife, and the other woman was too easy to pick up.

What he doesn't know is, that the wife knows and no one has to tell her. There are always the tell-all signs, but he can't see them. I know. I was there.

···→

I believe lovers cheat because they are lonely. I don't think that one will cheat because the other has done them wrong.

For instance, maybe your partner has gone away and will be gone for quite a while. You try and try to remain "faithful" however you get this feeling of loneliness and just want some company. You think everything will be just fine after their return. Nevertheless, in the meantime you still want to feel loved, and cared for. You simply can't obtain that from being by yourself.

So you go out and find that friend that somehow ends up giving you more attention than you bargained for. But you can't let it go because it feels so divine. And you think to yourself. . . "When was the last time I've felt this great?" So you provide what your body needs in the meantime.

After a while, you stop thinking about it as cheating and start referring to it as substitution. You know, like teachers. And you do this so you aren't left feeling guilty, when you really are.

···→

I have been cheated on by a man that I would swear to you is my soulmate. We dated for two years before I found out about the affair, which had been going since six months into our relationship.

He told me before we started dating that he had cheated on every girl he had ever dated, but I thought, like other women before me, that I would be different. Not so. What hurt most was that we were planning on being married some day. When I found out my entire world ended. I left him. There were no harsh words, only hurt and resentment. I loved him so much that I only wanted to see him happy.

In the last year, since I found out, he has proposed to me twice. Both times I kept my resolve, and I became a stronger person for it. Without him there to cloud my vision of my inner self I was able to discover my true calling in life, and I have since set out on the path.

He has recently returned to me, still lying and cheating on his now ex-fiance. I can rest assured that my decision, though the hardest one I have ever made in my life, was the right one.

He has entered counseling and may eventually be a better man, but I wasn't there to get stepped on while he went through his realization that he was wrong. I was busy building myself up.

My philosophy is simply this: let him/her go. If you are important to them they will some back willing to change. Be strong enough to see whether or not they are sincere. If you doubt at all, stay away. If you know that they are changed, still proceed with caution.

It can be worked out if, and only if, both partners want it very badly. My best advice is this: search your soul. The answer lies there.

⸺⸺▸

Some people do not believe in fidelity. They try to excuse it by saying that "it didn't mean anything." When the other women come back to me (after he fooled around on them) and seem so surprised that he did it to them too, I ask them, "What makes you so special that he won't do it to you?"

Someone who cheats never really stops. It doesn't matter how pretty you are, how thin you are, or how intelligent you are. That person will always find a reason (in their mind) for what they do.

⸺⸺▸

I've been cheated on before and I took him back numerous times. He promised he'd stop fooling around, that he would be faithful, that he loved only me and that he didn't mean to hurt me, he won't do it again, etc.

After a year of him cheating on me with several women I finally woke up to myself and told him to hit the road. I'm a better person for leaving him and I'm happy for the first time in my life.

····➤

I think that some people cheat because they fear committment and when they feel themselves getting too involved they try to escape the bonds of love by subsituting the relationship.

····➤

I haven't cheated, but I do sometimes think about it and could if I so choose. But I have restrained. Why? Because when it comes down to it, a relationship involves a certain degree of trust. And it would pain me to think that I have hurt my love.

But then you could say why do you think about having sex with someone else? I think about it because it is exciting, fun, dangerous, etc. One gets a certain rush when having sex for the first time, and it abates over time when you are with a partner.

So that is why I think of it. I don't wish to hurt my love in any way, I just would like some extracurricular fun, if you will.

····➤

I've been with the same man for almost ten years — we dated for five years and then got married. I have cheated on him with two different men, one a one-night stand and one a four-month affair.

I have also just flirted with a few men, and I enjoy the reaction I get from them. I have never told my husband about either and never will, since I know it would crush him.

He is a brilliant and mercurial man, and I love him very much and will never leave him, but sometimes he will get so wrapped up in some project or his work that there is no energy left for me.

When he and I are happy and getting along, he is the most wonderful man alive and I would do anything for him. But when he gets busy and withdrawn, I feel like I'm being deprived of all light and warmth, and long for his attention.

My lover was very sensual and adoring, like my husband when things are good. He tried to get me to leave my husband for a relationship with him, but I wouldn't.

I don't think I would cheat if my husband was less of a workaholic, but I don't blame my problems on him — even when he is busy he manages to keep me wonderfully provided for and make me feel that he does care.

I will never tell my husband that I cheated on him — he would probably not leave me, but would brood on the hurt for years, to the point of being self-destructive.

I feel unworthy of him a lot of the time, because I know he would never cheat on me. He has spent every night of our relationship sleeping next to me, aside from business trips (which he despises). I know he doesn't suspect me. I wish I had the strength to be less selfish.

····→

I think lovers cheat because they're afraid of intimacy they get from one person. If they cheat, then they would be sharing themselves with someone else and another person won't be able to get too close to them.

····→

I've been cheating on my wife for about two years. She will not give sex so I got caught twice. She promised to be a better wife and that's been a year and it's still the same. I will keep on doing it until things change.

I expect she is doing the same but it doesn't bother me because I feel we are just roomates. Yes, I do love her. Maybe I'll stop in time

····→

My girlfriend of nine years is still demanding mariage, and for a new twist, she says that if I was really committed, I'd buy her a house. Now, let me get this straight. I spend nine years (eight and a half faithful) of my life with her and the children, and she doubts my level of commitment? I really don't get it.

As for the children, it is not about whether I love them or not, because I do love them dearly. There are some very serious problems that their mother refuses to help me address. The oldest has always been a problem, never accepting me as a parent even though she was only 4 years old when I moved in, she still puts her real (deadbeat/absentee) father way ahead of me.

My girlfriend also has trouble understanding the importance of work in any man's life. Men are most productive at work between 30-55 years. Anyway, the other woman is still (occasionally) around, although it seems that if I get thrown out (yes, thrown out) I will probably end up alone. At least I still have my job. The next time she asks me to leave, I just might take her up on the deal.

····→

A boyfriend of mine cheated on me about 5 years ago and it has affected me ever since. I was extremely hurt and devastated when I discovered that my boyfriend had been having an affair with one of his roommates. It made me sick to think they were together and that it had been going on behind my back for some time.

I felt stupid, violated and sick to my stomach. I wanted to kill her and I felt like ripping his heart out and stepping on it. I got over it (sort of), but I have never forgotten that pain.

It unfortunately has affected most relationships since then. I have a hard time trusting my partner, I'm very suspicious of any women he does business with and so forth. I feel I am being unfair when I question him or indirectly accuse him of possibly cheating.

I wish there was some magical way in which I could forget it all. I have great self confidence and am usually a positive thinker. I guess the only good thing about it is that I will never inflict such pain on any partner. It's unfair and immature.

⋯➔

People cheat because they are selfish and are only thinking of themselves. My husband of 9 years had a two year affair. I found out about it from his ex-slut friend three weeks after I had a baby.

She was pissed because he broke up with her so to get back at him she called and told me all about it. We have been in counseling ever since. Though things seem to be working out I don't know if I will ever forgive him or trust him again. Without that I'm not sure how we can have a future.

People sometimes just don't think about how their actions will effect others. I am so hurt and feel so betrayed I didn't think that he would ever do such a thing to me; he just didn't seem like the type. Guess I'm a bad judge of character.

He is full of remorse and says that he loves me and would never do that to me again. Would you believe him?

⋯➔

I think that people cheat for multiple reasons. Some of them are insecurity, some are lack of excitement. Some are socially related, involving our culture's tolerancy of untidely ended relationships.

When divorce was not an option, people who got caught cheating had to live with their spouse for many more years as well as with the wrath of the community in which they lived.

So, the answer is psycho-social. The amazing thing is that such wonderful people will cheat. You never know who'll do it next.

As for me, I'd rather stay single than cheat on someone or be cheated upon.

⋯➔

I think that lovers cheat because they cannot make up their minds what they want. They are somehow flawed emotionally and insecure. So rather than make a decision that will save additional heartache to the one they are cheating on, they procrastinate, and then when they are discovered, the decision is made for them by the other person.

I think that a person who handles a situation this way is a coward, and a liar. It just makes a bad period of life harder and more difficult to get over.

Falling out of love, or changing your mind is easier to accept than deceit, especially if the one being cheated on never has an explanation and does not receive closure from the relationship.

···➜

Why do they cheat? Magnetism, body over mind. It doesn't mean you don't love your spouse. Your body sometimes can be stronger than your mind.

···➜

To even begin to understand what makes a man stray means that you first have to accept that men and women are completely different creatures. They have different objectives and different goals. They thrive and learn to survive off of different things.

If this is true, then it also must be true that we (men), as different creatures, not only develop relationships differently, but also expect different things from a relationship.

One of the key differences in our relationship outlooks is in the department of sex. Whereas a woman generally relates the act of sex as an expression of or a gateway to Love, a man looks at sex as just that — Sex. Call it intercourse, love making, fucking or whatever. To a man, it is all sex.

This is not to say that a man is incapable of love. There are many men who are in love with the person they are with and engage in monogamous sexual acts with that person. What I am saying is that most men can be in one or several sexual relationships for the remainder of their days, and never even begin to entertain the idea of love.

Women, on the other hand, generally speaking, will become emotionally involved with anyone that they are giving themselves to, thus leading towards love. It is like a situation of give and take. A woman gives of herself. A man takes all that he can.

I have heard many women say that a man who claims to love a woman but cheats on her doesn't actually love her. This is nonsense. One has absolutely nothing to do with the other. A man can be in love with a woman completely. A sexual act with another woman could and often does mean absolutely nothing. Nothing at all. So why do it?

A man has an ego that needs to be stroked. It's part of his daily survival kit. Men are taught from birth that they have to be strong, protective. They have to be the providers. The status of the family is dependent on the success of the man. All these things are burned into their sub-conscious from the beginning.

As he grows older, he becomes accustomed to a certain amount of stroking. He receives stroking from friends, peers, loved ones and especially from the opposite sex. He then develops a need for it. This need to be stroked generally outweighs his need for a relationship. Therefore he will take the stroking anytime.

This isn't to say that he will fuck anything that allows him to. Stroking can come in many forms. A second glance at the stoplight (the first glance doesn't count), a kind word, a hug, a cuddle (they are definitely different), a kiss, sex... you get the picture.

Usually though, it starts as harmless flirtations. The problem with these flirtations is that sometimes they can go too far. It starts very harmless, but all the while there are seeds being planted. If either party takes hold of one of these seeds and starts to cultivate it, then the flirting has gone too far.

So what then? Can a man take hold of the reins and slow his roll? Sure he can. Will he? Most men who choose to be faithful, do so because they value what they have and they don't want to risk it. But a man who is not afraid of getting caught, or has no concern for the ramifications thereof, 99% of these men would keep moving forward. Because again, it's just sex.

This is not to say that a man is weak and cannot control his hormones (because I know that is what you are thinking). It's not a matter of being weak and lacking control. These are both situations of choice. For a man who has no fear of getting caught, being unfaithful is a choice. There is no strength or weakness involved.

See, there are two types of men in this world. Those who do cheat. And those who can't. Recognize that there is a big difference between do and don't; and do and can't.

Before I explain this, you have to understand that there are very few men in the world who can withstand seduction. I don't mean just an offer of sex. I mean real seduction. I mean a situation where you don't know her and she doesn't know you. There is absolutely no chance of getting caught. There's no hiding, no lying, no remorse, no work, no guilt and no problem. Once the event is done, it's over. Never to be spoken of again.

I would be hard pressed to believe that any man would pass this type of situation up. This applies to any man. If you can understand this, then you have to understand when I say this. All men will cheat!

Now for those that do, they cheat more often than they even know. This is because cheating is really a mental situation. A man who is in a relationship, but is willing to stray at the first opportunity, cheats on his mate every day of their relationship. This man cannot say that he is faithful.

A man who doesn't want to cheat, who has never thought about cheating, who couldn't fathom being unfaithful, but ends up a product of that seduction, or even has a bad day and ends up with someone, has still cheated. He has not been faithful.

Then there are those that can't cheat. This man is actually willing to cheat, but is very unlucky in his efforts to find a partner who is willing to be with him. He has not slept around due to his rotten luck. This man cannot say that he is faithful.

Lastly let me just say this is not meant to be a justification for a man's actions. I don't expect any man to get busted and use any of this as a means to justify his infidelity to his woman. This is simply my opinion of the long asked question of why men cheat.

···→

So why cheat? For some people, having just the one person around is just not enough. They want more validation, more sex, more attention, more anything than they think their current spouse or significant other is giving them. You could be giving your heart and soul 110% but it will never be enough.

These people who need more will always bounce around from person to person, being unfaithful, always cheating, always on the lookout but never leaving. They even make it difficult for their spouses or significant others to leave. They never leave until the spouse or significant other leaves them but even then they already have someone waiting in the wings.

Watch out for these people! You can spot them easily enough; they will tell you what happened to them in the last 10 years in the first 10 minutes that you meet them. It sounds impressive at first but it really is a pathetic attempt to impress less experienced and sophisticated people and trap them.

Then you have those people who hook up with the wrong people and mistakenly think that they can make things better. They stay on in the relationship even though they know deep down that it is a mistake. They truly think that they can make a difference. By the time these people stray, they are desperate to make up what is lacking, to have normal human contact. They are looking for attention where they are currently being ignored. They are looking for praise when they are currently being criticized. They want someone to hold them instead of looking at an empty bed and wandering where their loved one is and slowly going crazy.

They want joy, warmth and wanting to know what they have done counts instead of despair, coldness and being dismissed. They lack the strength to leave but they, too, are looking for that first toe tingling flush of attraction.

You can spot these people easily enough too; they will know more about you than you do about them. You have to earn their trust but they sometimes may never leave.

Two forms of insecurity, two plausible explanations but you know that there is always more to it than that.

···➔

Cheating is a overused word. People are in affairs because there is a lack of extended love. If a person could love two people at the same time, what's wrong with that? Love is beautiful. If it doesn't work, at least you tried.

···➔

First of all, I would like to declare that I have never cheated on my wife of 20 years. I have considered it, though.

People cheat because something is missing in their relationship. It may be sexual or the need to feel wanted. My relationship with my wife is sexually unfufilling. We don't make love more than once per month. I get the feeling that when we do, it is only out of a sense of obligation that she will do it.

I have a sense that she is seeing someone else but I don't really want to catch her at it because I still love her deeply and feel that having this exposed would damage our relationship possibly beyond repair. She is bored with our relationship. I have tried everything which I could think of to restore the romance which once existed between us.

I am considering having an affair so that I can receive the message that I am good and that I can please a woman. The reason which I have not gone forward with it is that it would not be fair to the other woman to be "used" like this. If the potential affair was more than a physical thing, it could spell the end of my marriage.

···➔

I think that lovers cheat when someone is getting too comfortable in a relationship and letting little things get away.

···➔

I cheated on my husband because he was not passionate or affectionate and did not satisfy me in bed. He was just okay at first in our marriage, but then he started drinking more and was unable to perform.

I was young and in need of affection. I was tired of talking about it and begging for it and seducing him and reading books on how to get him to be a better lover. I regret that I didn't leave the marriage before I cheated and now that I am older and wiser, would never do something like cheat again.

--→

I'm a voluptous divorced female who was 100% monogamous during a very bad, abusive 7 year marriage. One day I had enough and filed for divorce. That was a year ago. Now I am single and childless; and loving it!

I have missed out for 7 years on my youth, and for what? At least I can say I never cheated on the ex-spouse. But now? I have five boyfriends. I sleep with three of them. I've had one-night stands. And slept with ex-boyfriends. I love the thrill, the sex, the attention. I feel free, sexy, and young (I'm not yet 30).

They all think they are the only man. I smile and continue my games making no promises to any. Does this make me a cheater? If it does, I say I deserve to find romance, thrills, and excitement. I love this. I am happy. I know I'll settle down one day again, but not anytime soon. Meanwhile, I'll play and laugh and live life to the fullest. What's the harm? As long as you are honest about why you cheat and you hurt no one, go for it! Best sexual move I've ever made!

--→

Why did I cheat? It's difficult but at the same time easy to explain. My ex and I had a relationship that in essence had ended. We loved each other but couldn't stay together any more. We grew so far apart and didn't even realize it.

At one point all we could see were each other's faults and we had forgotten about the things that brought us together. We had fallen into what I call a dependent state. We didn't want to be with each other but didn't want to let go.

I felt as if I was falling down a deep hole and couldn't stop. I felt as if the air was sucked out of my lungs and I couldn't breathe. I was suffocating. I needed air and I found it during an affair.

Was I right? No, I was wrong. I should have ended the relationship I was in first and gotten my life in order before I got involved with another person.

I believe people cheat for many reasons including boredom, character shortcomings, and also just to see if the grass is greener. Usually when people are dissatisfied with a relationship they don't want to break off cold turkey, so they try a new relationship to see if it shows promise before they lower the boom on you.

⋯→

I think insecurity is a major reason why men cheat. Women cheat if they aren't getting enough attention in a relationship, but insecure men seem to want to prove themselves desirable to other women.

⋯→

I think I have a really big decsion to make in my life for the first time and that is move on with my life because I feel unwanted, unloved and I've been cheated on. It is still not over between this other and my mate until I see it with my own eyes

⋯→

I think that cheating reflects that something is lacking in a relationship. It should also be the end of the relationship. However, if the cheating is going on and the significant other is unaware of this, the one doing the cheating must tell the significant other, and let them decide to continue the relationship or not.

I also think that people cheat because they cannot withhold sexual desires to a new partner. I can honestly say that I have never cheated on any of my girlfriends and am proud of that.

⋯→

I am a white male. I have cheated so many times that I am am seeking professional help. My wife did not do anything wrong. All my needs and wants were met by this beautiful lady. I had no reson to cheat. I was in love. I certainly felt it was a rush to have sex with different women and thought it was ok.

I am a sex addict and I may never be able to have a relationship with anthor woman. I cheated because it was a rush and a high. I hurt my wife and now she is gone and she can't have a relationship because of the shit I pulled on her. I think you should be out of the relationship first before you go on with another person.

⋯→

I found out my fiancee' (at that time) had an affair with the mother of his children. She took great pleasure in calling me after he'd ended it and letting me know about it. This was because she found out I was pregnant and she had been told to stop calling our home late at night.

I never expected this man to cheat on me in a million years... I thought he loved me too much. I especially would have never guessed he would have been with her. Needless to say when I found out it felt as if he had physically punched a hole through my chest, grabbed my heart, threw it on the ground, stomped on it, ripped it up in many pieces, and threw it in my face.

The rest of my pregnancy went terribly. I had depression most of the time. I was under so much stress my last trimester had to be spent on bed rest. My baby ended up being born early.

I felt as if he had no regard for myself or my child that looked up to him. He could have just as well broken up with me to be with her if it was like that.

I think people who cheat are selfish and stupid. They have no though of how many lives can be affected by their behavior. To this day he hasn't given me a reason for why he did it. He just promises me he'll never do it again. Do I believe him?

····➤

In my opinion cheating has to be looked at on a case by case basis. I try to be a faithful and honest partner. I've been with my significant other for several years. I love her very much and hope that we will be together forever but honestly I've felt cheated by the relationship for a long time. The longer we're together the more selfish and confining she becomes.

Until recently I was completely faithful to her, but due to her jealousy she couldn't see it. She would continually accuse me of cheating on her though I had not. It got so bad that at one point I tried to convince myself to cheat on her and make it true.

I've had several opportunities but passed them up because I knew that all the time I had been faithful would be cancelled out by one indiscretion. However, I've heard from many that if someone accuses you, without reason, they have likely done so and fear you will do the same. I hope this isn't the case with my wife. As I am out of town right now I would hate to think that she is or has done anything even though I almost did myself.

I know I was wrong and am plagued with it every day in my heart. However, the only thing that would make feel worse than I do now is if she's been doing what she so often accuses me of.

I'm not a cheater by nature. I love the marriage concept, though it's far from a reality in this society. I just hope these developing doubts can be supressed until I can speak with my wife face to face, so that I don't do something I know I could regret.

····➤

At the time I was married to a nice guy. He had wanted us to be involved in a 3-way with another girl. At the time I thought it was wrong, we were married to each other for love, respect, etc. I would not do this. So what does he do? Has a relationship with this girl, brings her home to meet me, then they go off with another friend of hers, and, well you know the rest of the story.

I packed up what I could that night, called a friend, stayed with that family for a couple weeks, never saw him again, saved my money and moved home.

I feel that if we give our partner enough rope that it will happen, no matter how hard we fight it. It is not right to hurt any one this way but face it, it happens.

He would not divorce me, saying this way I'll always belong to him. That was until he found someone else he wanted to marry. He paid for it. A divorce was a wonderful birthday present for me. Girls, be careful

···➜

I have read many of these responses. The one thing that I'm tired of reading is "People cheat because there is a problem in the relationship". Has anyone heard of communication? If there's a problem in the relationship talk to your partner about it. If, for whatever reason, the problem cannot be solved, the right thing to do is agree to end the relationship before moving on to another one.

In my opinion people that cheat don't love themselves. When you love yourself, whatever you don't want done to you, you don't do to other people. If people that cheat would stop to think about how many people they hurt when they cheat, not to mention what goes around comes back around, maybe they would reconsider.

I was recently hurt by a man that cheated on me. I thought he really loved me. Then I find out the main reason he cheated was because he didn't know how to communicate.

Your partner cannot read your mind. If you don't talk to them and tell them what your likes and dislikes are, they'll never know. So people don't cheat only because there's a problem in the relationship. People cheat because they don't know how to communicate. Knowing how to communicate involves maturing.

Basically what I'm trying to say is men and women that cheat simply need to grow up.

···➜

I think people cheat for the thrill that they might get caught. It adds a sense of danger to a relationship, that it might not be there anymore.

I've cheated and been cheated on and I know that sex wasn't the only reason. I think that people need to feel in control of their sexuality when in reality, they are not.

⋯→

I don't even like the word "cheat." It minimizes the impact of what is happening. My wife decided it was important for her to be sexually active with men other than the one to whom she was married. It wrecked a 15-year marriage and is still sending shockwaves through my life, the lives of our children and the families on both sides.

There is no integrity in the soul of those who cannot hold to a vow. I fight hard against impulsive behavior in order to be a man of integrity who can look at myself in the mirror with no shame. Even when I was a youth, I would not even consider asking out a girl whom I knew was dating another man. It just wasn't done.

These days, men and women seem to think little of abandoning the vows they have made to a spouse to take a roll in the hay with someone else. Personal integrity and accountability is at the heart of this issue.

⋯→

I'm married and have been for 16 years. I have a man other than my husband that I am very much in love with. We've been in love for the last 5 years. We are apart by miles and our relationship is still going strong. He is married too, for 26 years.

He and I didn't want this to happen it just did. We started off as friends and before long we were lovers. I feel that he is my soul mate. He feels that I am his soul mate. Our plans are to be together and married to each other within the next 2 years.

We both have a lot to lose if it doesn't work out. We are both willing to take the chance just to be together, but the timing has to be right for both of us.

Things like this happen I guess, when you least expect them to. Love happens! Even if you are happy in your marriage, and love your spouse. It is not impossible to fall in love with someone else.

⋯→

Men cheat because women become stale after a child is born. Women become insecure about their bodies and men have yet to discover the magic formula to bring them back.

Women cheat because the man is either a lard-ass dud or simply because she is a skank, looking for a better cash-cow.

⋯→

Changing would be a better word than cheating. Some people realize they are changing, or that something is not right, but they do not have the ability or communication skills to express it or deal with it, so they throw themselves into another person's arms.

People are people, some are more suitable to us than others but all of them have their own quirks to iron out.

I think it comes down to loving yourself, accepting, caring about yourself, doing things for yourself and not relying on a relationship (another person) to fufill the missing relationship with yourself. It's good to be married and have relationships, but it's not so good to use them as something that will save you.

···→

I think people usually cheat for ego gratification, instant gratification, and selfishness. So many couples have formed for the wrong reasons in the first place and are not always based on a spiritual foundation.

Anything that is not based on a spiritual foundation is doomed to fail at some point... relationships, the world... everything. Just take a look around. I think, for the most part, men's reasons for cheating are very different from women's... not worse... just much different.

···→

Having been cheated on and been the cheater I have many a conclusion on why someone would do it. Here is my list: they're not ready for the big C (commitment); they don't respect the person they're with; it makes life more exciting and less monotonous; they use cheating as a type of mask so as not to get hurt; they're not satisfied in the relationship and are too scared to do the right thing (breaking up with the person); it's more convenient to sleep with someone and not say anything while not hurting anyone in the process (except themselves) so as not to create conflict; they do it out of selfishness; the list could go on and on and on.

It's all individual, but it is true that once a cheater, always a cheater until that person spends time on their own to get to the root of why they are the way they are. It's almost addicting.

It's also really important to know that it's usually not a personal thing against the person being cheated on.

Every relationship is different, though. People will do what they want to do and if they don't they're usually the ones getting cheated on. Saying it's wrong is both true and false, too, because in some cultures, people can have up to 7 or 8 spouses, maybe even more.

I was livid for a year and a half because my boyfriend at the time cheated on me the whole time. I knew most of the time, but I "loved him too much to let go of him." That was my lullaby.

I had no self-esteem when I was with him. He walked over me all of the time and I ended up cheating on him as well because I wanted to give him a taste of his own medicine. I never told him because I didn't want to hurt him even though he was constantly hurting me.

I did end up breaking up with him, but it was almost too late to restore anything. I am better without him, though, as is anyone in the same situation. It's a dog-eat-dog world sometimes. People do things they don't mean to all of the time. What more can be said?

···→

A lot of people cheat simply because they have fallen into a rut with the person they're with. They want to experience something new and different. There are two people in a relationship and you can tell if you have fallen into this rut. It's important for both people to recognize the problem and for both people to fix the problem.

You should try and make everything as exciting and interesting for your partner as you would have your partner make things for you.

···→

I think people cheat to get out of relationships. I think people make too much out of sex. Just because your husband or wife sleeps with someone else doesn't mean that they love the other person.

···→

I think they cheat because they have never been cheated on themselves and don't know how it hurts.

···→

I was married for 20 years when I discovered that not only had my husband cheated but he had a teenage son with his lover! I found out when she sued him for child support.

My world has been turned upside down. I cannot put into words the devastation, pain, betrayal, loss of self-worth, etc., that has been the result of his affair.

Our family has been forever changed. How my husband lived/lives with the shame and humiliation of the entire world knowing of his years of lies and deception and the fact that he now has a child with this woman is beyond me.

Of course he realizes now that what he did was very selfish and the worst mistake he could make. It almost cost him his family which he professes to love.

Even though I still love him and want our family to be together, my heart has been shattered. He will never know how much he has devastated me. As for the whore, she still is not married and has children from different men. I am curious to know if it was all worth it for her.

····→

I think people cheat because they have no respect for the person they are with. Actually, all people involved have no respect for themselves.

My daughter's father currently has a live-in girlfriend. He has slept with me, making promises that I know he will never keep. I have finally realized that he is a snake. I also realized that by being with him, and falling for his lies, that I had no respect for myself. More than anything I want to tell the girl he is living with about this game he is playing.

Anyone who is with someone that is involved is a fool, and the person doing the cheating is not only untrustworthy but selfish.

····→

We waited two years after we got married before we started our family and had a great marriage, lots of passion, though I was sort of quiet. Then, our babies came two years apart and we had four. After the last one, my wife, a young Liz Taylor look-alike, wanted to work. She needed an intellectual challenge.

So, I helped her get a job and used my influence to help her advance. Along with the advancement came the usual corporate gatherings, parties, conventions, etc. She enjoyed the parties more than I did and there was always laughing, joking, alcohol, kissing, dancing and hugging. In time, she asked me to stay home with the kids for I was so "bored" with those events.

She had her first affair almost immediately. He was the complete opposite of me. I caught them in a motel convention room when one of the children was ill and I panicked. She denied it.

We were divorced in a friendly divorce soon afterwards. She and this guy married for a few months, then they divorced. She came back to me then and for a few months, it was like before.

Then, her job pulled her from our relationship and she began to go from one limerance situation to the next. Now, she wants to get back together.

How may I trust her? I will always love her but feel what drew her to affairs before still exists and sooner or later, she will have to go again. She is addicted to limerance. I want the long, slow burning, lifetime love instead. Thus, we are incompatible. Right?

····→

I think people cheat because there are things they want to do and their partners won't allow them. I also think that cheating is a result of not trusting your partner fully.

····→

I feel that people cheat when their relationship with another person is lacking certain elements, such as trust and understanding, or when they are just not completely satisfied with what their significant other is giving them for whatever reason.

My opinion is that this is most likely due to a lack of personal, emotional, physical, or mental support. When you find that you aren't being supported, or appreciated, you tend to leave your options open for others to come and "fill in" what the other person isn't giving you.

Cheating is not always a matter of just simply wanting to do it for selfish reasons. Sooner or later, it just becomes a little to hard to try to ignore the fact that there are people out there who actually do understand, trust, and appreciate you, and you "fall." You end up cheating, not because you wanted to, but rather because you sort of felt that you "had" to.

And why does it become cheating? Because no matter what you still love the other person and would rather be with them.

Sometimes it seems that this is the only way in which you can find what you really want in a person... by finding it in two people and having the best of both worlds.

····→

I think that most men just don't have it in them to love the same person forever, because they don't love the way women do. They are incapable.

····→

My question is, if a person that you are involved with is cheating on his other significant, why is he doing this? Also does this mean that his marriage is in trouble? And will he eventually leave his marriage and come to me?

····→

I have been cheated on, and it hurts like no other pain in the world. I just wonder if the pain and hurt will ever go away. I was my husband's first, meaning he was a virgin. We have been together for almost 12 years, and married for 3 years. It hurts like heck.

····→

I think women cheat because they are not getting something out of their current relationships, whether it be attention, affection, or what not. I think men cheat because men are not meant to be monogamous, and always think they are missing out on something better. Also, they are generally the more sex-oriented of the sexes, and may not be getting enough of it at home.

When women cheat, they are looking for an emotional attachment, while men usually are looking for a physical one. At least that has been my experience.

····→

I think men and women cheat for different reasons. Men cheat because they don't want to be tied down to one woman, even though they want to be your one and only, they want you to be faithful to them, they just don't want to be faithful to you.

Women cheat more for the cause and affect. Either for a man to prove that they love her, or because a man has cheated on her in the past and she is somewhat tainted by the experience.

····→

It's elementry. Marriage (as well as any similar relationship) is an archaic institution that no longer works, but we stupid romantics keep trying anyway.

Look, if you eat filet mignon every night, some night you're gonna kill for a hamburger! Too bad we all can't enjoy relationships like the ones we have with our best friends who would rather say good-bye than to see us participate in a restrictive life-style.

····→

I can't speculate on anyone's behavior but my own, but after I did the unthinkable deed I took quite a bit of time to try and figure out why I cheated. It all comes down to that basic need for justification so that I could look at myself in the mirror every day, but I did come to some conclusions.

A virgin until I was 20, I was always really shy around women. I was in a long relationship with this girl when I was 22 and she was 19. We had been having problems, but it was more me wanting to get out of the relationship than her.

I was away for the weekend, and went to a bar with a couple of my friends. I hadn't been in the bar very long when an older woman came up to me and let her intentions be known without any doubt. She was very attractive, and so even without thinking I let her take me back to her place and so the story goes.

I must say, however, that I am glad that it happened. The sex was very unfullfilling, and that opened my eyes to the reality that sex without love is pretty much worthless.

If I had not been having second thoughts about my relationship would it have happened? I cannot say. All that I can say is that now that I am older and wiser, I can handle situations in a much more mature fashion. I cannot guarantee that I will never cheat again, but at least next time when the opportunity arises I will think twice.

····→

Couples should pray together, be honest about their feelings toward each other and communicate, communicate, and communicate so that if any differences are present, they will have a chance to be worked out before anyone's feelings get crushed!

····→

I think true love and committment is a thing of the past. I was so hopelessly and blindly in love with my husband that I could not see that he was busy bopping everything in sight. Finally, one gray day it all came out when his current lover decided to enlighten me with the story of their romance.

We are still together. I don't know why. We don't make love anymore. We don't touch each other even in a casual way. I wish I could forgive him and move on with my life. Instead, I decided to punish him and wound up punishing myself even worse.

I became involved with someone else. It lasted for 4 years. I realized that it was going nowhere and I was only hurting myself. My husband is my friend after all. I just don't feel love anymore.

I don't want anyone's pity. I know I made this mess. Just because he was doing it was no reason to sink to his level. I can control my actions. I can't control his. One day soon I think I will leave this marriage. I want to find peace and quiet without a man.

····→

People cheat for different reasons, mostly selfish ones. It has been my experience that cheating mostly stems from lack of communication. Two people who love each other should be able to be honest about their feelings, fears, likes and dislikes.

My advice to anyone considering cheating, try to see past the moment and remember that you are not only hurting your partner by doing it, but you are also hurting yourself.

····→

Women are very sensual people. They love to be romanced, spontaneous, and very affectionate. This is from my perspective, being of sound mind, body and soul and also a woman.

I have been with my husband for over 11 years and have never cheated on him. I have my fantasies and desires as well. He is not a romantic and likes things the old fashion way. Nothing new or exciting.

We broke up several years ago and were separated from each other for about 7 months. During this time we both dated other people and I was given all the pleasures I fantasized about from the man I met. He wined, dined and gently caressed me. I was in heaven but we never slept together. Sounds unreal right? It's so true.

My husband and I have decided to get back together but nothing has changed and since I was able to explore the romanticist in me, I realize that my husband and I are not made for each other. He is not interested in me but because there are children involved, we continue to stay together.

I've been thinking about "satisfying" and maintaining that past relationship in order to keep inner peace between my husband and I. So you see all reasons for affairs are not completely selfish.

⋯➔

I recently met a man in his forties. Here I thought was a mature man with a great job and great personality. He had a girlfriend that is very career-minded and treated him badly. He would give me the sob story of how bad she was and how upset he is and how confused he is because he has feelings for both of us.

This started out as friends but I feel something for him. I know not to get involved. He cheated on his wives and now on this girlfriend who simply adores him.

It makes me mad to think people use people as far as feelings are involved. I have ultimately made the decision to leave him alone and not answer calls or acknowledge him.

⋯➔

I have personally been cheated on more than once and I have done my fair share too. My very first relationship was based on lies -- he cheated throughout our two years together.

I felt like I wanted to get revenge with every man that I dated. Every guy I dated I cheated on. I guess I never thought of the consequences until now.

I am in a wonderful relationship and I am starting to believe in "true love." He is my "knight in shining armor" and makes me feel what love is supposed to feel like -- not the way I felt before.

I grew up with the misconception of love created by my first boyfriend (who, I might add, was abusive in every way). If you love someone with your whole heart then you will never stray. Love is love and lust is lust!! It takes a real person to decipher between the two.

I have cheated. The first time was due to neglect. This was resolved and I thought I did it because I was young and not sure about what I wanted. Today, it's totally different. I realized that something in the relationship is missing. Therefore, I searched outside of the relationship for what I thought is missing.

I discovered that the other man is everything I want, but I cannot end the present relationship or I don't know how without totally breaking his heart. He would be totally devastated and it would break my heart to see him hurt. Therefore, I continue to keep the outside relationship undercover, but I know that I have to make a choice soon.

I was married for 14 years to a man I believe cheated on me the entire time we were married. He was very discreet about it but in retrospect, he left plenty of clues to his adulterous lifestyle.

I feel like a fool for trusting in him and not cheating like he did. I absolutely despise him and would like to see him hurt the same way he hurt me.

I've been told by my husband of 12 years that he was unhappy for many years. Two weeks before I realized what was "up" he was telling me he couldn't imagine his life without me!!

This was his second affair and I had one also. The difference: his first was because he was too young (his reason), his second because he was unhappy for years (his reason); mine because I was stupid and only thinking of my own feelings (my reason). I should have left instead of stooping to that level. I apologized and have been sorry ever since.

I have to live with my decision but there is no justification for the pain that is left afterwards for a moment of lust (call it romance if you want).

If a person realizes they are not going to be able to resist cheating they should share the info and/or walk away first. This would hurt enough but not like loving, believing, and trusting in someone only to find you've been deceived and lied to. It is very difficult to trust anyone after this.

First of all, individuals who cheat do so for various reasons. It depends upon the individual. I only know what happened to me. I cheated on my marriage. My husband is a very good man, and I am still trying to figure out why at this time I did. I know a lot of it had to do with feeling attractive, and the man I did this with I was attracted to emotionally. He was very attracted to me, and showered me with compliments; he was a very funny and intelligent person.

I realized after two years that I never truly cared about this man, and ended the affair. The man I loved all along was my husband, and I am devastated by what I did.

The reason I am writing this is to encourage people who are thinking about going into an affair to evaluate the dilemmas within themselves, because they are the ones with the problems, not the spouse (of course, there are exceptions). If you think you truly care about this other person, re-evaluate your own situation. You may just be getting yourself into a predicament where you are wanting to validate your own self-worth, and this is a quick-fix.

You will have to live with what you have done for the rest of your life, and the guilt is so tremendous that nothing could ever be worth that.

····➤

I have cheated. I wanted to test the water before leaving my marriage and, yes, I found I was comfortable enough to go back dating others. I am now the other woman and have been for over two years. But it suits me for now.

····➤

I think back to the time it happened. It was only a few months prior that I proposed to my girlfriend. She said "yes" (but it was the second time I tried asking). That fall was rough for us. Disagreements abounded. There were times she'd even get upset at me and give me back my ring and leave. She'd come back eventually, but the ordeal was frustrating, and it happened several times.

Christmas rolled around. It was to be our first Christmas together. Maybe not. She opted to leave town to be with her family instead of me. I felt rejected. It was very lonely without her. I didn't go to my family's; I was totally alone. I remember going to a convenience store to buy a TV dinner for my Christmas meal. A few days later I got a call from an acquaintance. She said she was lonely too and invited me over. Well, we had sex. Afterwards, I regretted it and said nothing more.

I was so glad when my fiancée returned to town. I didn't tell her what happened. Last fall she found out — was told by the other woman. My fiancée has resented me for it ever since. I want to put it all in the past and be forgiven. I regret what I did and want to know how I can make her forgive me, to not bring it up anymore and get on with our lives.

We always want more and more because we are all human beyond being man and woman. We aren't satisfied when we find the "good" and continue to look for "very good." Although we are happy and are satisfied with our relations, we look for something different, something beyond the realities that can make our life so colorful.

We look for magic in our lives because we always want excitement and challenges. And we know very well that one day, in any case, in the most perfect relationship we have, the excitement will reduce. Love is a long line and passion is a small point.

In short, as long as human beings need a third dimension in their life which is beyond the reality and full of magic, we will continue to run after it to catch it. So cheating is inherent in human character.

I think if you find someone else attractive and you are in a relationship, you should not cheat but just tell your spouse that you want to be with someone else.

I cheated on my ex and when he found out he broke up with me and I was the one with the broken heart, not him. I have also been cheated on and I didn't like it very much. It hurt a lot to know that my boyfriend was with some other girl, meanwhile he was telling me that he loved me.

So do yourself and your spouse a favor and just get out of the relationship or don't get in one and date different people.

I think that when people cheat it's because you don't get all the attention that you need from your partner. The guy I've been seeing cheated on me, but I felt that I couldn't leave him so I just cheated back on him. It made me feel better, but I know that others don't agree with the choice I made. The only thing is that he didn't know that I did it. Oh, well.

I have a philosophy based on the adage, "fool me once shame on you, but fool me twice and shame on me." I don't give someone the opportunity to fool me twice. After you fool me once, I don't want anything to do with you again, ergo you won't fool me twice.

He cheated on me because he thought he still wanted me, but he didn't, not enough. He knew if he had asked I would have agreed to it. But he didn't want me to have the power of approval.

He also didn't want to hurt me! He was confused, and feeling horny, but not for me. He told me she was younger, more beautiful, and smaller than me. Bless him and her for these facts: She is older, not as beautiful, and larger than I am. I really like her! We have stayed friends and lovers.

He will never cheat on me again. I am wounded and hurt and a bit angry and frustrated, but in the same thought I also understand. Our boyfriend/girlfriend relationship was fading, but it is hell for both of us to face the end of the bonded part of such a passionate relationship.

She offered him a transition. A chance to end his primary relationship without feeling undesired. He is a darling and very sexy, and will never be "undesired" but it is harder to feel that, and part of what makes him desirable is that he doesn't feel he is "God's gift to women."

·····➔

I cheated on my husband shortly after we were married because I had fallen in love with another man. I married him for all the wrong reasons and we just weren't compatible. I got a legal separation 3 months into the affair, to be fair to both men. Unfortunately, my boyfriend left me soon after that. Perhaps he got cold feet. Perhaps he wasn't serious about me after all. There could be a million reasons why he left.

I was heartbroken, but life goes on. I am still going to go ahead with my divorce. I'm single and I'm happier now than I was when I was married. My affair helped me get out of a bad marriage so I have no regrets.

I've been cheated on too, and it hurt like hell. All I can say is -- don't do it. It's bad for your soul, bad for your conscience, bad for your reputation. And whatever reasons you can come up with to justify your actions, they're just excuses and you know it.

·····➔

My husband gave me gave me the expected excuses for his affair: I'm too fat, he lost love for me, he didn't like my attitude anymore, he was weak, etc., basically putting all of the blame on me and my shortcomings. I knew better than that, but it was still a great shock to my heart and self-esteem.

We talked about this with some very close and loving friends. Neither of us got any pats on the back or all of the blame. After that, my husband came to me and wanted to talk. He cried like a baby, which is not his style, and he told me that he did have the affair but that it had nothing to do with me, it was never my fault.

He said he was being selfish and inconsiderate. He said all that talk of my being fat was just a smokescreen because of his guilt, it made him feel better to think that I had part of the blame.

Now, it crushes him to see me hurting and he can't do anything to change what he has done to ease that pain. You see, honesty is the only way to get back what you once had together. It was killing his macho pride to point the finger at himself, but he did it and I give him a lot of credit. Now, I think the real healing will be able to begin.

I forgave him a long time ago, I'm still here aren't I? It's the acceptance that is the most painful and difficult part. Praying to God every day for a big enough throat to swallow all that I must in order to get past this mess.

For those of you thinking about doing this, please think twice. You have no idea how devastating this can be to the one who loves you. Today is but a moment, you have the rest of your life's worth of tomorrows. Whatever your problems are right now, they can be worked out if you only try. Remember why you fell in love to begin with and all of the history you share. Then ask yourself, is it really worth throwing it all away?

⋯➡

I cheated on my husband once, due to a severe lack of emotional support and intimacy in my marriage. The man I had an affair with filled the emotional void. It was not about sex. The affair enabled me to stay married longer than I would have. I left him a few years later for other reasons, not the man I was seeing or anyone else. I ended the affair when I left my husband because he was also married, and it would have changed the dynamics.

⋯➡

I have cheated, and never been cheated on that I know of. When I cheat it is because I am not happy in the relationship, I am either mad, hurt, or confused, and use that as a way to get even with the person I am with even if he doesn't know about it.

Kinda stupid when you think about it. I am just learning now that to go out and cheat on the person I love, is just a way to degrade myself, and justify my feeling bad.

We learn, we grow, we discover that the answer doesn't lie in the neighbor's yard. The grass is not greener on the other side of the fence. The same problems exist there, except when we look over the fence, we don't see that, we only see where the sun is shining, and not where the manure is piled.

⋯➡

I have cheated on my spouse because he cannot satisfy me sexually. I love him and have no intentions of leaving him. I am very discrete and practice safe sex!

Most of my liasons are with men who are friends and it doesn't interfere with our friendship because it is spoken from the start that this sexual occurence is just that, a good romp and no strings attached. It keeps me happy and I in turn can be a more loving wife to a man who is an absolute dud in bed, but a good husband in every other aspect.

····➔

I was cheated on by my husband of 16 years, and it is the biggest letdown that anyone can feel. Forgiving is hard but if the love is there and you are willing to work, and he is willing to open up and work together it can be done. It worked for us and it can work for you.

····➔

I don't think there's any worse feeling than to honestly know you've given your all to someone and you get nothing in return. There's absolutely no excuse for cheating. None! If you don't want to be with the person for whatever reason tell them!

To those "men" that are reading this and have cheated, is cheating or thinking about cheating, whenever something happens you're quick to say, "I'm a man." Well this is your time to prove it. Real men are honest and can accept responsibility for their actions. Being a male doesn't make you a man.

The same goes for those women who think they are so great, being a female doesn't make you a woman. People who cheat have absolutely no consideration for the other person's feelings. Actually they don't give a damn about their own. When you have respect for yourself, then and only then can you have respect for someone else.

These cheaters need to find themselves first before they try to be in "so-called" relationships. Once someone has cheated on you, you can't honestly look at the times they made you laugh or the times you thought everything was fine and say they were real.

When the truth comes out and you get the full picture that he or she has cheated on you, you realize that among those "good times" he or she was cheating! So can you really look at those times as honest times? No, you can't.

Trust is something that's earned. Once you've broken it in any way you can't just go to the grocery store and buy another one, it's gone! I'm not saying that it can't ever be replaced, but the person that f---ed up has to work extremely hard.

Now, you're talking about a person that cheated in the first place working hard to make what they wronged right. Seems kind of impossible doesn't it? Don't get me wrong, I'm not saying people can't change, because I believe they can. But only if they want to.

All I'm saying is go with your heart. Only you know how much you can deal with. The problem with that is you'll never know until you try it. So you have to ask yourself, is it worth it?

Maybe he or she has changed or you may be in for another rollercoaster ride. One that may be bumpier than the first one. But just like life, it's a chance you have to take.

To those people that think cheating is cute, or something you do "just because," I feel sorry for you. However, I also know for every action, there's a reaction. It's only a matter of time.

····➤

I have been cheated on by a man I loved very much. There were warning signs but I didn't believe them. I felt that I loved my man with all my heart and should give him the benefit of the doubt. Well, my gut was right. I found a letter from a woman asking my boyfriend for more than their current sexual relationship.

Most people who cheat are insecure about themselves and need to feel confident or desirable. The most important thing to remember is to go with your instinct. If it tells you something is wrong, then believe it, not the person that you are with. If I had done it when I felt something was wrong, I would not have spent two years in anguish.

····➤

With each day that goes by I feel less and less pain. The healing has begun and we still have a log way to go. Someone told me once that sometimes a marriage can actually get better after something like this in that it forces the two people to open their eyes and see what they really have in their partner.

I'm not sure I agree with that idea, but I do know how much better my husband and I are communicating and relating to each other now compared to before. Reconciliation isn't for everyone because not everyone can stand the pain. I just want to be one of the ones that beat the odds.

····➤

As embarrassing as it is to admit, I was the "cheater" in all of my relationships. I'm now single by choice for the first time since I can remember! I suppose it was my insecurity about being alone that drove me to find someone to take the place of my partner, just-in-case.

Sadly enough, I was 80% certain that the relationship I was in was not going to make it much longer. However, I would vascillate between guilt over cheating and guilt over wanting to leave, thus, prolonging the misery for all of those involved!

I think that if you are married to a person that loves you and you cheat, and get caught, you cause great pain and distress that can totally mess up someone's world.

My husband cheated on me while I was pregnant, denying the situation even till this day. I subsequently had a miscarriage and was devastated, but thanks be to God I am still here. My suffering period, feelings of insecurity, loneliness and anger and then the loss of my child was unbearable. But I'm here! A survivor, still healing behind the wounds, but thank you Lord, I'm here!

I don't think that if you have someone that you have promised to share a life with, you should take that lightly. If you then go out and meet someone else, you should end the relationship before you hurt, damage and in some cases, destroy, another person.

In these days, we shouldn't play with folks. You don't know what another person's breaking point is, what their enough is. We should be careful. I speak this as a woman who knows firsthand what kind of pain that is and I will not put someone else through that. Besides, I'm scared to death of my punishment that I know God will put on me for deliberately hurting someone else. You know what they say, "payback is a b—h," but I add to that "But when it's due you, it's a M——F——r!"

····→

Cheating happens sometimes when not enough time is spent with the other person or someone doesn't feel as though they aren't important enough and possibly taken for granted and no communication is in the relationship. Also, beauty is hard to turn away from.

····→

I don't believe in cheating because I haven't and he has and he is also abusive. So why do I still love him even though behind his back I have applied for divorce and he'll never know it. But, if he would be honest I would go back in a minute. But he hasn't, and now I am lost in a new and lonely world.

····→

I think all men are predisposed to cheating. That's why I only make romantic relationships with women now.

····→

I've been cheated on in a past relationship and think the same thing is going on in my current relationship.

I believe that people make choices for themselves and no matter what, they can choose to cheat or end the current relationship before they move onto another relationship.

I wish these men would have the guts to get out of the relationship before they look for something else. It really hurts to find out you have been betrayed in such a way.

I made the mistake of bringing the baggage of mistrust into my current relationship (based on being cheated by someone I trusted completely) and now either I am really paranoid or my current partner has found someone else. I've confronted him but he denies it.

I was a fool once to believe it wasn't happening; I'm afraid of becoming a fool again. I would never cheat on my partner, I'd end the relationship long before I could hurt another person in that way.

···→

I was cheated on in more than one relationship when I was just dating. But then I got married and my ex-husband cheated on me with my best friend.

I have come to the conclusion that men cheat, or women for that matter, because they are lacking something they need. Whether it be attention or sex or just some pillowtalk every now and then, they were not completly satisfied in all areas of the relationship.

···→

People get tired of having sex with the same person all the time and they go out and cheat. Like after years of being with someone the relationship goes sour.

···→

I think people should try to find new things out about each other to enhance their relationship and sex life. After all doors are open if they are still bored then it's time to end the relationship.

···→

In my situation, he cheated on me to feed his ego. He had to constantly have another woman's attention to feel like he was a "man." I guess he just didn't believe I truly loved him.

Funny that now I ended things and took away his children and my love, he says he would do anything to have his family back and that he would never hurt me again.

···→

Man are really polygamous by nature .They don't know how to really love a woman. They were not actually looking for love but lust so they tend to shift from one girl to another.

Have pity on them! I know a lot of men who take advantage of their girlfriend and wife, even my male friends do it so I have a concrete basis on why I say this.

⋯→

It is not only the men that do the cheating. I was married for nine years to a woman who cheated every chance she got. I wanted to try to make it work because we had kids but I couldn't handle it anymore.

We have been separated now for two years and I just got served with papers today. I tried to love but got my heart broken over and over for nine years. Some women just can't handle being loved and cared for by a real man.

⋯→

I am a beautiful woman. My husband and I have been married 15 years before he cheated on me. I do believe people make mistakes and it should be forgiven.

As far a why? I still don't know. My conclusion is that he is selfish and could not turn the temptation down due to lack of sex when I was ill.

My eyes are open now and I will never be taken advantage of again! He could never say it was as lack of trying new things as we had a great sex life (except for when I was ill).

I think you have to have the willing push before a good person gets involved in this. A one time thing is not the same as a long time relationship (affair).

⋯→

If somebody cheats you, you should wait until you get a chance to do the same thing and then decide whether to leave that person or not.

⋯→

I have cheated. I walked into a bar one night with someone I had been seeing for six months and the guy I had been seeing for about a year was there.

Both of them picked up on the fact I was caught doing something, they just weren't sure where each one stood as part of my life. I talked my way out of it with both of them and today I am still seeing them both.

⋯→

People cheat because they are not getting enough at home. They see the forbidden fruit, taste it and it is good and they just can't leave it alone. You keep going back.

⋯→

I am cheating on my boyfriend. We've been seeing each other for three years and have lived together for two years. In the two years he won't have sex with me more than maybe two times in a month. I'm cheating with a married man whose wife is not interested in sex anymore. There's no commitment. Only the needed sex satisfaction.

⋯→

People cheat for different reasons. It is unfair to blame your partner for something you have done willingly. Your partner is responsible for their actions only. If you feel there is something lacking, think it through, discuss it with your partner, decide if the problem is within your relationship, or just an excuse to be free. You at least owe your partner that much.

When you cheat and get caught, the first line of defense is to say the relationship lacked something, love, sex, attention. This is so unfair of you. Take it from someone with experience, the person who has been cheated on will beat on themselves over what they should have done differently. There is no need to add insult to injury. People that cheat do out of lack of something in their relationship, they lack something within themselves.

⋯→

I guess it comes down to what is your idea of cheating. Is it flirting? Is it being emotionally close to somebody else? Is it having sex? I used to think that it was having sex. Then I was cheated on.

It was not with someone I know. They were people that my friend meet on chat sites on the Internet. There were phone number and pager number exchanges. There were telephone calls, e-mails and maybe some meeting. There was no sex.

By my own idea of what cheating is, there was none. I still was hurt. I found out that cheating is really the emotional withdrawal from one's partner. It really does not matter the reason for the withdrawal. Once it has started it never stops. You can never get that closeness back. That's my view on cheating

⋯→

I think that once people cheat they will never change, no matter what they say. I have had a few lovers cheat on me and when they say they will change I have believed them. It's not fair. Cheating is not right, whatever people say.

···➔

I started the relationship with a man at work, a man that I always wanted to be with since the first day I saw him. At the time he was engaged to be married so I never followed through with my feelings until several years later when we were both married with children.

Now I have been with my boyfriend for a year and am totally in love with him as he is totally in love with me. I look for the attention from him because my husband is an alcoholic. I was neglected by him for the first two years we were married I was looking for a friend, a lover and I found that in another man.

I do feel bad about hurting my husband the way I did and still do, but I am so much in love with this other guy, if it wasn't for the children we would be together right now. I have no regrets. You only find that kind of love once in a lifetime and if you find it never let it go.

···➔

Men cheat because they want their significant other to be every woman: friend, lover, mom, confidant, intellectual challenger, playmate, slut—but they can't accept anyone as fufilling all of these roles.

···➔

I discovered that my wife of over 20 years was having an affair. This discovery was the biggest shock to me. I was devastated and, at first, even felt guilty for having "caused" this to happen.

But time is the great equalizer and teacher. Eventually I benefited from my wife's affair in that I began to see how we both were at fault for the demise of our marriage. But, nobody made my wife cheat, that was her sole decision.

At this point I know 2 things: she has demonstrated the ability to cheat on her spouse, which does not bode well for her future mates; and that I am much happier without her. How ironic. I almost want to thank my soon-to-be ex and her boyfriend.

···➔

I've read both sexes accounts of cheating. Guys blame women and vice versa. Listen to the country western songs and you hear the same. Been there, done that.

My ex-wife acquired a boyfriend when I was out of the country on a Navy ship. I felt betrayed, as I had opportunities in other countries but stayed faithful as I thought both of us were. I went through anger, depression, blamed her, blamed myself, blamed her boyfriend. Finally figured that we all had a hand in it.

I could have paid more attention, kept the romance going. She could have done the same. As for the boyfriend, well, I could still shoot that a--hole, I know what he wanted (and got).

The two of us get along better now, since the divorce, at least. We talk, which is good since we have a son from the marriage. We're friendly, though I would not want to remarry her because the hurt is still too great.

I guess before anyone starts pointing that first finger too much, they should look where the other three are pointing as well.

···→

I know both sexes cheat on one another, and everyone does it at least once. My current boyfriend cheated on my best friend with me. I cheated on him when I was pregnant with his child.

The reason I cheated was because I was not sure of my feelings for him. I cheated with an ex-boyfriend who I still had feelings for and whenever I saw him old memories surfaced of the good times we had together.

My current boyfriend and I broke up, and I was with my ex for awhile, trying to deny the feelings I had for my current. Eventually I got back together with him and now we are planning to get married very soon.

I think I just needed closure in the other relationship, a chance to find out if what I thought I was feeling was still there. In short, I cheated because my current boyfriend had changed and I didn't like the new him. He changed back and now we're happy. I think he cheated with me because my friend wasn't giving him what he needed (love, affection, honesty). She cheated on him before he got with me. She ignored him and spent more time with my boyfriend at the time (not the same ex).

I think men and women are looking for the same things in a relationship: love, affection, honesty, a sense of security, and passion. We are not all that much different, although there are some scum-bag womanizers out there. And vice-versa.

···→

They cheat because it's possible to genuinely love someone and want to stay with them but still want to have sex with another. It may not be the traditional definition of love, it may not be a kind of love your partner is willing to accept, but it happens nevertheless. I know, because I really do still love my mate but still want to cheat.

···→

I am the one that cheats. I cheated on my first husband many times and ended up marrying one of the men I was seeing. Now, after six years of marriage, I'm at it again. I like the feeling when someone wants me. It makes me feel special. I need a lot of attention and my husband doesn't give enough.

I have tried to be faithful but then someone special, not just anyone, comes along and I lose control. I don't know if I will ever change. I try to but I'm weak. Do cheaters ever change?

···→

I've had an on-again, off-again "affair" with a married man. I am not married. We have known each other two years, but only slept together over one weekend. Ours is truly an affair of the heart.

He will not leave his wife out of a sense of obligation and duty, yet we can't seem to stay away from each other. We feel that we are soul mates. Our relationship consists of tenderness and love, not sex. This is probably the worst kind of cheating.

···→

I ran around on my wife several times, because she never put any love or affection in her lovemaking. I used her body and was always left feeling empty and unsatisfied when we were through. When I would take her out to dinner and dancing and get home after what I though was a very nice evening and ask if maybe we could make love, she'd look me in the eye and tell me "you know I hate it, why do you ask?"

A man needs love and affection not just sex! A clean house, a hot meal, we like to get felt up once in a while, too, makes life a lot more worthwhile.

I am married again to my first love and she keeps me humping (no pun intended). She lets me know I'm wanted, needed, and loved. I still look, but I'm hers for keeps. My ex misses my paycheck, but that's all.

···→

I cheated on my live-in boyfriend because we got too emotionally close and we were planning a marriage. This added to and intensified my childhood sexual abuse issues so I had to sabotage the relationship.

I am a workaholic and always have been (one of my coping behaviors from childhood) and I didn't want to face therapy yet. I just wanted to run.

I loved him and he loved me, but I didn't feel "in love." However, I don't know what real love is. I have a low opinion of myself, that is why I work so much.

I feel terrible about everything that transpired. I lied to my boyfriend until he finally caught me, then I continued to lie to him and I didn't give him closure or any of the reconciliation he needed. Like I said, he was a caring and gentle person, but I couldn't handle that. Someday I truly want to get help and stop running.

····▸

I've been cheated on so many times it's a shame but now it's my turn to do the same to him to see how he'll feel. Women have feelings just as well as men. I wouldn't cry less if he cheated on me.

····▸

I cheated on him because I was starving for emotional love and he refused to give it to me. Sexually, he could not satisify me, but I enjoyed being around him.

····▸

There may be underlaying problems in the relationship, one partner may be ignoring the other, the person cheating may like the "chase," the affair may not be indefinite therefore a feeling of impulsive/temporary security, or the cheater's self-esteem is zero, which is probably the most likely.

····▸

Yes, I've cheated, but not for sex. I cheated because my male friend was a couch potato. He never wanted to take me anywhere, so I found someone who wanted to do fun things. I know that it was disrespectful, but he made me feel alone even when we were in the same room. I though about his feelings and I still felt like I was loosing out on my youth because he just wanted to keep me inside. So I loved him, but I loved me more!

····▸

I feel a relationship devoted to committment on both ends is essential to its longevity. However, if something is missing in the relationship after quite a few years, it's flattering to have a friend, co-worker or whoever give you that little something you may be lacking in your relationship at that time. And of course on the sneak.

····▸

My lover has cheated on me with his ex. He says he loves us both and I believe him. But how can you love two people? I think he is confused about us both. We can offer him two different worlds and he has his cake and can eat it, too.

····▸

Lovers cheat because of the sexual urge to experiment. The main reason people cheat on someone they love is because they don't think they will get caught so they can have their cake and eat it too. Usually a cheater does not have a guilty conscience unless they have more feelings for the person they are cheating on besides lust. Lovers cheat because for the moment of pleasure they are thinking with their heads not their heart.

····→

I believe there is a person destined for every person. If you are with your "soul mate" you will not cheat. Plain and simple. Not because you restrain yourself for the proper reason, but because the one you're with is so wonderful in your mind that no one else can really appeal to you. If you cheat, you do not belong with that person. So hold off the major commitments until you know you've found "the one." And as cliche as it sounds, you really do just know when you meet them.

····→

I have been cheated on, and the way I feel is pretty much neutral. It is one of those topics that is so "wrong" yet you hear about it happening all the time. If you cheat, you are obviously not with a person you respect, at least not enough to save them from that heartache.

····→

I think when people stop showing the attention and love we all need it causes the neglected person to seek happiness in other places. I think they don't end the relationship due to selfishness and the security of the other person.

Though security isn't the only thing we need to survive, the safety net of the other person is still there. It isn't fair to the person being cheated on, but did you ever wonder why the cheater did it to begin with?

I feel it's very hard to satisfy any person fully, but when one doesn't care to try it, becomes a hopeless battle. I call it a head and heart thing. Your head says not to, but your heart isn't fullfulled. That is not fair to either of the people invloved.

If telling your lover doesn't cause them to try harder, what is that saying? It isn't easy to be everything another needs, no effort is normally a failing proposition.

····→

What is cheating? Was there an agreement, verbal or written, or just assumed? Without a meeting of the minds there is no "cheating." What about the person who withholds affection and sex, are they not "cheating" also? Why is the male supposed to be "understanding" when he is "cut off" and yet be satisfied?

Cheated, is a promise deliberately denied. She wants sex, he won't. Or power struggle: he sits down to watch the game then she gets amorous when only an hour ago she acted cold? What gives?

Lack of respect lack of boundries, power struggle, bad information? What?

⋯➔

I cheated, because I fell head over heels in love. And this was possible because I was no longer "in" love with my spouse. I loved him, but it was more like a caring, sibling kind of love.

⋯➔

I don't buy the line that men are inherently polygamous and women are virtuous. I know men who would not cheat because it isn't their emotional make-up or value system. On the other hand I know more women who have cheated, me included.

I refuse to blame the relationship or my husband and assume all responsibility. My husband is a great provider emotionally, sexually, physically, financially. He is the only man who can make me happy. Yet I have had three men while with him. And they couldn't even hold a candle to him.

I do it because it's fun, I'm making up for lost time (I got married too young). I don't know when it'll end. I hope when I have a baby because I have to stop this addiction sometime. It is undoubtedly despicable and irresponsible.

⋯➔

It's so hard to be in this kind of situation, and so easy to tell people to just leave, give your partner the boot. Honestly, it's never that simple, that black and white. There are feelings, history, and sometimes family (children) to be considered.

Ending a relationship isn't always the answer, although for some I'm sure it is. Bottom line, no one knows your relationship better than you. It's time to step back, look at your life, take inventory of the situation, and do whatever needs to be done — counseling, separation, divorce, whatever the case may be.

I don't feel it's fair or compassionate for others to degrade the "cheatee" for wanting to try to work things out, if that be their choice. Everyone is different, and the ability to overcome is different. Instead of bashing these people, they should be applauded for trying to save what they have. I have overcome that pain, with love of God and family. It can be done.

⋯➔

My husband developed high blood pressure and while medication controlled the blood pressure, it has left him impotent. We have not had sex of any kind in two years. I have told him that there are things we can do that do not require his being able to penetrate and that I want us to be able to have some sort of sexual relationship but he does not seem interested. He is very loving otherwise.

I enjoyed very much the sexual part of our marriage. I haven't cheated, yet. What do you do in this sort of mess? I love him but am starting to feel more like I am not in love with him. I think he should do something to satisfy my needs or expect that some day I would look elsewhere. Is this cheating or survival?

····➔

My husband announced a month ago that he doesn't love me anymore and he wants a divorce. He can't seem to understand that I still love him. The pain is so unbearable.

At first friends and family hoped we could work things out. Now they are telling me that I need to accept this and move on. How do I do that? I have three young children and I still want to stay married and keep our family together.

I wish they would outlaw selfishness. I wish I didn't love him. He tells me that I'll get used to it and we need to work out a friendly divorce to save on legal fees. How can I work out a divorce I don't want?

····➔

I was cheated on. First time she said it just happened. Last time booze played a strong factor in it! Also she claimed boredom.

····➔

Is it really cheating when your wife has a stroke and loses all desire for sex, and you love her but have desires that you would like to satisfy? Natural, normal desires, but you do not want to leave your wife? I know it is wrong but is it really cheating?

····➔

I cheated only after I was separated (if you count that as cheating). I cheated with someone who is married. We started to see each other after his wife moved out of the state.

It was never a "real" relationship, just really good friends. He was someone I confided in. I eventually "fell in love." Then, nine months after seeing each other, he had to leave (work related) and join his wife.

Although I knew "we" would never be, I ended up getting hurt. He does travel back every few months, and we still get together to talk about things and have a little one-on-one.

It's been a little over a year since he left and I still care for him tremendously. I'm not dating and at this point, don't care to. I'm trying to enjoy the single life.

····➔

There is no one answer. Some evolutionary psychologists suggest an evolutionary pressure in which men who were drawn to multiple partners and impregnated as many women as possible passed on their genetic tendency to have multiple partners. Perhaps, though this does not explain why women cheat.

Evolutionary psychology aside, there are still many reasons why people "cheat." Some people may not ever have had the type of psychosexual mega-bond with someone which would make dalliances with other lovers meaningless and boring. I am talking about the type of experience in which trust, vulnerability, fidelity and passion make lovemaking a blindingly powerful spiritual experience.

About these people (or their partners) we might say "They just don't know what love is about." Which may be true, but apparently there is some need or desire not being fullfilled in their relationships which impel them to keep on searching. There is just "something missing" in their relationships.

Then, there is the garden variety of cheaters, by which I mean most of us. Yes, I have cheated. I have spoken with many women online (and off) who find themselves married to men who are unable or unwilling to meet their emotional and/or sexual needs.

There are men and women whose spouses criticize them, try to control them, refuse to validate them, the list is long. Over time, they kill "That thang called Love."

For these men and women, the desire to be with their spouses has been systematically and thoroughly destroyed. The causes of this are many. Childhood issues, issues from previous relationships, (transference is the popularly accepted psychobabble term used to describe this phenomenon).

Then, there are just the plain old life stressors, kids, finances, religion, politics, sex, etc.

Lest you think that I am dodging the question entirely, I do believe that there is one element, which if missing, will inevitably lead to the disaffection which sets up extramarital affairs. And that is trust. Trust. One word.

Once we begin to feel criticized, uncared for, invalidated, our ability to open up with our partners emotionally and sexually, our ability to be vulnerable with them, once this is gone, love is gone. And the search begins to find someone else we can trust enough to be completely ourselves with. Someone we can open up to, be vulnerable with, someone who accepts us for who and what we are, without reservation.

And someone for whom we can return that gift. Because it must be mutual if it is to last. Trust is built over years, and can be destroyed in an instant. Once damaged, it is never quite the same. More's the pity.

In my case, trust is the biggest issue. I could say that it was because of the difficulties she has being sexual with me, but that would be an oversimplification. Lovemaking, in all of its wonderful and myriad variations, is a symptom of a good relationship.

Prior to the day we married, things were wonderful. On the night of our marriage, things started to deteriorate. Now in year four, that part of our relationship is long gone.

In my case, cheating is a pale substitute for a real and fulfilling relationship. Love, and life, are lived in the day to day, not just in stolen moments.

···→

People cheat because they don't like themselves or are insecure in themselves (they may not be consciously aware of either). As a result, they are incapable of giving themselves and of themselves totally and completely, to one relationship.

People cheat because they are in a "safe and comfortable" relationship, but one that lacks raw, visceral passion and magic. Safe and comfortable is fine as long as they don't meet "that" person. If they do, well that's why this question exists, isn't it?

···→

Lovers have affairs, or cheat because there is something lacking in their own relationship! I had an affair on my wife (who I love dearly) because I felt no love or affection from her. That doesn't make it right, I hurt her deeply and she may never forgive me for it!

All I can say is, keep your partner happy with whatever it takes. You won't regret it!

···→

Yes, I've cheated a few times. I am 26 and have been married for almost 10 years. I think getting married at a young age has something to do with it, but I think the real problem is neglect.

When you love someone and give them your all they take advantage of that and abuse the relationship. It becomes a roommate kind of thing. My husband and I are actually roommates. He comes and goes as he wishes, and leaves me out of everything. We stopped doing things together a long time ago. We don't even say we love each other anymore. I used to give it my all until he started to ignore holidays and birthdays. Our anniversary is a joke; we try to pretend that it means something, but it doesn't.

145

I don't go out to look for men, it just happens. I see things in these guys that I want and I can't help myself. The more I am around them the more attracted I get. Right now I have this thing for this guy I have known for a long time. I was always attracted to him, but I was able to control that then. Now I think of him all the time. He is nice looking, has a good personality and is fun to be around. The most important is he is caring.

I lay awake at night and imagine how I would change as a person if I were to come home every day to a person that cares about what's going on in my life. Someone that has feelings for me and returns the love that is given.

····➔

I cheated once. I saw the pain in her eyes when I told her, and it killed me. I've not cheated since that time almost twenty years ago. Communication of honest and open thoughts to your partner as well as trying to pay attention to your partner's feelings and desires will keep you busy enough so you won't cheat. After all, when you've got the best, why mess with another?

····➔

I personally used to think cheating was wrong until I did it myself. It was a very long complicated relationship and abusive; I needed someone to turn to, and I did. So sometimes cheating isn't all that bad. It can be justified.

····➔

I have been married for 14 years and have four children. For the past two years my husband has been having an affair. Through counseling I have come to realize how I made him feel in our marriage. The kids always came first and what was left he got, which wasn't much.

I think sometimes affairs open your eyes to things you didn't realize were wrong in your relationship. My husband has been out of our home for nine months and now we are trying to get back together. It will be hard to ever trust him again, but I think it's worth it. Maybe our marriage can be stronger now that we both see our faults.

····➔

I personally have cheated. One reason is I had been ragged on all my life by men cheating on me and I had been faithful all along, but that didn't matter. So when I finally found a man that was absolutely perfect and something I had never had before and thought didn't exist, I was scared to get too close for fear that he would be like the rest and so I cheated.

The other reason for cheating is lack of attention and affection and the only time I would get anything sexual was to wait until it was convenient for him; my needs never mattered. By the way, the man I cheated on that was so perfect, I ended up marrying and he wasn't so perfect, cause he cheated on me many times with a friend of mine while I was at work.

···→

This is what I know... he did it because he was resentful and refused to communicate with me. He hated my job and he hated that he had to put the kids to bed.

I did it eight years later because he pushed me away for too long and I needed someone who wanted me. I'm not saying it's right or wrong, I am saying it happens and everyone who does it has their reasons. No one can understand unless they have been there.

···→

I cheated on my wife once. I did it a few years ago when our second child was born. She was having post partum depression and not giving me any attention. When this younger woman started paying attention to me, I never meant for it to happen but that is what they all say.

Women, keep a close eye on your man or it will happen. Every man has it in him, if that younger woman starts flirting it will happen.

···→

I have been married for 12 years to a wonderful man. We have two beautiful children. We are working professionals with college degrees. I say this because most would never believe that I would have an affair.

This affair has lasted two years. We live in different cities and though we don't see each other often, we talk at least every day. We have become very close friends. This affair developed out of a friendship that turned flirtatious.

We have very similar lifestyles, children, spouses and long-term marriages. The main attraction is sex, although a deeper affection has developed. We both have good relationships with our spouses, but have something missing.

For now, we have found in each other what is missing in our marriages. There is no intent to act further on these feelings as we have both made it clear that we are devoted to our spouses and families. However, we plan on continuing this relationship long term. Ten years ago I would never have dreamed this would happen to me, but it has and I have no regrets.

I have cheated, I've been cheated on and I've had relationships with married women. I prefer a relationship with married women because you get all the benefits without the bullshit. I intend to place an ad for a relationship with a married female.

It has been my experience that women who cheat have been cheated on. The husbands go ballistic when they find that their wife has been cheating. They, on the other hand, often think of themselves as a super stud when they are having an affair.

The wife is often left to wallow in her own misery about which the husband could care less. I prefer longer-term relationships rather than short-term affairs but I would not hesitate to date a married woman on a short-term basis.

My advice to men, especially the arrogant, egotistical boneheads, is that what's good for the gander is good for the goose.

···→

It seems to me that men and women who cheat have so many excuses. I wasn't getting enough attention, I was really attracted to this other person, I wasn't getting what I needed out of the relationship.

Whatever the excuse is there is always one common word cheaters share, "I!" They are very selfish people. If they took the time out to think about how their affairs affect the people they are involved with they wouldn't cheat.

Or they would at least give their spouses the common courtesy and respect they deserve by discussing the real issues at hand and deciding whether or not to end the relationship.

···→

I shared a wonderful relationship with my partner for 16 years. For eight of those we have been married. Then I found out he had cheated on me just in the last few months. When I asked him why, he said because he couldn't be honest with me, not deliberately, because he was not in touch with his true feelings.

I think men cheat because they are self-centered. This one was certainly self-absorbed and gave no thought to the pain and suffering he would inflict on the woman who was so totally and utterly devoted to him for 16 faithful years! She is now so totally and utterly devastated!

···→

Why do people cheat? Because the other person stops listening. Or maybe doing something as simple as taking out the garbage. They cut you off in midstream of your sentence, leave the room and leave the house. You are left to pick up the pieces because they no longer care.

....➔

I was the one that cheated, and is cheating. I needed to feel that someone wanted me for something other than cleaning, cooking, car pooling, etc. There is no long term commitment here, it is purely self-satisfying pleasure.

....➔

I have been cheated on — royally! After a twenty year marriage my "husband" left for a "lady" he met on the internet! Packed his clothes, signed the house over to me, took "our" new truck, and left without even telling his daughter good-bye.

....➔

We are not swans as much as we'd like to think we are, familiarity does breed contempt. People cheat on each other because they have forgotten how to put aside the everyday world and exist as one in a timeless space where nothing else matters but the senses.

They bottle passion and desire up with anger, hurt, and heartache. All the little things which make up the downside of every relationship, married or not.

One day you feel there is something missing and maybe you are not looking for it, but suddenly there it stands before you offering you a chance to spark the flame doused long ago by familiarity.

Most people think they need a change of partner when what they really need is to change themselves, the way they look at things, the way they feel. We could be swans if we try really hard.

....➔

I have cheated — when I was first married, with a close friend of my husband's. I did it because he wasn't providing me emotionally with what I needed — sex, and the excitment of exploring someone else's body. I am now, two years later, thinking of having another affair. What is wrong with me?

....➔

I think men cheat because women will not satisfy them when they truly need it. Once a week is not enough when it comes to sex.

....➔

I think people cheat because they are looking for something in someone else that their current relationship is not giving them. Or maybe they are tired of their current relationship but there is something in the relationship that they can't get rid of.

Let's say that the person's boyfriend or girlfriend is taking care of them and paying their bills so they stay with them, but in all actuality they don't have any feelings for them. In short, they're just using them for their money.

⋯→

I think that cheating is a complex issue that has to do with many other things besides that issue of cheating. Cheating is usually the result of some deep-seated issue with the partner that is not yet resolved.

⋯→

I haven't cheated but have tried but didn't do it. I wanted to because my wife has cut me off and it has been several years. Sometimes I think she wants me to cheat because she won't let me go out with any guys but when a girl calls up she just about pushes me out the door to go with them.

But that would just prove her mom right that men are nothing but slim. I could use some advice from someone on what I am supposed to do to fulfill my sexual needs.

⋯→

I think men cheat (on men or women) because they have doubts about whether or not they are satisfying their partner. This tends to be why they choose people who it's very easy to tell exactly what they want in order to be satisfied.

For example, a prostitute wants some money, a person of "lesser social standing" wants to move up in the world, an ugly person just wants some attention, a man in the bathroom wants the titillation of public and anonymous sex.

A woman, on the other hand, cheats for an entirely different reason. She cheats because she's comfortable with the non-sex parts of the relationship to want to get what she wants physically from another in order that she can continue that original relationship. That's why women, often in a stable relationship, seem to end up with very "virile" men, or exploring with very sexual women, or end up in a very sexual relationship, when they have a nice man or woman at home, who loves them very much and is quite reliable.

I think I have cheated because of both. Maybe that means that I, and everyone else, is a juxtaposition of man and woman, and we're all just trying to find balance.

⋯→

I don't have a problem going out with married men. Hey, if their wives can't satisfy them, they should go out and have fun with women (like me) who can. I'm currently having affairs with four different men, and I love every minute of it!

⋯→

I had an affair a few months ago. Why, I don't really know. All I know is that I love my husband very dearly, but he just doesn't make me feel very good about myself sometimes.

I have always been a very confident person and it takes a lot for someone to bring me down. Anyway, I met this other man and he is wonderful. He is the epitome of "southern gentleman." He always tells me how pretty I look, he holds doors, values my opinion, and is very, very romantic.

After the affair, I tried to stay away from him, but I think about him all of the time. He is the one I turn to when I'm not feeling very loved and he is always there for me. I would definitely say that my extramarital affair has very little to do with sex.

So, to answer the original question, I think people cheat to fulfill the emotional needs that are not being met at home. I feel that my life is very complete with two men in it.

···→

I now hate all men because the man I loved cheated on me and didn't even break up with me before. He was also married before this and I still continued to see him after his divorce.

···→

I've forgiven my husband but I'll never forget. That makes the relationship harder and the trust factor is very low. I've thought about revenge but two wrongs don't make a right. Besides, I still love my husband.

···→

People cheat on their partners for various reasons. There are so many opportunities out there. I personally think if you truly love someone, you will treat that person the way you want to be treated.

If you cheat it's your fault. No one else is to blame. Maybe if people realized that each day could be their last on earth, really thought about it, then they would spend more of the day thinking about the person who loves them the most.

Cheating is a purely selfish act. In this age we live in it's easy and cheap to get a divorce. So there is no reasonable excuse to cheat.

···→

I think when something is lacking in the relationship, be it physically, mentally, or emotionally, the person who cheats is actually just turning to another person to give them what they need.

I've cheated in the past, and it was to fulfill what I wasn't getting in my current relationship. It's almost a survival tactic, because I have problems with being single.

···→

I cheated once. It ended up showing me that I made a serious mistake in marrying the gal that I did. I discovered the hard way that many people get into relationships and wear a mask that may take years to drop off.

The cheating ended up as a full blown affair, and it continued into a relationship post divorce. In a way, the affair became a thing to blame for my ex, she never had come to the conclusion that I just couldn't handle her (short) temper, abusive language, and how I was the cause for every problem.

The lady I met was super sweet, and I would have married her in a heartbeat. She eventually confessed to me that she had a substance abuse problem, and that she could not live up to what she felt I deserved (her words).

Needless to say, my "other woman" gave me the gift of showing me what a loving caring relationship could be, and she gave me the emotional support to get through the divorce. I will never stop loving her, wherever she is.

Cheating is a symptom of a problem, and is a problem in itself. If you cheat, look inside yourself first and see why. Then ask yourself if the price is worth it.

···→

I cheated once shortly after our wedding. I felt that my husband married me because he thought he had to. He had put off the wedding for several years and I worried that he didn't love me as much as I loved him.

I turned to the other man out of loneliness and pain. Shortly afterward I told my husband of the one night stand because I wanted to try to repair our marriage. He was very angry for a while but he forgave me. I have worked hard to regain his trust and he says that he does trust me again. We are more in love and happier than we have ever been.

Some people say that once a person cheats, they will do it again. I don't believe that is true. Not for me. I believe some people cheat because of a problem in their marriage, once that problem is fixed the cheater no longer wants to cheat.

I almost lost my husband once, I will never cheat on him again. He is the love of my life and I will spend the rest of my life proving how much I love him.

···→

In my opinion I find that the number one reason is the different languages opposite sexes speak; it takes skill to learn how to communicate well to one another.

The second reason is that people get so caught up in all the feelings they feel at first and skip the negative aspects of their loved one so they can live in an everything's perfect fantasyland and hope love will always be strong enough to overcome anything.

Sweet, but reality is what it is and I think if people really took the time to get to know each other better, we really could see things like this coming before it begins. Lack of a little communication, openess, close friendship or knowlege of the human body will no doubt leave open doors for someone else to fill.

All in all, I think we are selfish and lazy in our intimate relationships, and I think it's strange how we make sure our bodies have an abundant amount of unnecessary, unhealthy foods daily, but our mind frames of love are so directed, and, well, boring.

····➤

My husband didn't "physically" cheat, at least, I don't think so, but he did have an online, graphically sexual affair. I suspected something and confronted him, at which point he lied about it.

Years later I have discovered the truth. I don't know which hurts more, the "affair" or the lie. My trust in him is shattered. He says he is sorry and that it is over, but I am the one who still hurts about it.

····➤

I believe people cheat because they are unable to end their current relationship. They have feelings of fear and guilt and do not know how to express these feelings properly. I suggest they look inside themselves for the truth and live by it.

····➤

I am a young woman and I think that men cheat just because women accept that they do. When a man cheats on a woman, we say "that's a man for you," and then remain with that man knowing he will more than likely do it again.

Most men will not stay with a woman if she cheats. It's not macho. His friends will call him weak or "whipped" if he stays with her.

····➤

I think people cheat because they're unhappy with themselves. Some moral attribute is lacking in their self-esteem that causes them to find perceived happiness in someone other than themselves.

Most people attempt to find happiness from something or someone else and only end up in a temporary relationship, wondering what happened.

Self perseverance is the key to finding happiness from within yourself. Once you are happy with yourself, then, and only then will you be able to identify with the pain you've caused others, by cheating.

Heed this warning: If you have cheated or been cheated upon, then you must change your focus to change your results. Never lower your standards to be comfortable in a substandard relationship, the signs are always there.

If you wouldn't leave your child with a substandard baby-sitter, then why leave your heart with a substandard mate? You inherently look out for loved ones, so now begin to look out for yourself.

⋯→

I think that you cannot predict if you will cheat or not, until you find yourself in that particular situation. I personally believe that I could never do that to my husband but I do know that if I were to be in that particular situation I might be confused and have the temptation to cheat. I strongly believe that once you commit yourself to one person you should honor and respect that one person.

⋯→

I have been married for 27 years. During this time my wife cheated on me most of that time, with her friends, my friends, my employees, etc. During this time she always said she really cared about me, and etc. Finally I am dumping her. She has never really made a commitment to me only.

Guys: don't let your girl get away with this, if you forgive her, she will not stop. The Bible says: "an adulterous woman can never be righteous." You are just wasting your time hoping that she will some day change.

⋯→

"No matter how you 'slice it,' it all boils down to fear!" Be it fear of intimacy, needing validation that one is still desirable or attractive, fear of being alone or any other negative stereotypes one might be identified with. Inferior, unlovable, incapable, immature.

Even when one uses the excuse "I don't want to hurt his/her/their feelings," it stems from one's own fears and insecurities of loss and character associations.

A final fear I will associate with the "cheater" is loss of property, money, material status, image associations and friendships.

That's right, you "dishonorable manipulators," what you really are, are "wimps." Your need to control is a glaring sign of your own insecurities. Just remember the law of Creation, "What you put out is what you recieve." And, Gods Will that you "Do unto others as you would have them do."

It's no wonder you seem to have trouble with believing anyone is trustworthy. I think you're usually those people who can dish it out, but you sure can't take it!

···→

I am not sure why it is done. I used to cheat here and there until I found the one I love dearly. Now that we have been together I personally could not be with anyone else.

To love someone the way I do, could never be again for a long while. He is the one I love and love to be with sexually. To have him near is dear, my eyes see nice looking men and think he looks nice but never to be with him in the way I should not be. I like that feeling, it is great. But for the other times that I have done it I am not sure why. It is different for everyone, no answer is the right one.

···→

I have been cheating with a married man and am looking for other women's end results. I am also married, but both of us are unhappy. It has been going on for seven years. I think I am ready to divorce, but he is worried about his and my kids.

···→

There are many reasons people cheat. I have found this in many relationships including myself and others. When people are not happy they look for happiness elsewhere.

Many people live in fantasy. They see other couples together and they automatically think that their relationship is perfect without any flaws. I have done it myself.

We fear hurting the other person so we don't break up with them. Instead we let the feelings of wanting to be with someone else build where it ends in cheating. This is another form of miscommunication.

No one can stop another person from cheating. The best to do is if you're not happy, try talking with the person and if that doesn't work it's time to move on.

···→

Cheating is the stupidest thing to do. Not only is one cheating on their partner but also on themselves. Truth will always reveal itself in the end, and when it does, it will only bring an end to what could be a beautiful relationship. After all, there's an old Chinese saying (literal translation) "Paper can never wrap a fire."

···→

If your man is cheating on you the best thing you can do is laugh it off and act like it doesn't bother you. Some people cheat just to see how badly they can hurt you! Trust me, been there and done that. My ex cheated on me and now he's got his ego crushed because all I did is laugh at him when he told me. Trust me, it works!

•••➔

Most people can't help but cheat. They are less evolved. This idealogy entails the fact that the human is another animal. The more evolved ones have more self-control and discipline, others act on impulse and upon a temporary solution. All animals have a natural instinct to survive. But in this day and age, humans can ensure their genes to go on with just one female, but humans have that desire to find stronger genes.

Perhaps your husband or boyfriend isn't the strongest. There is a reason why you would go for a physically stronger male or a curvy female. But subconsciously when we cheat, this is what we are truly going for.

If we remember the true reason why we are cheating while wound up in such an act, we would stop ourselves when we get attracted to someone else. And if the person is so infatuated, then why not break up first? Humans, being mammals, tend to form strong bonds that last for a lifetime more often than not.

•••➔

I am a female involved with a woman and she has cheated on me in the past. She said she did it because she was afraid of being "labeled" differently from her friends. I have major trust issues now although she swears she will not do that again. She is a lot more open in public and with her friends about our relationship.

Sometimes I get mad and throw it in her face about cheating and she says we will never move past that if I don't learn to let go. It is really hard for me. I want to believe her.

•••➔

I personally believe men are all the same. I once slept with a married man while his wife was out of town and his kids were up in bed sleeping. It was fun and exciting.

•••➔

I'm a male, and I don't believe in cheating or being unfaithful, I believe in honesty and doing the right thing, and that stems from my view of Love. I believe that Love is doing the right thing or doing something good for your neighbor, and cheating is not good.

I think men and women cheat because their view of Love is not sound, it's not empowering and it's not good. They have learned the Love that Hollywood, the press, the media, etc., teaches when the only Love, true Love is Biblical Love. And that would be action, action, doing something good for others.

It's so simple and clear but people have not gotten it! So in conclusion, people cheat because they reject, or have no moral standards that they respect.

···→

I have been cheated on and it is the worst thing I've ever been through. I love my husband and we decided to stay together. This happened nine years ago and he is sorry and learned his lesson. I can't seem to let go of the past.

···→

True love should be a commitment with the person you're with. It should be based on trust and being faithful to that person. It was never meant to understand a male's way of thinking or a female's way of thinking. If we could understand the opposite sex, things would be too confusing.

The Bible says that committing adultery is an act of sin on God. If you're truly in love and committed to that person then you should have trust in that person. All you need to suvive a relationship is trust and love. The reason that people cheat is that they are self-conscious about themselves. Think about their feelings and yours when or if it ever happens.

···→

I think that people cheat because sometimes temptation becomes too great or the marriage is getting on their nerves and they want a new pace of change. It's always because the spouse became bored or discontented with what they had so they turned to someone else to boost their ego.

···→

I'll never forget the day I found out about my wife's affair with her boss. a man who's older and less secure. But I'm searching within myself, because it does take two for a loving relationship. But I can say, I have always been faithful. Gosh it still hurts.

···→

To those who think it's okay to cheat... think about how you would feel or possibly have felt when you found out that you had been cheated on. Anyone with any empathy and normal human emotion would feel devastated to think that someone else was receiving the attention/love/devotion from their partner with whom they thought a deep emotional connection had supposedly been established. Think about it.

There are few things more painful than to think that perhaps you don't measure up in some way to the standards of the one you love and adore. Beside the wide belief that it is a sin and morally wrong as well, it just hurts! It makes for very cynical people who find it hard to trust others, especially in love.

No wonder that the "institution of divorce" is now more prevalent than that of marriage.

····➔

Why are you people cheating and then trying to get back with your partners?! If you felt compelled to cheat before, what makes you think that everything's going to be alright after? It will only be worse! The trust between you has diminished assuredly if not completely been lost altogether.

You people take monogamy and fidelity so lightly it is frightening to think where our moral standards are headed. On top of the emotional issues, let me make another point people tend to shy away from... STDs!! That's right folks, STDs. Ugly isn't it?

I have heard more than one story of a one-night stand gone awry only for the cheater to go home and have to tell their spouse (whom they still love very much) that in order for them to have sexual relations, the spouse will now have to either take their chances or use protection to avoid getting herpes!! HERPES... that's one ugly word! And that's just one STD.

There of course are all the curable ones like chlamydia, syphilis, gonorrhea and other equally unpleasant diseases. Then we have the aforementioned incurable STD (herpes) that stays with you for life (try explaining that one to a potential new partner) and other incurable diseases like venereal warts and the almighty death sentence... HIV/AIDS. Is this something to take lightly? If you think so, then you've never been through it. And it *can* happen to you, don't think it can't!

There is a reason for fidelity and monogamy and morals that go beyond even the emotional aspect of hurting someone's heart. It is disturbing to think about such an unpleasant subject but that's why we need to think before we act.

····➔

Yeah, I cheated. Sex was good until my ex-wife and I had two kids. After that, I can't remember once when she ever approached me for sex. I spent the next nine years begging for it.

When you're in that situation, you are powerless. I was walking on eggshells all the time. If we had a disagreement, no sex for months. If I didn't buy her jewelry or flowers, no sex. If I didn't help her with her chores, no sex. She held grudges, so when we did have sex, she would bring them up in the middle of it and spoil it all. Then she would say "I just can't get into it," or "I need more foreplay." I would give her foreplay for an hour, but she would still not get into it. She was full of excuses.

I really wanted to be close to my wife, but it just wasn't happening. When I told her I wasn't happy, she gave me this lame line "Then just leave--I can't make you happy. You need to be happy with yourself."

She just wasn't into sex or me anymore. She claimed she was a warm-hearted person, but she was as cold as ice to me. I was always hoping for someone to show interest in me -- to want me so I could leave. I found a few women to have sex with a couple of times which helped a little, but there wasn't enough there to have a permanent relationship with them.

Finally, I met a woman I absolutely adored and wanted so I decided to end my marriage and try for her. Unfortunately, it didn't work out because she decided to patch things up with her boyfriend she was fighting with. But I guess it helped me to take action and get out of my empty marriage.

I'm struggling now, I miss my kids and I am kind of lonely, but maybe someday I will meet someone who will want me as much as I want her. Then we'll be on a more equal relationship. I just pray that I don't end up with someone like my ex again. I don't believe that marriage should be sex-less.

⋯➔

He had no reason to cheat. He made up a reason for her to make me look bad. We have three children and a home. And had a nice life until then. He has done it twice in 11 years. So I cannot tell you why he is back here with me when I know in my heart he will do it again. I did everything for him and then some and this is how he repaid me.

I cannot tell you how bad I hurt. He has been back 9 months and things are not the same. I don't know if I am in love with him or not and this is all due to him running around with trash.

⋯➔

I think men cheat because women act so sexy when you first meet them. But after a while, they cut you off and have sex less and less. Then when you can't stand it anymore because they are just bitching at you all the time, you go out and find someone new to have fun with again until they turn into a bitch.

Why do women have to bitch and nag so much? Why can't they keep it fun all the time?

→

I have not cheated -- but am often tempted to do so. I see young attractive women and wish I were free to be with them... at the same time I love my wife and do not want to do anything to hurt her or our marriage.

→

I thought this was going to be a much more scientific type of survey from the way the previous page was presented. However, I will say that I have been cheated on and that I have also cheated in the past. That is the key to it all, it is in the past.

Shit happens and life goes on so you just have to suck it up and deal with it or let the depression roll you over like a Mack truck.

The trick is to learn from the pain of it all, that is why my lover and I are looking into swinging with others rather than doing anything behind each other's back.

→→→

Infidelity Q&A

As part of the research for this book, I set up a private online forum and accepted a small group of volunteers who agreed that their responses, stories and comments could be included in this book. Everyone who participated had first hand experience with adultery whether they were the one who was betrayed (the majority), the betrayer, the other person, or a combination of two or more roles. Most of the participants were women.

Identities have been changed, and personal stories have been edited as needed to further insure anonymity. Otherwise, the responses that follow have been edited very little from the way they were posted in that forum.

Each person's responses come from their particular experience and current viewpoint. For some, the betrayal is fresh and their feelings are raw which is evident in their answers. Others are working to repair their marriages and have moved to a vantage point where they are able to respond with a little less raw emotion and a bit more forgiveness.

····▶

Will adultery happen if everything is right in the marriage?

Does a partner commit adultery because their marriage is having problems? Or do they cheat because of an inherent flaw in themselves? Or, is it that their "good" marriage just isn't meeting some important personal needs of their own?

Raquel:
We had a good marriage. We still have a good marriage. My husband told me he was looking for sexual variety, nothing more. Hence the many one-night stands. He has even said that he thought those encounters with other sexual partners were good for our sex life. Of course, I never got to vote on that one!

He also said he was surprised when he got emotionally involved with the other woman. I told him he did all the things one does when one is looking for a new emotional relationship -- dating, having sex, sharing experiences.

To some extent, I think my husband was a bit naive. I think he truly thought he could handle a casual relationship with her while still being married to me. For a long time, he also insisted the only problem was that I found out. Sometimes I think he still thinks that.

Dana:
For married people to seek others outside of the marriage would require there be something "missing" in their marriage. I have heard of long-standing marriages where the husband and/or wife cheated, and neither spouse knew about it. The marriage lasted, probably because the cheater was so good at maintaining that dual-personality. Either that, or the betrayed spouse really was clueless.

This one is a hard revelation for me as I am hearing-impaired, my husband is not. I'm sure he thought it would be easy to cheat on me, as I couldn't hear his side of phone conversations. As someone said to me, it was easy for him to cheat on me, in front of me, which made him the ultimate asshole, taking advantage of a "poor, handicapped person" ...not!

The only problem for him was my sense of perception and interpretation of body language is very keen; when you lose one sense, all the others seem to magnify to compensate for the loss.

I truly believe he needed to "talk" to someone, and didn't feel I measured up, because I couldn't hear. Never mind my intelligence, never mind that I've been told by others that I'm a great listener and conversationalist. Some ingrained part of him probably believed that I couldn't give him what he needed in that department.

So, if everything was "right" in the marriage, would there be adultery? Who the heck knows? Maybe some couples are so good at hiding their imperfect marriage that the truth never gets out. I think what I meant to say was... everything seemed to be right in our marriage, except for the fact that I am deaf (in his perception).

Emily:

I think in most cases, things aren't right and so spouses cheat. But I believe my husband had a need to get affirmation and he cannot be loyal to one woman. I just don't think it is possible for him.

When I was pregnant with my first child, I was not able to do much because I had a problem pregnancy; he had already started. If someone pays attention to him and there is alcohol involved, he is very, very susceptible to cheating. I couldn't be there every minute so he strayed.

Helen:

I think if a person perceives a problem, the key word here being "perceives," then they believe there is a problem. Does that necessarily mean there is a problem in the marriage? No, I don't think so. I believe there are circumstances where one's perception is definitely skewed, i.e., depression.

Now, if a depressed person feels he is unloved or unappreciated, does that necessarily make it true? Maybe. But then again, maybe not. I believe a person's history sometimes provides a better answer than his or her current perception.

Beverly:

An inherent flaw is the problem with my husband. There was no problem 30 days into our marriage. He did not know how to keep a promise. He has no honor. He thinks only of himself.

I forgave him more times than I want to remember. We went to counseling many times. He could not tell the counselor one thing that was wrong with me. I never like to yell or fight. I would talk and try to fix anything I could.

I was willing to change to make him happy. It only made him mad. My never getting angry made him mad. My being calm made him angry. My willing to have sex anytime he wanted made him mad. It is my belief that he is angry with himself and not me.

I would give him a back rub every night at bed time. I told him what a goodlooking man he is to me. He would yell that I need to quit saying these things to him. He was not going to be nice to me. I was nice and he got mad. I was sweet and loving and he got mean. The hate poured out of him. Just like the counselor said, he needed a lot of help. I was not the problem.

I am going to be okay. I know that I am a good person and loving. I did not one thing to cause this affair.

Paula:

I think in the case of my husband it was not that there was anything wrong in the marriage, it was the sense of urgency he was feeling with aging, the thoughts of "is this all there is." He put too much effort into work, and forgot what was important.

Our marriage and sex life were great until he hit 40, and even after he began seeing the other woman we were still intimate. All he could see was the fantasy, and no one can compete with a fantasy.

So my answer to your question is: yes, adultery can happen even if everything in your marriage is right. I think his other woman made him feel sorry for her and the rest is history.

Something inside of him snapped and he became so unhappy where he was in his life that he started trying to figure out why he was so unhappy. Instead of looking within, he began pointing a finger at the one that loved him the most, me.

John:

Yes, I do believe that adultery does happen even if everything is going great in a marriage. It depends on that person and what is going on in their life.

Stats show that more men have affairs than women. I think that is because for centuries it has been a men's culture that affairs are okay to have, mostly with the wealthy and the powerful men. In today's society, affairs are very common in both men and women. Even more so now than it has ever been.

I believe that is because we have gotten to "if it feels good, do it" mentality. The big difference between now and back in yesteryear is that it is talked about now. Way back when, it was known, but it was never talked about.

William:

I doubt that adultery will happen if everything is right in a marriage. But, how many marriages are there where everything is right? If you cannot learn to live with your partner's personality flaws, you leave yourself open for problems. True married love is give and take, more giving than taking. It is a full time job. You must show your partner that you care. You have to communicate.

In my case, depression caused me to withdraw. It frustrated my ex-wife. She responded by showing her terrible temper. We quit communicating. She turned to someone else for comfort. And, she wanted to punish me.

Daniel:
First of all, I have come to realize that there is no such thing as a perfect marriage. Some are much better than others, but they all have elements within them that could be better. But, even in the best of marriages and relationships, adultery can raise it's ugly head.

I still believe that my wife and I had a good marriage. There were no overbearing influences within it to cause her to look outside of it for happiness. What I mean by that is, from all appearances, we lived an idylic life. Nice home, good neighbors, great kids, free of credit card debt, all in good health, and financially strong.

If I had any complaint, it was the frequency of our lovemaking (I wanted more). We had gotten into a routine where weekends were the only possible times to squeeze it in. My wife had always insisted on getting her eight hours of sleep, so school nights made it almost impossible to have sex.

My wife would not even consider having sex if she thought any of the kids were still awake, as she had heard her parents having sex as a child and she swore it "traumatized" her. Couple that with some nights we'd both be exhausted from the daily trials and tribulations of being parents, the thought of sex wouldn't even enter the picture.

All of these things relegated us to Friday or Saturday nights as our only possibilities. I came to accept this schedule as our "reality" and even though I made it clear I wanted more, I never demanded more.

I can remember a few years before we separated, a study on the sexual habits of married people came out. The results were something like "the average married couple has sex 2.4 times per week." My wife was aghast at that conclusion and vehemently questioned me as to "how" a couple could possibly have sex that many times per month?

This only served to reinforce to me, that she was quite content with our frequency. At no time did my wife ever negatively comment or complain to me about any aspect of our marriage.

So, if all of what I have written is historically accurate, what caused her to go outside of our marriage for sex and happiness? Well, perception is everything! Somewhere and something along the way, caused my wife to suddenly perceive that she was not happy. I believe that when that happens to a person, they tend to dwell on what they perceive as a negative and it festers.

They tend to overlook or forget all the positives and concern themselves only with what they feel they are missing. As time goes by, they begin to perceive other "problems" or dissatisfactions in their lives, and ultimately convince themselves that they are justified in going outside of their marriage.

I know that there are many cases of spontaneous adultery where some catalyst such as alcohol plays a dominant role in the decision to have sex outside of marriage. Those instances are just as reprehensible, but at least a little easier to explain.

I'm sure most of us here do not fall in that category. Instead, we are dealing with seemingly wonderful spouses who suddenly and without provocation jumped into bed with someone else. They justified their actions as being acceptable to them because of perceptions, and I bet not one of them ever really agonized over how that choice would affect their spouse and children. My guess is they were only concerned with their own wants and needs.

Over the past five years or so, I have read countless references as to how we have become the "me" society. As long as that type of thinking remains prevalent in humankind, the instances of adultery will continue to increase regardless of the strength of a marriage or relationship.

···→··→··→

Would an open marriage have kept your spouse (or you) from being unfaithful?

Several books on adultery suggest that we humans aren't meant to be "locked" into one relationship for our entire lifetime — that being in a marriage "with fringes" is beneficial for all involved. So, given that as a starting point to this question, if your husband or wife said he or she felt the need to have a sexual relationship with someone else — but still wanted to remain married — could you have accepted an "open marriage" arrangement — assuming you, too, would be able to have outside relationships of your own?

Miriam:

Well, maybe it's just my mood right now, but I do believe that if my husband had ever suggested such a thing to me, I would have shot him on the spot. And I can't even imagine what he would have done to me. So, no, I don't think screwing around would have helped us any. There was a little too much of that going on as it was.

As far as the fringe benefits thing, I don't really see that. It does seem to me that multiple partners in an exclusive marriage tends to breed contempt and distrust and well, apathy. Who do you love? Well, too much of a good thing, and who the hell knows?

Candace:

I was thinking the other day of a book I read in the 70's called "Open Marriage." I think it influenced my point of view to the extent that I thought both parties of a married couple should be free to have relationships outside of marriage, although I did not believe that those relationships should be sexual.

I think I was naive in those days to think that men and women could be close friends without that happening. And I didn't go back to the book to see what they said when your husband started spending too much emotion on the other person.

I don't think openness to sex would have saved our marriage. My husband was never looking for sex so having sex outside of marriage wouldn't have helped. He was looking for "love." Always has been. Still is. I think my husband's over openness to intimate relationships killed it. So much for open marriage. At this point I want more of an exclusive relationship.

I think that although we are not destined to love one and only one person I think it is in everyone's best interest if we limit ourselves to one love interest at a time. In the writings of a certain religion I know it is mentioned that theoretically people could be allowed multiple spouses if and only if they can treat them equally without any jealousies arising. Since this is only theoretical and not realistic, multiple marriages are not allowed in this religion. I thought at the time the fact that a religion would even mention that a man or a woman would consider another spouse was interesting. But no, it is forbidden.

Karla:

I don't share well with others! When my ex-husband mentioned swinging, I about threw up! How dare he suggest something like that to someone he claimed to love! But apparently he'd been thinking about it for awhile.

Raquel:

I had an open marriage and didn't know it! My husband had many secret one night stands during our marriage but that obviously wasn't enough. He still became emotionally involved with an other woman. So, my opinion is a resounding "no."

Dana:

I kind of think my husband would have liked to have an open marriage: keep me as the wife and mother of his child, and do all the other stuff with the other woman. Problem is, I don't share. Never have and never will. So the answer would be NOPE. Having an "open" marriage was not the answer for saving *my* marriage.

Dana:

During the time that I was suspicious of my husband having an affair, I had to serve on jury duty. The bailiff was a good looking guy, and during our intermissions and lunch breaks, he would come and talk with me. We struck up a friendship that lasted the duration of jury duty. He wrote me a few times afterwards.

I'd mentioned it to my husband, but he didn't seem to think anything of it, until one day (much, much later) during marriage counseling. The counselor brought up something about why I was having a hard time with forgiving my husband for having an affair.

I said that he never said he was sorry for having the affair, that he said it "was something he needed" and he would not apologize for it. I mentioned that he didn't seem to show any remorse for hurting me. Then my husband comes out with, "Well, you were seeing that cop!" I looked at him and said, "What?" He said, "I forgave you for seeing that cop." I started laughing, and said, "I didn't sleep with him, it wasn't anything beyond someone to talk to during jury duty, and besides, you were fully aware of who he was."

Then the counselor asked my husband if I had been sleeping with the cop, would he have accepted that? My husband said, "No f**king way!"

So... what's good for that gander was not good for this goose. So, no, an open marriage, even if I was willing, would not have worked in our case. I suspect that my husband was not open to the idea of my having other relationships during the marriage. Probably would have felt too much of a threat to him.

Jeff:

I think we all fantasize about having sex with someone else... it happens. It's a thought which (to me) flits through the back of your mind from time to time. After all, isn't this why we (especially women) dress up and look good? So that others see us and appreciate what they see? We all do this, present ourselves to the rest of the world as best we can -- most of the time. What a wonderful sight! To see a woman that takes care of herself, and is proud of who she is! This is not always an "invitation" to "jump into bed".

When is an "affair" an "affair"? Thinking about it isn't in my mind an affair. Circumstances in our daily lives can lead to a sexual encounter -- it happens -- and I know I can hear moans and groans from some of you -- but unless you've been there, done that, how can you say otherwise?

Okay, so there's this sex encounter. Once a party attaches affection to the encounter, and afterwards, it becomes an affair! So... open marriages? I don't know, but it always sounded to me like Adam and Eve and the Apple. There's a sex bomb walking down the street, we meet someone at a conference, in the bar (what were you doing there in the first place?) and so on = The Apple. If we reach out it's big, huge, trouble! So we cockup. Now how do we handle this? Open marriages? Didn't we get married to love, cherish and all that, a promise we make, not to reach out for the apple?

I don't think open marriages can or will work. There has to be some sort of underlying current which hides some of the transparency which is supposed to be almost the forefront of all marriages. Isn't complete communication supposed to be the very essence of our bond?

Emily:

An open marriage could never have worked for our relationship. For the first five years of our marriage, my husband was more jealous of me and what I did, or thought of doing, than I was of him. He told me on many, many occasions in counseling and outside of counseling, that had I been unfaithful, like he had been unfaithful, that would be it. Period! He could never stay with me if I were unfaithful.

So, what was good for the gooose, most definitely was not good for the gander!

Alan:

My wife and I had discussed the "open marriage" concept. We discussed it at some length and with counselor and friends and decided it would not have worked for us. We are both too jealous. Now, of course, my wife still spends time with other men, but claims there is no intimacy.

I think an open marriage would work only if the couple was very much in love with one another.

Misty:

I do feel that *yes*, I could have saved my marriage if I agreed to an "open relationship."

The subject had come up about a year ago, the husband and I have two close couples of ours that have an open relationship and their marriages have not only survived but are strong. Looking at the couples, I have found that the number one reason this works is *communication*. They are so honest with each other and I guess they have figured out that they cannot be everything to each other and don't try to be.

I don't think that the situation would work if it was only sexual, one couple has had the same other woman and other man for over 10 years. The other couple, the husband has been with his other woman for a long time, the wife feels the need to change more often, they do tell each other what is going on. They respect each other and it works.

When my husband first brought the concept up about a year ago, I was totally against it. I figured that he was just trying to have his cake and eat it too. We discussed it a few times and I was warming up to the idea after discussions with my friends, but then it just never was discussed again. Life went on.

My husband and I had been friends a long time before we became intimate with each other and had dealt with a relationship where we dated others, so I did see how it could have worked. There were times where he cheated on me, but he was honest and I accepted it and we worked through it. Looking back, the marriage could have been saved, but my husband forgot one really important thing, *honesty*.

Of course we're dealing with hindsight, but if my husband would have been honest with me before he had the affair, or soon thereafter, the situation may have been very different. Do I think I could have slept with another man? I don't know, but I would have had the option and eventually who knows. Once he stepped over the line of not being open and honest, I lost respect and there was/ is no going back.

He had been living with her for three months and I never even knew, so what would have been the difference? In one of those last ditch efforts we made to save the relationship, I did bring up the idea of him staying in the house and having his girlfriend, too, hey you're a part-time daddy, why not a part-time husband?

I was serious and considering it until, two things happened. One, we were intimate and I had the vibe that he was feeling guilty for "cheating" on his girlfriend and two, my mother said I was being silly that he was a good husband and I should put up with him having a girlfriend (a one-sided street). I was livid. I guess it was the way it was said and the knowledge that he was with someone else and had lied to me about it.

I have since found a wonderful man and have been intimate again, so does that mean we are living the open marriage? We both know about each other's relationships and have even discussed some aspects of them. I do not want to save this marrige now, I have been so damaged by the lies, but it definitely could have been different.

Lora:

I also know of a couple who have an open marriage and it works for them. They do everything together. For some it can work, for others, it can't. In my case, no, an open marriage would not have saved my marriage.

1.) My husband was the only one with the desire to be with anyone else.

2.) No matter what he says (that he doesn't get jealous), I know for a fact that if I ever were to be with anyone else, he would lose it!

3.) My skin crawled at the idea of another woman's hands touching him.

I'm sure there are other reasons, but those are the ones that hit me at this time.

Ashleigh:

My spouse never hinted at wanting an open marriage but he would have been perfectly content to keep me in the dark and performing all of my duties (secretary, money manager, property maintenance, etc.). But, I have male friends, one of which I speak with on a daily basis. He hated it, didn't understand it, was angry because he made me laugh. About a week ago he actually told me that if that man had attempted to see me while I was in the hospital he would have punched him out.

Nope, an open marriage would not have worked. He denies being jealous but he is. I am not jealous but I think if your marriage is in trouble then adding fuel to the flame serves no purpose.

I agree with whoever said that an open marriage could only work if two people were deeply in love with a penchant for multiple partners.

Angela:

I had an "open separation" -- or rather two of them. And, I hated it. But, that is what Lee Raffel recommends in her book *Should I Stay or Go: How a Controlled Separation Can Save Your Marriage*. I did agree to letting him "date" other women (which he certainly did!) but I felt I agreed under extreme duress.

Our marriage was somewhat open, too, in that he did have other sexual partners from time to time. Of course, I didn't know about those encounters. So, the idea of an open marriage gets a great big "no" from me. It wouldn't have worked for us. I don't share well. Also, like my husband found out, some people can't keep emotional imtimacy out of sex with a long term partner.

Alan:

Well, I now have an "open separation." I don't think it is going to do anything positive for our marriage, if there is anything left of it, but I must say I am having a great time.

I am now sure that an open marriage is not for me.

····➤·➤·➤

Why did you suspect your spouse was having an affair?

Was there something specific that made you suspect an affair? Were there tangible clues, solid evidence such as lipstick on a collar, perfume, unexplained expenses? Or did a change in behavior, mood, or schedule make you suspicious?

Miriam:
It was combination of things that built up over a long period of time. I always knew my husband had a "propensity" for women. I knew he liked women, knew he liked being a "hero" to women. Even so, I, in my arrogance, thought that my husband would never step over that line because he knew I would never accept an adulterer (or I thought that anyway) and, he would do nothing that would upset his little nest, as he had it pretty good and he knew it.

But after a time, I came to suspect that he was keeping secrets from me. It was very intangible. The way he answered questions (very defensive and almost "too" innocent, if that makes any sense). The way he looked at me sometimes, at times very scared looking, other times very smug, as though he knew something I didn't.

Even the way he touched me felt "wrong." Sometimes passionate and grasping, as though he felt I was slipping away from him. Other times, I felt like there was something standing in between us. I could almost feel it. Or as it turned out... her.

I also considered the possibility that I was imagining all of it and I was just plain nuts.

Nevertheless, I started paying more attention to these things. The more I concentrated on it, the "wronger" it felt. I asked a few innocent sounding questions here and there, such as his views on fidelity and marriage and asked what he thought regarding circumstances surrounding others we knew who were going through affairs and losing their families because of it.

He seemed as though the issues at hand didn't apply to him. As though he were "above" it somehow.

I listened closer to him when he talked about women at work. I started looking through his jackets and actually, one time very early on, found a note to him written by somebody. A very vague note, in feminine writing, but nevertheless, it had a personal tone to it. I became suspicious then.

It was hard to pin down because he was home so much. But he also worked a lot and he always had an excuse for his late hours, sometimes very defensive, angry excuses.

I kept looking. I found a cell phone I knew nothing about. All hell hit the fan. He swore he needed it for work and he didn't tell me because he didn't want me calling and disrupting work. I knew that was a lie. He knew I rarely did that anyway. I didn't argue. But I did remember it.

I started looking for other evidence. I came across a check from a separate checking account from a jewelry store. It was marked simply "gift." He had given me jewelry before, so I could not be sure. This time I didn't say anything at all. I made a copy of the check and kept looking.

He was getting nervous. He kept trying to please me, taking me places and such, but it seemed the more I confirmed my suspicions and reaffirmed I wasn't crazy after all, the angrier I became. I started disappearing myself. Sometimes it was just to get a grip on myself, and sometimes to think it all through so it made sense. I truly felt I was losing it. Was it real?

And I just kept getting angrier.

Then one morning, something told me where to look. And I found it all. Hidden files of checks showing gifts for lingerie, more jewelry, you name it, there it was. Things I had never gotten. Ever. I looked for cellphone records, but they were not detailed, so it didn't help any. I made copies of them all.

I felt so cold. No feelings at all. Just a growing seed of rage than even then I knew I had to keep tightly controlled before it got the better of me.

Karla:

What made me suspicious? Well, he was stand-offish. Quiet. Glued to the TV. Then he would come home from working at the bar later and later, that's the joy of an indigo watch.

The one time I was invited by him to the bar, he and the other woman were in a corner discussing something ear to ear. While I didn't think anything of it at the time, my sister sure did. Then I would hear how this woman and her husband's counseling wasn't helping, how she wasn't coming home until 7 am, how unhappy she was. I was curious as to why he knew so much about what was going on with her, well I guess I know now why!

The day after our divorce, I called her husband. I asked him if they were dating, and he told me that was his impression. I asked him if there was any chance of them reconciling, and he said no. Needless to say the "you know what" hit the fan when my ex-husband found out I called her husband.

Then I had men he worked with asking me about it! They had seen him around town with some other woman and they knew it wasn't me and no one had the nerve to ask him. Then he decided to brag to a very good friend of mine about his new girlfriend and her kids. She pretended she didn't know anything about it.

Then it was finally confirmed the day of the other woman's divorce when I saw both of them walk out of the courthouse after her hearing. She had the nerve to wear black like she was the dumped spouse!

Dana:

We'd had the type of marriage that taking someone of the opposite sex to lunch was not a threat, or so I thought. When my husband was promoted to a managerial position he ended up with a female assistance and, of course, they worked closely together and went out to lunch quite often. I became a little concerned when it seemed as if every time I turned around, it was always "A" this or "A" that. I tried to tell myself it was normal, she was his assistant after all, and that they do work together.

One office party, I noticed "A" was spending a lot of time with my husband, dancing with him, leaving her husband alone at the table. I asked him what was going on with the two of them, and he said they were just very good friends and that he was thankful for having such a great assistant.

Wanting to believe him and thinking I was just being over-reactive or over-suspicious or whatever, I buried my head in the sand, pretty much gritted my teeth and bore it, until I'd had surgery a few months later. I was in the hospital for three days, and on the morning that he was to pick me up, he didn't show until I had a nurse call him to come pick me up. He dropped me off at home, and said he had to go to "A's" house for her son's birthday. That's when it hit me, that she seemed to be getting more important to him than I was.

I knew that his assistant's husband was going to be out of town for a week and, sure enough, my husband said he had a business meeting one day during that same week and that "all the managers and assistants were going to dinner afterwards." He did not return until 3 in the morning. I waited up for him in the dark, and when he came in through the door, I startled him with the question, "So, are you guys physical now?"

He asked me what I was doing up, and I said, it doesn't matter, are you guys physical? He said, "What kind of a question is that?!" and I calmly said, "Just answer the question." He gave me the answer that they had kissed on the cheek but that was as far as it went. I pretended to accept that answer, and I went to bed.

They ended up moving to another state and I was ecstatic, because at this time, I had been very suspicious but had no concrete proof there was an affair. I thought with her gone, my husband and I could go back to just each other with no "outside distractions." But, soon after she left, my husband kept getting suspicious calls that he would take in another room. I would ask him who the calls were from and he would answer, "It's just work."

One night while my husband was asleep, I went out to his business car, and searched through the whole car. I found letters, pictures, little gifts, etc., in his briefcase. One letter, in particular, was a sort of "good bye" card, and it started out with: "I will always hold on... to the memories of time we've spent together... as partners, as my confidant, as friends and as lovers..."

I literally "whited out," felt a powerful blow to my chest that knocked out my breath for a few seconds. I just sat there and shook my head, no, no, no. I don't remember how long I sat there in the car in the middle of the night, but it sure seemed like a long time. It was one thing to suspect, and quite a whole other thing to actually confirm all your worst fears.

I drove to my work at 3 or 4 that morning, made copies of all his letters (from her and to her), the pictures, the receipts of gifts to her, his cell phone records. The next day, I asked him to meet me at a park near his work for a picnic lunch. I met him there with my daughter, and while she was playing in the playground, I asked him if he heard from "A."

He said he had not heard from her since she moved. And I said, oh yeah? And pulled out from my purse all the copies I had made. He was totally shocked. I don't think he thought I would ever really find out. And *that* was the beginning of the end.

Raquel:

I was so incredibly trusting that I had no suspicions at all for a long, long time. Even after he became very depressed (due to her leaving the country on an extended trip) I put it down to job-related problems. It was not until after he insisted there was no other woman that I started to notice how much contact he and she were having on the internet, contact that he didn't even bother to keep secret!

I slowly started to put the pieces of the puzzle together but, even then, I couldn't believe he would actually have an affair. But, something deep down inside me told me that I had to face the truth.

Imagine my surprise when I found out some time later he had had a series of one-night stands throughout our marriage!

My husband certainly liked women and got on well with them. I even knew that he flirted with them and liked some of them more than he should have for a married man. But, I never thought he would step over that line.

I also knew he had always had commitment problems but even those seemed to fade as the years passed. Our marriage appeared to be working despite what I viewed as the kind of problems I could overcome by being a "superwife."

In retrospect I was far too trusting. And he was far too willing to take advantage of that trust.

Angela:

I became suspicious because of his emotional involvement. And when he talked about her every day. Regarding his Internet affair, I had also come across a chat message that was a little too intimate for "friends." About the real deal in town, when it became obvious that she and her family were his priority.

In both cases he also pulled away from me emotionally and our sex life died away. I was making all the moves and he wasn't really responding. That was a big sign for him.

Candace:

My husband always had friends who were women. During the early years of our marriage most of them were my friends, too. I implicitly trusted both of them although there were times I was suspicious because of how close they were. I thought I was just being jealous. I ignored or tried to ignore.

More recently my husband started making friends with women independently of me. I didn't know them. He would take them out for coffee and not include me. I didn't like that and complained. He invited me but then it was always awkward because he wouldn't talk at all. He felt uncomfortable and so did I.

He started giving lessons to one woman. I stopped by one day when my grandson was visiting, and my husband thought I was "checking up" on him. I wasn't, but it set an alarm off that maybe I should be.

I watched body language and I noticed them sitting in adjacent desks, body parts almost touching, and eyes gazing. That was it. The romantic love between them was a betrayal even if there was no physical relationship.

My husband's behavior continued with intimate e-mails to her, time spent away from me to be with her. I started looking for more concrete evidence and found it one day when he left his e-mail box open and I saw 15 letters from her. I admit, I read one... or two.

Vivian:

There were no tell-tale signs. Nothing, nada, zip. He will forever be the "great pretender." I discovered a rather full grocery bag of correspondence while cleaning the attic. This bag had been hidden behind a stack of boxes. I was totally shocked as I read each and every card and letter from the other woman.

Shortly after my husband and I married, we moved into our new home. His best friend since childhood asked if he and his fiancee could be married in our home. We were delighted. Like many young couples, we shared vacations together, having and raising children, the "ups and downs"... everything.

We had two beautiful children together. He was, and still is, an excellent father. He had a wonderful career, and was active in the community and church. He involved himself in the children's activities, and mine as well. He encouraged me to be a "stay at home" mom and supported my talents as an artist. Perfect is the only word I can think of to describe our family.

The two of them began their affair eight years into our marriage and my discovery happened during the third year of their affair. It was devastating. It's true, "I was the last to know." I was a zombie, I felt as if I were on auto-pilot when it came to day-to-day tasks. I was losing everything I had worked for.

I filed for a divorce only three days after finding and copying the contents of the bag for my attorney and for her husband, my husband's best friend. When I confronted my husband with my discovery and that I had filed for divorce, he said nothing. He simply packed his things and moved into an apartment across town.

Throughout the separation I asked him many times, why? He never answered me. For the sake of the children, I never denied his requests for visitation or participation with the children while the divorce was pending.

The divorce took almost a year to settle and during that time I became familiar with the intimate details of their affair. I learned that her third child was actually fathered by my husband.

Since the divorce over a dozen years ago, I have thought about that whole ordeal over and over again. There were never any clues! I had no reason ever to be suspicious.

The other couple went into counseling and are still married. My ex-husband married a lovely woman a couple years ago. Since both of our children are on their own, there is no need for he and I to communicate. I am now engaged.

Rob:

I actually fill more than one role as I was cheated on by my first wife and I wound up the cheater to my second. In between I was the other man to a few out of pure spite.

What made me suspicious of my first wife? Well, she left where we were living to supposedly take our child to a doctor in her hometown for a check-up. After she was gone a couple of days, I called and she told me she was not coming back. So I ended up moving there because I didn't want to lose my marriage and family. I got my old job back and went to work on a Monday only to come home and find a note on the table.

We went round and round when I finally found her at her mother's. She moved into her own place and we were seeing each other and I finally moved in with her. A lot of my friends used to stop by for a beer or three and the thing that tipped me off was when a guy needed a ride home and then she didn't come home until the next morning. I looked for them through the night, but they were well hidden. Thank God I didn't find them.

I left after that (she also hit me a few times during the arguments leading up to my leaving with her balled up fist and yes, I slapped the dog sh*t out of her after taking all I could). I lived with a guy I knew until I caught them together one night. I was at a friend's house playing poker and drinking beer when I decided to try to talk to her again to try put things back together.

They had left his truck somewhere and just her car was there. She wouldn't answer the door, so I came through the living room window and sometime during the time I was knocking and then coming in the window, the guy went to the back of the house and got dressed and she was out there talking to me in her underwear. Well, this guy comes out and I lost it. I wrecked her house and came as close to killing two people as I ever want to.

I believe, looking back on it now, that lack of communication was a big, big factor in all of it. And being far too young with many bad circumstances surrounding that relationship.

···►··►··►

When you suspected your spouse was cheating, how did you gather evidence of the affair?

You may have had a "gut" feeling that your husband or wife was cheating but you needed actual proof of the affair to confirm those feelings. What did you do to get evidence? And when you found tangible evidence, how did you feel?

Jeff:

When I noticed the "attitude" and got the "speech letter" — I was left thinking "who in hell" had encroached in *my* marriage?

Cell phone -- most obvious! I called for all the accounts since day one! The trail was long, wide, and very littered with huge "evidence."

Her current "toy" lived in an "apartment" and I asked some of the people who lived in the complex, and they knew all about my ex-wife and her toy, how often she had been there, what time of the day, weekends, etc.

So I got it all. But, why? What was I going to do with this info? Nothing! It was just that I needed to be sure, and it is a whack in the head once you find out!

The odd times of getting home, 4 or 5 in the morning was nothing! "I've been having coffee with a 'friend'!" What had happened to my IQ? What was she thinking? I saw them "having coffee" hand in hand and all the other stuff, why?

Again, to get it clear in my mind that her reasons for wanting a divorce were not what she was telling me. She was hiding the fact that there was an other man, and in the trail I found there had been many other men! Talk about blind!

Other than that, it's not like I wanted to "catch them," more to make it hit home in my head. Funny enough, I was not mad at all, I just couldn't believe I was being betrayed! I had to make sure that this woman I'd loved, committed to, cared for, that was my very being, was doing this, and making it all my fault!

Once the "road to divorce" was on the cards, I decided that at all costs I'd retain my dignity and manners, and not lose it, get mad (externally) or rant and rave. I wanted to walk away with an amicable friendliness, but, she had other ideas. She screamed and flamed until the last day.

Yes, I was hurting inside. Yes, I was mad inside. Yes, I went through all the emotions, but was determined not to show them.

I guess it's a man thing - yes?

Miriam:

I "knew" but had to have the evidence, in black and white, irrefutable proof, before I got enough guts to do something about it.

I was very angry. You know that kind of black rage where you get very quiet and just kind of cold inside? That kind. I scared myself a few times because I knew, beyond a shadow of a doubt, that with the right explosive circumstances, I was quite capable of hurting him. So I kept a very tight rein on myself. I had to know, to see it. I guess I thought I would be able to make more rational decisions.

Searching for the evidence of his adultery gave me a focus for my anger. Kept me searching and thinking, rather than brooding. I knew how to check on bank accounts, how to handle jewelry store clerks, etc., without them being suspicious of my questions, knew how to secure cell phone bills (although they didn't help me, weren't detailed, but the amounts were very high).

During this time, the black rage settled down to a kind of contempt, I think. Not only of him and what he had done, but of what I had deliberately let myself not see. How could I have been such a fool for so long?

So I gathered evidence. And then I gathered materials to protect myself, such as property assessments, made pictures of everything we owned, money funds, all of it. All before I was ready to do anything about him. A long time before.

Dana:

I searched my husband's car one night and found letters, little gifts, pictures, receipts of gifts to her, a whole stack of incriminating "evidence" which I then copied so there was no way he could deny anything. She and her husband had moved away at that point.

She moved back almost five years later and less than a year later, my husband gave me "the speech" and moved into his own apartment. He never mentioned that "she" was back in town so I checked on her, went by her place of employment to check that it really was her, followed her to her apartment so I knew where she lived.

I asked my husband if she was back, and he acted like he didn't know. When he pulled his "all nighters" at work again, I knew something was up. This time, he was pretty careful. I never caught them together or had any other proof that he was seeing her until one day after church, over a year since I heard she'd returned.

I thought I'd stop by my husband's apartment with our daughter to say hello and to see if he wanted to go to breakfast with us. This was about a month after he moved out, to "find his space."

As my daughter and I were walking to his apartment, the balcony came into view. She was there on the balcony, and we saw each other at the same time. She literally ran into the apartment, so I went up to the door and knocked, but of course, no one would answer the door.

That was the irrefutable proof that she was back in his life, and there was no going back. My trust in him was completely and irretrievably severed from that point on.

Candace:

My husband covered up his actions under the guise of service and friendship. I felt uncomfortable about this kind of service but I needed something more specific. One day when the computer went online his inbox was right there for the gawking. I saw about 15 letters from her. I read some.

I didn't need anything more but looked on ICQ to just see if he wrote to her there. I didn't turn anything up but found notes to other women about her and other young girls who I thought were just friends, too! I cut and pasted and left them on the computer. Not as smart as photocopying. Then when I showed them to him he forcibly removed the evidence.

I also checked the phone bill which I figured out how to read and noticed numbers that I didn't know. When questioned, he had no answers. That was good enough for me.

Raquel:

My husband covered his tracks well. His other woman was one of several young women who socialized with several of the men in his office. As far as I knew, he was out with the group when, in fact, he and the other woman were having their own private parties. Of course, most of the group were "in" on the deception. I didn't suspect anything until she actually did go out of state and he became very depressed and very angry.

Since he didn't get along with his new supervisor at work, I assumed at first that this was the cause of the change in his demeanor. When I finally asked what was going on, he denied the existence of the other woman and, like the naive and trusting person I used to be, I believed him.

But, at some time in the following weeks I started to realize that my honest and trustworthy husband was not as honest and trustworthy as I thought. I didn't have any hard evidence but I began to suspect that the communication between them, although he didn't hide it from me until later, was far more frequent and detailed than it should ever have been between a supervisor and a former female employee thirty years his junior.

So, I confronted him without any real evidence and he did admit that he had "some feelings" for her. They supposedly broke off their relationship at that point.

My search for evidence only started after this admission when it became obvious that he had not broken up with her. My search, at different times, included:

- looking at ICQ history since he always deleted his conversations but didn't realize that I could find even deleted messages. Although he didn't talk to her on ICQ he did talk to others about her and his feelings for her.

- looking through his pockets after he took a trip from one city to another to break up with her. It was what I didn't find that was significant. He had thrown away his motel receipt, something he never does or never did until he had something to hide.

- finding and using his Hotmail password where I discovered what amounted to the "last straw" that led to our first separation. This was almost a full year after I first realized that something was amiss.

- looking through his camera bag where I found his secret stash of gifts, letters and photographs. This was just before he moved out the first time. I don't know what prompted me to look. Maybe it was just a feeling there was even more to the story than he had already admitted to. Again, of course, I was right.

I think looking for evidence almost became an end in itself, a compulsion I found hard to give up even after our second reconciliation. It was almost as if I wanted to find more!

Alan:

I read my wife's journal and found out all kinds of stuff. I am not proud I did it, but it's too late now. I was just driven by this compulsion to "know."

Teresa:

I'd had my suspicions for a while but my husband had always made me feel like I was going mad. Everything was all in my head. I was some mad jealous woman finding problems where none existed. He had never ever cheated on anyone before. He was not that sort of man.

When I got the speech initially I veered wildly between being sure there was someone else, to thinking he was ill or depressed, and back again. I really, really wanted to believe that there was no one else but my sister and my friends all told me that there would be. My husband was incapable of going anywhere alone so absolutely no one believed he would live on his own.

When he was out I looked at his contacts in his electronic organizer. He had admitted to an affair before and then said he had only said that to hurt me and it had not been true. On that occasion the person he told me about was the one woman in his gang at work that he never mentioned.

Her name never came up at all. So when I went through the list of names I looked for a woman he had never mentioned before. I found one and he had all her phone numbers, home, work, mobile, and "mum & dad" (entered as "mum & dad," not "parents" or "Mr & Mrs x").

I looked through the bin and found a receipt for jewelry bought for cash the day before Valentine's Day. It was my birthday a week later so I waited to see whether I would receive any jewelry but I didn't.

When I confronted him he told a pack of lies and I still really wanted to believe him. However, again everyone around me told me to get a grip and face up to the fact he was having an affair. I finally believed it when I went to a site on the Internet that gave all the signs of an affair and I could tick off most of them (i.e., his mobile phone which had always been switched on before started to be switched off and he had put a bar on it so I couldn't access it. The phone bills no longer arrived at our house, etc.).

I looked for further evidence in his car, briefcase and clothes but never found anything else. I researched her on the Internet and found out where she lived and that she had recently changed her name.

I contacted a private detective and arranged for him to follow them but I pulled out at the last minute. I decided to stop as I felt like a mad woman out of control. It just wasn't healthy and I "knew" anyway.

Once he left there were a lot of clues, things he would never think anyone would pick up on. He would send the kids presents with cutesy fluffy notelets (not his sort of thing at all).

He got an attorney in the same town as she lives, miles from where he lives. The kids saw a great big cuddly dog in his apartment which he said he had bought himself to stop from feeling lonely.

He had fancy candles around the apartment (feminine touch). He mistakenly put her hometown down as part of his address rather than the town he is living in. The list is endless and so easy to see once the rose coloured specs have come off.

Karla:

I downloaded his personal ad. I wanted to tape it to the doors in the women's restroom at his club, but I didn't think about it until later. After that I would snoop through his wallet, pockets, etc. Not a proud moment in my life, but you do what you have to do.

⋯▶⋯▶⋯▶

How did you handle the confrontation with your spouse once you had proof of infidelity?

If you were the betrayed, did you confront your unfaithful spouse? If so, what was the outcome and would you do the same thing again? If you were the betrayer, did your spouse confront you about your affair? If so, what was the outcome and what was your reaction to the confrontation?

Raquel:

As I believe is very common, the first time I asked my husband if he was involved with an other woman, he denied it. His exact words were: "I'm not seeing anyone at the moment." My husband has a way with words and he knew that I would take that to mean there was no other woman without him actually lying. How was this possible? His other woman at the time was living out of state so he couldn't actually "see" her.

However, that deception lasted less than six weeks as it became more and more obvious to me that there was an other woman and even who she was. So, I confronted him a second time. But, it took me several days and a couple of beers to work up the courage to do so. In fact, we were walking home from a night out at a bar at the time.

What I said this time was: "I know why you said you weren't seeing someone else. You said that because she is in xxx and her name is xxx." This time he didn't deny it at all. I think he was so totally blown away that I had figured it out he didn't have time to think of a way to wiggle out of the truth.

He then told her I knew and she, in turn, immediately tried to break up with him. As a result, he became extremely upset. Being the nice person I am, I consoled him and held him while he cried over her! Of course, they didn't really break up at that time or for a long time after that, but that's a different story.

Miriam:

When I was thoroughly sure that I had been lied to and betrayed and that my husband was cheating on me, I decided to see if, when backed into a corner, he would, (a) tell the truth, or (b) continue to lie. So I invited him out to dinner.

I had the copies of the checks, etc., in my purse. When dinner was over, and we were sitting there just finishing up drinks, I looked him in the eyes and asked: "Are you cheating on me? Blonde, brunette, redhead, married or single? Are you cheating?" He turned white as a ghost. He stuttered and looked away. He turned back and said, "No babe, when in the world would I have time to cheat? I work too much. And I love you."

I said nothing for a minute. Then I said: "You know that to find out you had betrayed me would destroy my love for you, don't you? Not to mention what it would do to me. I could not live with it. Nor you."

The rest of that evening was spent with him desperately trying to find ways to please me. But it was too late. I was already gone, at least emotionally, and planning on how and when to let him know what I knew.

Looking back on it, from the comfortable viewpoint of several years down the road, I realize that I put him through a lot of pain in worrying about what I was going to do during those months of letting go on my part. He was panicky during those days. I remember once walking into the bedroom, and finding him in tears. I never asked what was wrong. I just turned around and walked out.

He knew I knew what he had done. But he was desperate not to have to face it, and in doing that, he made a horrible situation worse in that I was given no choice but to make us both face it.

When I decided I was strong enough, I had the evidence out one morning when he came to the table for breakfast before work. It was a Saturday morning. He sat down and looked at me, and I think he could tell by the look on my face that something was up. He didn't say anything.

I handed him the copies. I said: "I deserve better than this. I deserve better than you. Get out of my home." He wanted to tell me about them, explain what they were for.

He even tried to tell me they were for his brother's girlfriend! Then he tried to stroke my hair. I smacked his hand away and forbade him to touch me. I told him I didn't want to hear lies anymore. He then got all prideful and said "well, we'll just sit down and divide everything up."

I started laughing. I said "I don't know what you think you're going to divide up. All you're taking with you today is your underwear. The rest the lawyers can sort out." I don't think I have ever seen such a look on any man's face before.

I know I was a real bitch, but being mean was the only way I could keep from breaking down. I started to walk out. I turned around and said "I'll be gone when you get back today. You be gone when I get back tonight."

So started a very long three year journey that I suspect is not quite over yet.

Dana:

After I confronted him with all the evidence I had, there was no way he could deny it. I had him tell me how long it was going on, why it happened, and what did he want to do from here on out.

It had been going on for a year and a half so the whole time I was suspicious, I had been correct in my feelings. The reason he had the affair was because he "needed it." It was "something he needed at the time and that's that."

He wanted to work on our marriage for the sake of our daughter, so we attended marriage counseling for about seven or eight months. The following four years, I thought we had been working our way through it. Our marriage supposedly stabilized, we saved up money and bought a new house. We planned on putting down roots in a new town.

Meanwhile, my sister was keeping tabs on "A" in the other state. When I discovered "A" had left her husband and returned to our hometown, I waited to see what would happen.

My husband started exhibiting the same sneakiness and I knew he was seeing her again, but he totally denied it, pretended he didn't know she was back. I don't know what happened to his brain, he didn't seem to remember how I was able to "find things out" that totally spooked him.

We are in the process of divorcing, and he is now living with the other woman. It was a long, hard four years from the beginning of the end!

Angela:

Affair #1: His depression and the e-mail I found a month before finally clicked in my brain. I felt sick to my stomach and lightheaded. I almost drove to where he works and confronted him, but I knew that it really wasn't safe for me to drive in the shape I was in. My kids needed me alive. So I waited until the next day and left work early with the excuse I was sick. I certainly looked and felt sick. Several people commented on it. I went home, woke him from a nap, and just nailed him. He told me the affair had busted up the week before and he wanted to make us work.

Affair #2: Fast-forward about four years later. He had been pulling away talking physical and financial separation. I finally realized he wanted out and he really was involved with who I though he might be involved with. I had also gotten the speech eight months before, but he had waffled big time telling me about three months after the speech he didn't want a divorce and then sliding away again emotionally.

I didn't know it was physical until it busted up and he then spilled his guts to me. I also had no clue until he admitted that it had been going on for two years. I wouldn't have been surprised about a year but that two years did wake me up.

The only reason I was willing to try again after #2 is that I sensed a real change in him and I wanted to give it a chance. I have to admit that I was a bit skeptical at first, but he hadn't treated me this well in a long, long time.

Dana:

It took me a while to confront him with it, though, when you consider it was a year and a half of suspicions. I was only able to get concrete proof of the affair a couple of months after she left. It was my own cowardly fault for not confronting him right away, also, he lied so convincingly I really wondered if I was going nuts.

I wanted to believe him, and I fooled myself into believing him. Getting that "evidence" gave me the "backbone" to confront him, because then he had no way of lying to me. If he had lied to me right then, there would be no doubt that our marriage would have ended on that day.

Looking back, I wish I had done it with strength, anger, contempt, and a total cutting of all ties. That might have been the best way to do it. Might have had a different ending.

Candace:

I knew my husband was having relationships with women that were far more intimate than I was comfortable with but I didn't know if I had the right to demand that he stop or if I was being "jealous." I went a long time feeling that I was being childish. I confronted him a lot with those feelings and, of course, he told me how jealous and immature I was being.

One time I sent him a bunch of quotes about family unity and that it was more important than my maturity. They were religious quotes. He never responded in writing but moved out of the apartment that day. I wish I had done that sooner. That was before there was a physical relationship between them.

When I found Internet evidence of a physical relationship I had the stupidity to show him and he just destroyed the evidence, quite angrily. But we had both seen it and he knew I knew. And from that evidence I learned there had been others. At that point, though, I desperately wanted him to come back to me.

We separated but I was hoping that without me he would just give up the other women. At one point he and I went for coffee and I asked him to step out of himself and give me advice as an impartial advisor and he advised me to leave him! Then right away he made the switch and started defending his actions. I wanted to stay so I listened to the second guy not the first. The final time that we did split there was no confrontation. I saw the evidence and I said "that's it."

I had an intimate internet relationship of my own but it was well after we separated. When we were married, or trying to be, I would have done anything to keep that marriage together. I was so careful not to do anything to him I perceived as hurtful to me.

I had a brief relationship before my lover. I was separated of course. But I had a son at home. One time my "friend" posted something very risque and my son saw it. He told his father, my husband. My husband's response to our son was: "I had my chance at romance and it failed. Now it's your mom's turn."

Daniel:

Certain events caused me to ask my wife point blank, if she was having sex with someone else. When she responded that she was, I remember feeling as if someone had cut my legs off below my knees. Not just because of her answer, but also the manner in which she answered.

There did not appear to be even a hint of remorse in the tone of her voice. And her eyes, they were as cold as I had ever seen them in my life. I felt as if I was talking to someone other than my wife. If she had started crying, or at least appeared somewhat remorseful, I probably would have reacted differently than I did.

Her callousness infuriated me even more than her reply to my question did. So, I reminded her of what you call a married woman who sleeps with someone other than her husband, got in my car and drove away.

Raquel:

We had two confrontations. The first was after he had blown up at me for accidentally putting scratch in the door in our bedroom trying to swat a wasp because he has a major fear of them.

It was the culmination of about two months of building hostility on his part coupled with a distancing of himself from me. I had first thought it was due to stress at work but I soon came to realize that there was more to it than that.

I asked him if he no longer wanted me and if there was an other woman. He denied there was an other woman, stating, "I'm not seeing anyone at the moment," but he did admit that he had been wondering if he wanted to stay married

Things continued on a similar level for about six weeks at which time we went on a disastrous holiday on which it rained and he insisted on having the kind of sex I really don't enjoy that much.

I had been mulling everything over in my mind since the first blow-up and had pretty well decided what was really going on, but I had no evidence other than a strong suspicion that the closeness he had with one of his former associates was more than it seemed. So as we were walking home from the train station I said very calmly, "I know why you said you are not seeing anyone at the moment. You can't see her. She's out of state right now." He didn't even try to deny it. All he asked was how I had figured it out.

William:

My wife filed for the divorce for irreconcilable differences. I went into severe depression and was court ordered to leave the house. For the next three months, I tried to get her to reconsider but she was so cold and indifferent.

Then, an anonymous caller informed me of the affair between my wife and a married co-worker. I just thought I was suffering from depression until that day. The only thing that could hurt me worse would be to lose a child, God forbid. The affair had been ongoing for two years. I was pretty blind.

I immediately called her and confronted her. She admitted it in that cold voice that I will never forget. Our divorce was final six months later. She and the other man continue to sneak around until his divorce is finalized, then they plan to get married! My ex-wife has yet to talk to me about it. I know that she cannot face me in person. She is not the woman I married 19 years ago.

Vivian:

When I confronted my ex-husband with the evidence (and the divorce papers), he said absolutely nothing. He went and packed his bags and moved to his mother's home. I asked many other times during our separation, still no response. After the divorce was final, I just didn't care anymore to know.

Misty:

The moment of truth... I was sitting in front of the computer. He was "working" so much, he was never here, and was not acting like himself. So I changed his password on the email account and there it was, so beautifully formatted in a calligraphic font: "I love you now and forever."

The email was not to me, needless to say. I sat there staring at the screen for I can't even tell you how long. I was just numb and felt like my heart had been ripped out, but that was nothing compared to what would come next.

I was going to wait for him to come home to confront him with it, he was away on "business," translated helping her move in to the house they are living in (which he bought?) I would later find out. Well, he couldn't log on to AOL and found out that his password was changed.

He called me on my cell phone in the middle of a parking lot. He called me every name under the sun, for being untrusting of him. Said she was a friend going through a tough divorce and he was sending her support. No, he was in our house sleeping with his wife, sending his girlfriend love notes.

He still didn't admit to anything, until he finally "left." I accessed his cell phone messages and there was one from her, "Hi Honey, I'm glad you're safe and on your way home, I love you." I erased the message and replaced it with mine, "I know that you are in love and living with someone else, be a man and face me with the truth, you owe me at least that after 13 years."

That was my final separation point, up until then I had a glimmer of hope he would come back, he had before. This time it was different, I heard another woman telling my husband "I love you."

Angela:

There were two affairs. When I confronted him about he first affair I realized it was an "emotional" affair and that he was "in love" with her. I came home after he was off his shift, woke him up and confronted him. Being totally unprepared and half asleep he didn't have any mask on and he admitted it. Also it was over at that point and his depression was a result of that.

He had withdrawn emotionally from me and I hadn't realized what had happened. We did use that as a springboard for communication but when I got my new job and it took more time, he felt neglected.

So then woman #2 enters the picture, a neighbor who was separated from her husband. She needed my handy dandy guy to help around the house a bit. She also asked him to scratch her itch for her. Anyway they had a good alibi. It was perfect. My husband could come over, scratch her itch, and do work on her house and she paid for materials. The only problem was that he got involved emotionally. Then it felt like our marriage was done.

When I finally got suspicious enough he had his mask in place. Oh, no, they weren't involved. She was like a younger sister to him. I knew how single women with kids made him feel (like he wanted to rescue them.)

Until the last two months before it blew up she was still buddying up to me and he was still bragging and showing me the work he was doing at her house. Funny how her family kept coming first in his life. He was so needed there.

Anyway it wasn't until I realized he really wanted out that I had no doubts they were involved. Our kids were very suspicious too. When he finally admitted it none of us were surprised.

···✦··✦··✦

Why wouldn't you think you had the right to demand that he or she stop other relationships if they made you uncomfortable?

If your spouse was "just friends" with someone, why would they put that person's feelings first if you said you felt threatened by the relationship? Did your husband or wife do anything to prove to you that their relationship with the other person wasn't a threat to your marriage? Did they ever try to include you in the friendship?

Candace:

Good questions and I wondered myself what my rights were as a wife. When we got married my husband told me that he loved me but he would always love God more. I could live with that. At the time I didn't belong to the same religion but I respected his choice and God seemed more important than human love.

All of my husband's relationships with women were garbed in some kind of notion of service to God. So that is why I always doubted whether my feelings should change something. When we first started having trouble I looked desperately for a counselor of the same religion as we were because I really didn't think that what my husband was doing was really what our faith was all about.

I knew he would listen to someone of our faith telling him that family unity was more important than the service he was supposedly a part of. But there was no one available until about two months after the last time we separated.

We found a psychiatrist/psychologist married couple of our faith. We went to them. Yes, they said family unity was more important. But guess what? That is what I heard but my husband did not hear it! So when we got back from counseling he made no attempts to change. If he had, I suppose I would have reconsidered our separation.

As for him trying to make me feel okay, one time after his physical relationship, but before I knew about it, I only knew they were emotionally close, they arranged to meet in our house. They sat on the love seat, giggling and talking while I was in the bedroom trying to be unobtrusive.

That was his attempt to make me feel better about his romance. Looking back it seems like more of an attempt to throw it in my face and hurt me than to help me. I think he is a sick man.

If a married/separated person goes with a single person is it adultery? I think that it depends on the status of the separation. At the very beginning of a separation a couple may need to be apart to explore what is going on and decide whether to divorce or try and reconcile. If either person has another love relationship during that period then it is very distracting to the purpose of the separation.

After a given amount of time the purpose of the separation changes. After a while you know whether or not you are trying to reconcile or make the separation permanent. In my case I could not get a divorce due to residency issues even though timewise I had been separated long enough.

Karla:

My ex-husband always had a certain female friend, usually someone I had met, but that I didn't really know and usually didn't like. I got tired of him taking her to lunch, I never got a lunch date, I mean he would go and pick her up from work!

Did I demand that he stop going to lunch with her? That's a laugh! No one demands anything of my ex-husband! If he wanted to show me there was nothing going on he could have invited me to join them.

Finally it was her boyfriend that put his foot down, told her it was inappropriate for her to have lunch on a regular basis with a married man, period, end of discussion. All I could do was tell her boyfriend "thank you."

···◆·◆·◆

Is it adultery if neither person is married or if there is no sexual relationship?

Are we splitting hairs when we try to define what is and what isn't adultery? Does physical sex have to occur before an outside relationship turns into adultery? Here are some definitions from Webster's Dictionary:

Adultery: *voluntary sexual intercourse between a married person and someone other than their spouse.*

Infidelity: *1) marital unfaithfulness, 2) disloyalty.*

Cheat: *3) to practice fraud or deceit, 4) to violate rules or agreements, 5) to be sexually unfaithful, 6) a person who cheats, 7) a fraud or swindle.*

Unfaithful: *1) not faithful to duty, obligation, or promises: disloyal, 2) not accurate or reliable.*

Using these definitions you could put marital cheating in the adultery/infidelity terminology and all other betrayal in the cheat(ing) and unfaithful terminology.

I know it hurts to find your lover has cheated whether you're in a marriage or a non-marital relationship that you believed was monogamous. The difference is that it is easier for either of you *to walk away when there is nothing legally holding you together, which is probably the biggest reason people in "committed without marriage" relationships might try harder.*

Miriam:
While allowing the premise that there is a wide chasm of gray area between legal adultery versus emotional/physical adultery, my response would still be: nope, I do not disagree.

Candace:
Where does the concept of adultery originate? In the Bible? Everyone is not Christian nor of the Judaic faith. Is it a religious or legal concept?

Dana:
Looking at it from a legal standpoint, it is adultery if one or the other is married. But how about those relationships that have been monogamous for years and years with no legal bindings (i.e., marriage license)? I'm sure the betrayed will tell you it's adultery, while the betrayer will say it's not.

I believe it is adultery when one steps outside any committed, monogamous relationship to seek another relationship(s) with a different person(s), whether emotional or physical, at the expense of the original partner's trust.

Miriam:

People in long term relationships, and who have come to trust and depend upon each other feel no differently when that feeling has been betrayed. It feels like adultery. The pain is no different. Maybe just the way that some others look at it... you know, hey, if you're not married, anything goes.

I was reading an article recently about married couples versus live-in couples, and it was interesting in that it said research has indicated that live-in couples tend to dote on each other more, and stay "lovers" longer, and one of the reasons for that had to do with a fear of being left or replaced. Apparently that commitment factor was missing.

With married couples, the "spark" tended to settle in faster, but the deeper commitment to each other was stronger. A feeling of "we're in it for the long haul." And, a feeling of acceptance for each other was stronger. Maybe another plug for marriage, I don't know.

The point is, I think that couples, whether married or not, tend to love just as strongly, but in different ways. I think in some ways unmarried long term couples may worry about adultery more than married ones. Ironic in some ways. I think all the terminology about married but separated, married but willing, divorced but committed, all of these may be just word play.

So do I think that committed couples, married or not, who stray are committing adultery? Yes. Don't care what the deal is. And why? Because if they had not brought a third person into the mix of their relationship, there is always the chance that the relationship can be healed. But if there is somebody else standing in the way, no matter how temporary or for what excuse, those fractures will just get bigger and deeper until one of the partners gets scared of hanging off the cliff and just walks away.

Maybe the relationship would have ended anyway. But it deserved the chance to be ended with class and compassion and caring, just the two of them, those two people who shared a love and a life.

When the goodbyes are over and the hurt is healed, that is the time to bring somebody else into one's life, not before. Otherwise, it just gets too damn confusing.

···▸··▸··▸

Could you, or did you, turn a blind eye to your spouse's affair in the hope it would end on its own?

There are many "famous" couples in which the other person is (or was) a solid third — Katherine Helpburn and Spencer Tracy; Prince Charles, etal; Jackie Kennedy and her married lover, to name a few. The "threesome" marriage seems to be given a stamp of approval depending upon the people involved. But is there anything that would keep you "blind" to your partner's involvement with another person on a long term basis? Or have you tried?

<u>**Miriam:**</u>

I tried my best to delude myself for a very long time in thinking there was nothing going on with my husband, so during that time, I guess, to be completely honest, I was indeed accepting the idea of another woman meddling in my marriage. I know it's not quite the same thing as actually condoning the presence of another woman in your marriage, but then, after all, the knowledge is there, isn't it, whether you pretend like it is or isn't, it isn't going to change what is.

Nevertheless, when I finally did get enough guts to admit it to myself and do something about it, I was positively certain adultery was not something I could live with, pretense aside. So I guess my answer in the end is pretty much what I started out with: Nope.

Everybody has their "straws"... you know, the one that breaks the camel's back. Mine was adultery. It may not be so for everyone. In fact, for some folks, their husband or wife having somebody else in their lives may take some of the pressure off them as partners, freeing them up to do more or less as they please.

<u>**Dana:**</u>

The affair was going on for about a year and a half, and I'd had suspicions with no proof. I couldn't leave the marriage with just "suspicions" and by the time I got concrete proof, the other woman was already gone. You could say I stayed in the marriage on the basis of that. But when it started to happen again, I was better "prepared" for it, and when I knew she was back and he was seeing her, I told him to leave.

I'm far too jealous and selfish to share, and I would expect the same of my spouse. In the beginning of our marriage, jealousy was never, ever an issue, but I guess I developed that ugly emotion, along with everything else I hate in myself.

Incidentally, Louise Tracy, Spencer's wife, had a huge picture of him on the wall in her office, and I wondered at the time why she did when I thought he was married to Katherine Hepburn! She probably stayed in that marriage due to the fact he was bringing in the money for her school and they had had a deaf son together. That could have been a reason why she turned the other cheek.

Candace:

I have read two fiction books in the last two years that had other women in them. One was "Tara" and I don't want to say who that was by because I am afraid I will name a similar but wrong author and the other was "Marrying the Mistress" by Joanna Trollope. In the first I think the wife knew but in the second she didn't until the end. Both are recommended books if you haven't read them. They aren't heavy at all.

I think it is dangerous to say "I would never do that." Life has a funny way of playing tricks once you say that. However, I would like to think that while I am willing to accept my man having friends outside our marriage I would hope he would have men friends and women friends. And I would insist that the intimate, romantic and sexual stuff came to me! The only scenario I can see me turning a blind eye is if I were permanently brain damaged and then I wouldn't know anyway so it isn't the same thing.

Raquel:

I really thought my "last straw" was adultery. I really thought I would never condone any kind of extra-marital sex under any cirucumstances for any length of time. I really thought if I were to find out that my husband had any kind of affair, I (or he) would be gone. When it actually happened, it wasn't quite that simple. We continued to live together for almost a year after I first confronted him with my suspicions.

Even six weeks later, when he had admitted he was emotionally involved with her (I didn't discover that they were also having sex until a few months later but I had my suspicions), we stayed together and continued to have sex. I even told him I couldn't believe I hadn't ended everything right away.

However, I made it clear from the beginning and continued to make it clear I was in no way condoning his behavior. I was, instead, acting on his assurances it was over between them. That he didn't actually break up with her for many months and continued to lie to me about their many supposed break-ups just added to my heartache and pain.

Yet, there eventually was a "last straw" that resulted in our first separation. One evening before he went out, he had carelessly left available his password to his secret Hotmail account. Of course, I couldn't resist! There I found a message from him to her begging her to continue to go out with him now she had returned home. I also found other e-mails to his male friends bragging about having slept with her on a trip he had taken the month before. Yet, on his return, he had sworn to me that, although he had seen her, he hadn't slept with her.

At that point I had enough. When he came home from the bar later that night (after trying unsuccessfully to get her to join him, although I didn't know that), I lost it completely. I cried. I yelled. I screamed. I hit him over and over again in the chest. I cried some more. He also yelled. He threw things. And, he drank too much.

He knew that my tolerance level had been reached. So, he volunteered to move out as soon as he could find a place to live. He was gone in less than a month. As we had already discussed the details of a possible Controlled Separation, we also signed that agreement before he left.

Helen:

I, too, said the "never" word. I would "never" stay with him if he cheated. I would "never" let another woman insert herself into my marriage. Yet, when it happened, it sure wasn't as black and white as I thought it would be. First of all, I had that wonderful denial thing going for me. I wasn't quite sure ... I couldn't really prove anything. Three months later my suspicions were confirmed. God, I loved him so much. I felt responsible for everything.

Immediate panic set in and I would have done anything to save my marriage. It took a while, but then things started to become clearer to me. Now, I was starting to think logically about my predicament. My first thought was you do not throw away a 20+ year marriage. My second thought was how devastated my children were going to be if we divorced. However, the longer he was gone, the clearer I began to see my marriage and my husband.

I may have been able to survive the infidelity in and of itself; however, along with the other problems, it seems insurmountable. So for me, his cheating was the straw that broke the camel's back.

I have come to learn a couple of things. I am very selfish in that I will not share my husband with anyone else. I am stronger than I ever thought I could be. I never believed I would be able to survive his infidelity. I stayed true to my core beliefs. I would be lying if I said I didn't love him (I do) but he is toxic, and does not seem to be able to stay true to what he claimed were his core beliefs.

Sheree:

I would turn a blind eye because then I could be free to do what I want. I probably wouldn't have thought this back when things were good, but now that we're going through this trouble, I would turn a blind eye.

Why ? Because it is easier to pretend that everything is fine and that we are one big happy family than to separate and devastate the kids. Maybe not a good reason, but nobody's perfect and no one walks in my shoes.

Ashleigh:

After I discovered and confronted him about the affair it took about a week for me to think I shot myself in the foot. I actually kicked myself for being so open with him.

In hindsight, yes, I could play the "blind" wife. Not for very long though. Just long enough for me to get my finances in order and begin thinking clearly without intense emotion.

Not a pretty thought but one I have had often.

Angela:

No. It's a good thing I didn't really know for sure about either one of them until they were over, or one of us would have been living elsewhere. I can't be in a relationship in which I worry about his promiscuity. It has taken me a long time to heal and I'm not going to knowingly live that way.

···✦··✦··✦

Did you keep your spouse's affair "your little secret" or did you confide in others?

If you were the one being betrayed, did you confide your suspicions to a friend or family member early on or did you keep your thoughts to yourself? If you confided to someone, what was their reaction and did they give you support? Did you ever regret confiding in them?

If you kept it to yourself, when did you finally tell someone else? Would you have felt "better" if you had someone to confide in who was going through the same thing? Did you ever feel that you were "betraying" your spouse by talking about the situation with someone else?

Miriam:

"*Did you ever feel that you were 'betraying' your spouse by talking about the situation with someone else?*" That's exactly how I felt, and I guess it was one of the reasons I kept it to myself for such a very long time. I didn't want anyone to know what he was doing, and God help me, it wasn't so much because of what they would think of me, it was because of what they would think of *him*! How pathetic was that?

So I kept it to myself. I felt like I was crying all the time on the inside, you know? The tears were always there, just under the surface, and sometimes I felt like a walking flood about to happen. The burden just got so heavy after a while.

One day, months and months into this, my mother came by my office to pick me up for lunch, and when she walked in, I looked up, and without even thinking about what I was saying, I said "I know he is cheating on me." And before I could stop myself, tears were running down my face, and I was sobbing just like a child.

She wanted to know how I knew, and I told her. I told her I couldn't live with this. It hurt too much. She didn't say anything for a while, and then she told me: "You were not a child that anybody could ever lie to. You always knew. And you always wanted to know the truth. I don't think you can live with it, either, because this is the kind of thing that can destroy you."

And she was right. I couldn't. Not even for him. And even after I confronted him, it still almost destroyed me. It took me a very, very long time to heal. And I'm still doing that, even years later. Sometimes the tears are still very near the surface.

After I told my mother, it was easier to tell my friends. Suprisingly enough (at least to me, anyway) they didn't seem nearly as shocked as I thought they should be. Which would have bothered me, I guess, if I had thought about it enough.

I tried a divorce group therapy thing once, too. A friend talked me into it. There was so much pain there, and when they tried to get me to talk, the tears started again. I ended up crying again, and if there is one thing I hate, it's for anybody to see me cry. I walked out, and never went back. I have never told anybody that.

Jeff:

Once I had "the evidence" I went to my best mate (who was also a family friend) and just poured it all out. Once I had spoken about it, I felt much better. All he said was that nobody could tell me what to do, nobody could give the right advice.

Raquel:

I was embarrassed -- plain and simple. I didn't want anyone to know that our "perfect" marriage wasn't perfect. I didn't want anyone to know that this awful thing had happened to me. I wasn't trying to protect him; I was trying to protect me.

I think I may also have been in denial, so to admit to anyone else that my husband was cheating on me was to make it even more real than it already was. However, the first time we visited my sister after I discovered the affair, we both had a chat with her and she was very empathetic having gone through two divorces herself. My husband was less than forthcoming with both of us at the time so neither my sister or I knew the whole truth.

At the time, the affair was supposedly over and we were supposedly figuring out how to pick up the pieces. What a joke that turned out to be! I continued to chat with her on the phone from time to time but the distance made any real closeness and helpfulness difficult. But, it was wonderful to be able to tell someone what was happening -- even if that someone was so many miles away.

It was my husband who convinced me that I had to find someone to confide in who lived closer. I finally talked to a woman who was near my age and with whom I was fairly close (we used to go out as a foursome fairly regularly).

She was the third wife of her husband and had only been married a couple of years (her first marriage) so, although she was sympathetic, she really couldn't empathize with me at all. We met for coffee several times and it was nice to be able to talk to someone but I wouldn't say that I saw her as a close confidante.

Candace:

I am a talker. I share. I talked to a friend that I believed was a quiet confidant and she was. She has seen me through the whole thing. She never gossiped. I don't think she even told her husband. She gave me someone to talk to and supported me through everything. Even the parts she was a little bit uncomfortable with.

The troubles with my husband came to the surface in the spring and I wanted to go for counseling in the summer. My husband said, "don't air dirty laundry in public." I didn't. That was a big mistake. I should have gone for counseling then. Instead we waited, while he got a little more serious with his friend.

I told a friend from early on, even before spring. But I didn't go for professional counseling until the following fall. I told my mom that spring, also. She gave me support without telling me what to do. I told other friends via the internet. One, I regret.

I told my husband's best friend. For months I had tried to get him to talk to my husband about "things," hoping that they would discuss women and the friend would help guide my husband. These guys don't talk. One time I got chatting and did tell the guy. I am sorry about that. Another long term friend, also a good friend of my husband, told me to leave him. That was six months before we finally broke up. I always think her advice was interesting.

Teresa:

Several years earlier my husband told me he had an affair and then changed his story and said he only said that to hurt me. I didn't tell anyone. At the time I was feeling very insecure and depressed with two very young children. He said it was over and I didn't want people to think badly of him.

After a while I started to doubt my feelings that the affair had ever happened. The jealousy and lack of trust remained but my husband insisted (and still does) that nothing ever happened and I started to doubt myself. Was I mad? Was I just seeing things which weren't there? I didn't know anyone to ask to confirm or deny his story so it just got sort of swept under the carpet but the lump was still there and I tripped over it many times during our marriage.

In the intervening years I grew more confident in myself. Whereas before when I suspected things I would get hysterical and lose it completely, I started to just get angry and withdraw. The lack of underlying trust had made me turn more to my friends and I built up a very strong support system. However, I still didn't tell anyone of my suspicions because the lingering thought I was seeing things due to my own insecurity was still there.

Once I got the speech all bars were removed. I told everyone, and I mean everyone. I e-mailed his work colleagues and his business contacts. I told everyone I knew and many people I didn't know.

My counselor kept trying to get me to look at this behavior and I wouldn't at the time but I realize now she was trying to get me to see I didn't really want him back. I think I was somehow unconsciously forcing the situation into a state where it couldn't be saved. I had been hurt so badly the previous time and by much of his behaviour during our marriage that the protective instincts came into play. I knew I was weak and would keep him if he showed the slightest remorse but I also knew I couldn't survive any more in the sort of emotionless and loveless relationship we were in.

For years I'd believed I didn't deserve to be loved and so for some funny reason his lack of attention and nitpicking seemed right and normal. The last few years I had become more at peace with myself. I had cut out of my life several very negative people who reminded me constantly of my childhood problems and I had really grown to like myself.

I stopped taking his comments. I withdrew into my own world. I started to fantasize about having someone who loved me for myself. Someone where every day didn't have to be such an effort. Someone who would give me compliments, find me attractive, make me feel sexy. Someone who liked my opinions, wasn't threatened by my studies, was interested in more intellectual things. I had always hoped that one day that person would be him but I realize now that was just unrealistic.

It sounds horrible but I think I had already left the marriage emotionally and I'm beginning to wonder if the pain I felt wasn't due more to breaking a longstanding habit. I still love and care for my husband but I realize he simply can't give me what I want.

Dana:

The only person I confided in at the beginning of this whole mess was my sister. She gave me a lot of support, and she even did a few "sneaky" things for me that I was unable to do myself (like calling the other woman and chewing her out).

Of course, the other woman denied everything, even when my sister quoted her chapter and verse from every letter that she had sent my husband.

For the couple of years I had suspected the affair, I did not confide in anyone for the very reason I thought I was just being insecure and "crazy," especially since my husband wouldn't tell me the truth. I only confided in my sister after I found out for sure, and this was a couple of months later when I felt I would just burst with holding in all the pain.

Because my sister was keeping tabs on her, when the other woman left her husband and returned to our town, I was the first to know (besides possibly my husband, but I'll never know) and I was ready to see what would happen. So when he got back together with her again, I knew that was it. I told my mom, my family, his parents, his sisters, my friends, his friends. Now that I look back on it, I think I did it to show others it was "not me" that ended the marriage.

The first time I didn't confide in anyone because I was embarrassed, and I didn't want others to think badly of my husband. In a way, I believed if people thought badly of my husband, it would reflect on me. That was my way of thinking at that time.

The second time I told everyone because I figured the first time I didn't tell anyone and my husband thought I would do the same this time. Guess what his mom said (everyone else was very supportive): "Well, you must have done something to make him do that!" I just looked at this woman I had known and loved for over 20 years (and I thought she had loved me too) and realized her son comes first.

Angela:

When asked if there was another woman I told people not as far as I was aware of, but that he had a friend who was a bit too close. I didn't share this information with everyone, only a few people who were acting as a support mechanism for me.

After he admitted it then it got wider air play, although we have not disclosed this information to our family. They live several hours away and might use it as ammunition in the future.

If we had split up and he had gone public then that information would have been extremely public.

···✦·✦·✦

206

Do men and women cheat for different reasons?

This question was inspired by a comment a man made on another forum. He said men cheat because they want more sex than women do. He was referring to frequency as well as variety. Let's take that statement as fact (at least as the man who said it believes it to be) for the basis of the following question: If men are assumed to be cheating to have a sexual relationship, why do women cheat? What do they expect to get from an affair?

Dana:

Love and affection, I would presume. Validation of their attractiveness. Especially when one is in a marriage where they don't feel valued as an equal partner in the relationship. That's only my opinion. While married, I never found myself actively seeking other men, but I have experienced a longing (for lack of a better word) for attention from the opposite sex.

Karla:

I think I have to agree. We want to know that we are still sexy, smart, wanted, needed, instead of being belittled all the time. It's like I would wait for any crumbs of affection that he would throw my way, like I was a bad dog trying to get the master's attention, but still leery that you still might get smacked. I never looked for another relationship while married, but towards the end, well, that's another topic.

Raquel:

Probably, but not necesarily. My husband said he was looking for sex -- different sex; not necessarily better sex. In fact, he once said that sex with me was better than sex with the other woman. (This was long before our first reconciliation when things were still very bad between us.) However, he also said that there was a certain sameness of sex with me and he was looking for a change.

I am sure the fact that she was young (30 years his junior) was a great attraction as well. He insists the emotional attachment to her came later but I still wonder about that. I think he was deluding himself about that and he was already emotionally involved with her to some extent before they had sex for the first time. This brings back memories I'd just as soon not have.

···◆··◆··◆

Is it possible to trust a spouse after they have betrayed you?

If you were betrayed, have you been able to trust again — either your spouse who betrayed you or someone new in your life? What do you think is the most difficult part of losing trust?

Karla:

Yeah, I trusted again and got royally screwed. I got screwed by my ex-husband too. Right now, I trust no one and I mean no one. Could I trust my ex again? No.

The most difficult part of losing trust? Feeling like I've become a cold heartless b-tch, which is something I don't like. But unfortunately, that seems to be the way of life.

Dana:

Now that I think of it, I was trying to rebuild my trust in my husband again, but still deep inside, I didn't trust the fact that the affair had been cut so short. The affair ended because she had to move out of state with her husband, not because of any willingness for either party to end it. I didn't trust her. I trusted my husband only as far as I knew that she was out of sight (state). I had the feeling of just waiting for the other shoe to drop. And it did.

Do I still trust? No. Not any more. Not my husband. Not anyone else. (Aside from my family, of course, and a couple of friends I've known from grade school). I've been the type of person that once you've gained my trust, you're in for life. Once you betray that trust, you're dead.

I think it comes from having a physical handicap (hearing impairment). Not being able to trust people to accept me for who I am, the way I am. Not being able to trust that people won't let me down in the end, by making fun of me. I feel like I've turned into a hardened b-tch, I feel very cynical about love and relationships, and I find myself not allowing anyone to get close to me.

Yeah, this whole thing did a big number on my trust issues, and I'm hoping to God that it's not irrecoverable.

Raquel:

Trust? I am really not sure if I even know what that means any more. Sure, we are back together. Sure, things are going well. Sure, I feel like I am in a real marriage. But, trust? Hmmm....

I know I trust him right now because he hasn't had any oppportunity to stray. And, I trust him in so far as I think he believes that he will not get involved with another woman. But, would I ever trust him as completely as I once did? I don't think so. In fact, I think it was foolish of me to have ever done so.

I think trust has to be realistic and I certainly wasn't realistic when I thought that he would never consider stepping over the line -- given the fact that he was always, in my opinion, "too" friendly with women.

I should never have been so trusting as to allow him as much freedom as I did to hang out with the group he hung out with which included the other woman. I even encouraged him to go out on Saturday nights since I had to work and he didn't.

I also trusted him to be completely truthful with me because he was apparently so honest and ethical in everything he did. I don't think I should have assumed that he would always be truthful. I wonder now if it is possible for anyone to be completely truthful all the time.

What I am saying is the kind of trust I had in my husband was so naive I never once questioned him about anything! I will never be that trusting again. And, I don't think that is a bad thing.

Miriam:

I don't know. I'm still working on it. I thought it was just me, my own personality, but reading some of the others' thoughts made me feel a bit better.

It's strange, the attitude my husband has, sometimes, though. He wants me so badly to trust him, absolutely, the way I did before. It's just not going to happen.

Sometimes I feel poised on the edge, ready for flight. "One wrong move, bud, and I'm outta here," kind of feeling. I know it's not fair, and probably not right, but I don't seem to be able to shake it. Then there are other times, when I am very happy, very content, and in many, many ways our marriage is so much better than it was before. I find that I can forget what he did for long periods of time.

There's so much talk about how bad "they" feel, how "confused" they are... well, let me tell you, it's a picnic in the park compared to the betrayed having to learn to trust "them" again.

In the beginning, I used to wonder what I would do if I had the opportunity to "pay back his work" as a friend of mine put it so succinctly once long ago. It took me a while. But I know I wouldn't.

There are some things I can live with, and some things I couldn't. That's just one of the couldn'ts. And God help me, sometimes I wonder how they can.

Candace:

I would never be able to trust my husband again. Even now he seems to be in a state of denial telling people that he did nothing wrong and he doesn't know why I am divorcing him. I think I could trust someone else. I have seen so many men who are trust worthy around me. I wonder though, if maybe I am a bit wiser at pointing out those who are not trust worthy. I might be wrong on that point.

Helen:

I will never, ever be able to trust again at the level I used to trust my husband, nor do I want to. Maybe I should not have trusted him that much in the first place.

Not trying to be the drama queen but he threw away a piece of my soul that I will never get back. Even if he came back and made our lives and marriage 100% better I would not give him (nor could I get back) that piece he threw away.

Now, could I learn to trust him again? Under the right circumstances, maybe. But never again at that level. Could I learn to trust someone new? Yes, but once again, never at that level.

I don't think those who betray will ever truly understand the depth or repercussions of their actions. Something inside of you just dies and nothing, I mean nothing, will ever bring it back

Emily:

What an odd question with an even odder answer. I just realized that based on my relationship with a prior physically abusive boyfriend, who I semi-trusted and found out I couldn't trust, I don't think I ever really trusted my spouse.

I knew there were some things he was telling me, from day one, that were lies. I knew that he quite often left things out, just so he either wouldn't hurt me or wouldn't have to listen to me b-tch about them.

So, although I trusted him on some levels -- I didn't in the deepest sense of the word. At one point in time, I knew he loved me so much and was so jealous of me having an affair, that I thought I could trust him. But I very quickly learned, that wasn't the case.

Do I ever think I could trust someone else? Absolutely, positively never, ever! Which brings me to another interesting admission -- I just wonder how much of me not being able to trust, is because I have such a low self esteem that I don't think I'm good enough to ever stay with forever?

By not trusting, are my "loved" ones just experiencing a self-fulfilling prophecy, because of the way I feel and what that projects?

Vivian:

Trust, that's the biggest 5-letter word on the planet. When my marriage ended in divorce due to my ex's infidelity so many years ago, I had two children to raise. I busied myself with their schooling and activities. I never dated. I was not going to bring another liar and cheat into their lives. I was shielding them from disappointment.

But, let's be real. As a result of "protecting my children," I was building the biggest wall of resistance around myself. Not only was it tall, it was also very thick. I trusted no one. I questioned everyone's motives. I became very withdrawn emotionally. I went from being very popular to people whispering, "I haven't seen her in so long, I thought she was dead."

Then it happened, empty nest. Both my children were in colleges in other states. I had lost my excuse, "I'm committed to my children." So, I went out, was fixed-up, and was invited to dinner parties where I was banished to the "singles table." I tried, really I did. But I never even went on a second date. I was very good at making excuses.

This went on for years. I had made up my mind and had made peace with the fact that I would always be alone. I was happy (relatively), had tons of friends, traveled, was active. My life was not that bad.

Then I met my fiance. He took months of me ignoring his advances. But, he just kept after me until, one day, I was able to peek over the top of my wall and say hi. He chipped away. At first little pieces fell. I would sometimes try to put the pieces back. But, he chipped away some more. And then, chunks begin to fall.

During this process, as he was chipping away, I saw his soul. I knew that he was "the one." It's not that I just wanted to believe, I honestly trust him, completely. This has made me a much happier person.

I sometimes wonder just how hardened I would have become had he not stayed after me. In establishing our relationship, we reflected on our past marriages (one for each) and arrived at a "formula" for a happy life together. It's simple actually: Love, Trust, Understanding, Affection, Honesty, Tolerance, and Loyalty.

So, yes, you can trust again. And, happily

Rob:

I found that after I was cheated on, I had no trust for anyone or anything. When I married the second time, it took me a very long time to trust and I am not sure I ever really did. I never opened up about the issues I had with this, thus lack of comunication, all on my part. Times changed and almost two years ago, I was being tempted with leaving, then I cheated. In that process, I not only destroyed another's ability to trust, I also destroyed my own trust in myself.

That is not a good feeling, but I guess it is a lot better than it not registering or no guilt at all. It made me take a good long look at myself and I knew that I would not be able to live with myself. I started doing the work and getting the help. I didn't know at that time whether my wife and I would rebuild or what, but we were on our way to divorce.

Along the path, I found some friends who were supportive and I dated some (after my divorce was final), but never had that spark. I knew that for any future relationship to work, I had to not only have a certain amount of trust in myself, but also the ability to trust whoever else was in the picture. Enter my current girlfriend, devastated by her ex-husband's shenanigans, lies, deceit and pure meanness.

We started out as almost dire enemies but we started emailing each other shortly after because she was looking for answers as to why her husband was the was he was. After awhile, we were emailing at least once a day, her asking questions of me, sometimes very difficult and soul searching and others not too bad. If I didn't answer one question, she would ask it again.

Most of these emails were very long and detailed about things either she or I were going through or feeling. Thanks to this interaction with her, I was learning to communicate openly and honestly about the things buried deep inside I never told anyone else. I was learning to communicate about happy times and dark times in my life.

Then I went to visit her and our relationship started to grow into what it is today. I trust myself again, finally. I trust her love for me. This long distance relationship has taught me the necessity of trusting. I know that I love myself now and I love her to the exclusion of everyone else.

The fact that I love myself now after much self-loathing is very important to me. I have made the decision, not only with my heart, but with my mind, soul and body to love her. To trust her love for me.

The "feeling" of love ebbs and flows like life itself and the kind of love that life partners, whether married or not (committed relationships), is that concious decision. Now I, we, have the kind of mature relationship that will last a lifetime. Full of love, respect and all else that goes with it.

I have learned to communicate everything with her and I value her input and feelings on anything, as she does me. We both value each other's total being, something I have not ever done before.

So, yes, trust can be rebuilt after the worst of things. It takes a lot of hard work on everyone's part. It takes a lot of honesty on everyone's part and most importantly of all, it takes loads and loads of open communication and emotional sharing between the parties involved. Will it ever be the innocent, childlike trust? No, definitely not and by the same token, I don't believe adults should trust blindly, as utopian as that seems.

···+·+··+

Can men and women ever be "just friends"?

Does every friendship between a man and a woman eventually end up turning sexual in nature? Is it possible for men to be friends with women without expecting a physical relationship to develop? Is it possible for women to be friends with men without expecting more? Or is the sexual attraction between men and women just too difficult to overcome?

Candace:

I met a man earlier this year. We were in a course together. We went out for coffee a lot and talked about the course. We did homework together in the coffee shop. We were friends.

On our last day I thanked him for being my friend. I told him that I was beginning to doubt that men and women could be friends without some kind of sexual overtones. Since knowing him I knew it was possible.

His comment: "the day's not over yet." Yes, he wanted more. I couldn't believe it. My radar was all off. Or maybe I just don't have any.

Before knowing him I doubted men and women could be friends without some kind of sexual involvement. And now I don't know.

I have some very good friends who are men. They are the husbands of my good women friends. But I would never "go out" with them alone except under the most special of special circumstances and then I would not do it secretively. And even when we are out we chitchat or talk about work. Nothing very deep or personal. I guess I am saying that they aren't the kind of friend I am talking about.

Can men and women can have a deep friendship without sexual feelings getting aroused? Or acted upon? Lots of questions. No answers.

Dana:

I have a male friend that I have been close to for almost 30 years and another one for almost 20 years. No sexual relationships involved whatsoever, and I can talk to them about anything.

I think when you form those friendships at a very young age, you *can* be friends with men. But I will admit it is hard, if not difficult.

It's when you're older, it's harder to form those platonic friendships ... it's not easy forming those when one wants more than what the other is willing to give.

Raquel:

I do think that, under the right circumstances, it is possible to be friends but, having said that, I must admit that most of the men who started out as my friends did eventually make some kind of sexual advances -- which I declined, of course. Some of them even remained my friends for a long time after I rejected their advances but many (most?) soon drifted out of my life.

However, I did have one very good male friend whom I admired very much and with whom I had a professional and then a palatonic friendship for many years.

Miriam:

I think it's most certainly possible. There are men in my life who I consider friends, realtime and virtual and sex is the last thing I'm interested in with them. But, having said that, the sexual tension is still there, and I try to be very careful not to give the wrong impression. I tend to keep men/women/sex jokes to a minimum, and I'm very careful about the touchy-feely thing.

When my first husband and I were dating, there was a girl in my "girlfriends group" who we all knew was a man-eater. "See a man, bed a man" was her motto. We all knew that. We liked her, she was a great friend, you just couldn't trust her around your guy. As long as the rest of us kept that in mind, we all did fine.

One day I came home, only to find her car parked next door at my boyfriend's apartment. All hell broke loose, let me tell you! The poor guy was all confused. "I thought you all were friends," he whined. "We are," I said. "As long as she keeps her paws off you!"

That was the last time that happened. She backed off because I told her the next time I was coming after her! I guess you just have to be blunt with some people.

Candace:

I had a friend, a woman friend, last year. Her point was that the issue of sex always comes up eventually between a man and woman and you set your boundaries. Sometimes it is unspoken but the issue is there.

The sexual tension between men and women is one thing that makes male/female relationships interesting. Let's not throw it out. I used to think that men and women could and should be friends without it but now I think it just needs to be acknowledged and controlled.

Love is universal. It comes in many forms. Lucky is the person who has a sexual partner to express it with. Without that we still have to love to be alive. I think it is part of what it means to be human. And we are going to love people of the same and other sex.

Learning how to love people of the other sex and still maintain a marriage is a challenge. It is possible. I have seen men and women who do it and do it well.

I don't want to close my heart to half the world because I am scared of a sexual confrontation. I need everyone's love to make personal spiritual progress and I am definitely going to take it. And give it. I will learn how to deal with the sexual part in a healthy way. That's how I feel today. I reserve the right to change my mind tomorrow.

Vivian:

I've really had to think about this one. Male friends. Well, when I was married, sure I had male friends. But, soon as the divorce was over, they fell into one of these catagories:

"His friend" - Never saw or heard from him again.

"Helpful friend" - Offered to help me with "honey-dos," and then offered himself.

"Concerned friend" - Here's my shoulder, and my arms and my...

"Kidsplay friend" - While the kids are outside, how 'bout we play house.

"New friend" - Saw the divorce in the paper, came sniffing around.

"In-common friend" - You're single now? Me, too!

My closest girlfriends' husbands are wonderful. Never a problem. But these aren't people I would ever discuss the intimate details of my life with.

We all know how differently men and women communicate. And, if I did ever talk with one of them in that way, they would probably forbid their wife to ever talk with me again.

Funny, aside from my fiance, the one true male friend, the one I can share everything about my life with, the one that is always there for me, the one that asks for nothing in return, is gay.

Jeff:

I have five male *friends* -- guys I can call on at 3AM for help -- 24/7, and I expect the same from them -- we don't see each other that often, but the bond is there. Those that know them and me, all *know* our status. There are other guys I meet, have lunch, do the buddy thing, but would *never* even dream of calling on them in a time of "need."

Now... *most* of my "friends" are female. I'm talking day-to-day friends. The kind of person who I meet at the coffee shop, see at movies, go shopping with, have dinner here at home, and at their place, and so on. Never, and I mean *never* has there been any discussion about "sex" or "bed." These girls probably discuss me with their friends, and I get to meet them at some time or another. These are friends that come to me for advice, and I ask them for advice reference "female things."

Lots of people ask me how I get it right -- to be -- just that -- friends? I'm not sure. But all I can say is that it works, and it works well. Somehow the unwritten, unspoken boundries are there, and I'm not sure where they come from -- but I don't have a problem with "overstepping" and nor do they.

Sure, for my ego, it's great, and all I hope for them is that they feel the same. I know a lot of people probably "assume" I'm "doing the thing" when they see any of us together -- but hey, it's their problem, not mine, and if anyone asks, I set them straight.

Rob:

I tend to agree that if the frienships were established a long time ago, then it is possible. I also think it is possible if the boundaries are set either verbally or however in the first place.

I think we all know that most, if not all, men will at least attempt to move a platonic frienship to a sexual liaison if given the opportunity and there are some women who will do the same.

Again, I do believe it all comes down to commitment to your significant other, communication and confidence in your significant other's love for you.

Angela:

I have male friends and my husband has female friends. We are both willing to discuss the conversations we have with them. I have always been careful because I know those relationships can change quickly and cross borders before you are aware of it. Not all of them necessarily, but it is something to guard against. Obviously he hasn't been as successful at not crossing the lines as I have been.

John:

I do have a lot of female friends that I would never consider having an affair with. I am not the typical male in this area. I find it a lot easier to talk to women about personal issues, and they find it real easy to talk to me about the same. I have always been a good listener, and a couple of times it has gotten me in trouble.

···✦·✦·✦

What questions would you like your spouse to answer about their betrayal?

Betrayal leaves a lot of questions unanswered. If you had the opportunity to ask your spouse anything at all with regard to their adultery, what questions would you want answered?

Teresa:

"Why couldn't you just say you wanted to go rather than needle me until I exploded sufficiently to suggest separation?"

"Why couldn't you be honest with me?"

"Why do you think I'm so stupid I can't see through the lies?"

"Why couldn't you say that you were unhappy?"

"Why couldn't you at least try to work on our marriage?"

"Why are you still trying to hold on to me as second base?"

"Why are you so surprised I didn't lie down and die?"

"How is it that after 15 years of marriage you hardly know me at all?"

"Why do you expect me to understand, to act with kindness and forgiveness, to not be angry when you know you would not act that way if the roles were reversed?"

Miriam:

I can vaguely remember seeing the other woman once, from a distance. I didn't realize who and what she was at the time, and I didn't pay a lot of attention. She wasn't anything much to look at, I promise, and I'm not saying that just because at a later point in time I wanted to rip her lungs out.

Anyway, I asked him once: "What in hell was so special about that?" (meaning her). No answer, just a hang dog look.

Once in the early days though, when I was particularly angry and had been really nasty to him, he said "You know what? She was younger than you." For that, he got hung up on and I kept hanging up on him for weeks after that.

I know he was provoked, and angry himself. But I guess he learned that keeping his mouth shut, in this instance, was the better part of valor. He never said it again.

That was a little later though, after the anger had set in. When I got my backbone back. In the earliest days, when I was a mass of tears, the first questions I asked were: "Didn't you know I loved you? Didn't you know I trusted you?"

At least I wasn't in tears by myself. His response was a tearful "I know."

Karla:

My one question is still: "How after 20 years could you just walk away and never look back?" Never got an answer, I really don't expect an answer, I guess I'll never know.

Beverly:

"You said marrying me was the biggest mistake of your life. Why did it take 32 to years to leave? How could I be the mistake? You have been the abuser from day one."

"How could you be unfaithful from the start of our marriage?"

"What was wrong with our sex life? I never said 'no' and enjoyed making love to you."

"Why did you want to blame me for your being unhappy? I did not one thing to make you unhappy. I loved you totally. Do you think that you will be happy with yourself?"

"Why did you not listen to the counselor and go to one-on-one counseling? All the counselors say to you that you had some big problems. That your problems were not marriage problems. Why did you not want to get better for yourself, by going to counseling?"

"Why do you want to blame all your problems on me?"

"How will she ever trust you or you trust her?"

Raquel:

"Why do you think that your needs and wants are more important than mine?"

"Why were you so surprised that you fell in love with her when you did all the things people do on the road to falling in love: flirting, dating, double-dating with friends, spending a lot of time together, buying each other gifts, having sex, etc., ad nauseum?"

···✦·✦·✦

Were the two of you able to discuss the affair and then work to repair your marriage?

Many marriages end, not because the betrayer leaves to be with the other person, but, because the betrayed spouse isn't willing to take a chance on being betrayed again. If your marriage didn't end after your spouse's betrayal, how did you handle the infidelity and rebuild trust?

Georgette:

I started "softly" discussing some issues that were bothering me. It was 2 am, and my husband is a morning person, hates late night conversations, and usually snores while I talk. For some reason he could feel that he needed to pay attention and he did.

He was a bit confused that I had anxiety. He thought I lost weight last year because I "wanted to," and really just doesn't understand the depth of emotional turmoil he brought into our lives. He's obtuse that way. A very black and white thinker. It's over, so it's over.

I have these marriage repair books we were reading together at one point and suggested we should continue. He gently suggested that my constant "reading" was causing me anxiety, and I just lost it. I went ballistic on him. What started as a conversation turned into a nasty argument about respect and love and loyalty. I literally brought up every frustrating thing I had repressed in our relationship that had not been resolved.

Just as I was blindsided by his affair, I felt this was happening to him while I talked. He was wide-eyed and shocked. He got angry a couple of times and made a few excuses for his past behavior but I couldn't back down. I made him acknowledge that they were excuses and demanded he address the problem.

I am not like this, at least I wasn't before this, but I was out of control angry. I knew I still had anger that hadn't been expressed, but I didn't even know this was coming.

A couple hours later he looked at me and asked me, "What's this really about?" I was beat and embarrassed by then and I almost gave up, but I recognized that there was an agenda, and just laid it out. This is what I told him:

1) With my new job I work a lot of nights and weekends and I have a sick feeling in the pit of my stomach that if he knows I'm not going to be home he will "sneak out" to be with coworkers. So I don't give him my schedule and I hate myself and him for the insecurity I now feel.

2) When he shares personal things about his coworkers I'm suspicious that he's making that emotional investment in their lives. Also, by sharing this with him that he wouldn't talk to me honestly any more about his work day.

3) That I lost weight and went on meds to handle the depression and panic I was experiencing over my failing marriage and his betrayal. Not because I'd found a diet that worked!

4) That I didn't feel he was interested in doing the work to help our marriage, and that he was glad the counselor didn't work out and had quit making any effort to keep "us" healthy.

5) That I was insecure when he left for three days last week, wondering if his assistant met up with him. She was originally scheduled to attend this meeting and it's the first time I didn't go along since our problems began. Also wondered if he slept with or socialized with other women when he went to other meetings.

I basically told him that I was now this "crazy" person, who had a wild imagination, and flashbacks. That I couldn't let go and just trust again and I don't know why.

I told him what I really want to do when I feel this way is "run." I am so afraid of ever hurting like that again it would be easier to just start over somewhere else.

He responded that he's very sorry he ever hurt me this way, that he's not "done" anything he feels is improper since way back when it all happened. That his conversations about coworkers was info he gained by them asking for time off or in lunchroom conversations, not private chats.

That his assistant did not go to the meeting, and if she had, he said, "you probably would have gone along." I reminded him I couldn't go and asked if they would have driven together if she had gone and he said, "I suppose."

I came unglued again. He just doesn't get that part. So I said, "Let me put it to you this way, if I worked with a guy I had cheated on you with, and we drove together to an out of town meeting for three days would it bother you?" He says, "I suppose so!" My response was, "Well, then, now do you get it?"

I couldn't believe I had to explain it. And I added, "By the way, if you ever get into a vehicle to go anywhere with either of those women again, ever, I will be gone." He said, "gone where?" I explained.

He did say he wasn't "avoiding" the books, hadn't gotten anything out of counseling, but had always been willing to do what it takes to make things better for us. (Everything but take initiative.)

He suggested I calm down, he was very confused, sensitive and concerned, but very lacking in communication skills. No indepth discoveries there, just a complete baring of soul for me.

I was embarrassed by my outburst and apologized for handling it that way. He said it was okay, and he would do whatever it takes to help me get over it.

Now, I just feel empty, like I've said it all. I think I released a lot of anger and that feels good, but now I feel tired and empty, and sad that he can't respond the way I feel I need him to.

I want to dig out of him what I'm not sure ever existed. How can we not know each other better than this after all these years? It's weird. Doing better, but not settled yet.

Emily:

I had those kinds of discussions with my husband. The trust thing was impossible for me to get past. I imagined him being with just about every woman imaginable. Every situation where I could not be with him and there was drinking and women around caused me to panic. Unfortunately for me, just about every time that happened, he didn't behave.

Now of course, he said "nothing" happened, but I would hear otherwise. I was just lucky I had a wide circle of friends. I even got that same exact statement, I have not "done" anything. I, too, felt like a crazy person. I, too, couldn't get past it.

Georgette:

We had a party at his office for a longterm employee who had retired. I swore I wouldn't put myself in the position again of being around the two other women, but I did. I swore that I wouldn't overreact to anything and end up with anxiety, but I did.

My husband was taking pictures of the event and I couldn't help but "think" he laughed and joked while taking pictures at the "wrong" table (with the other woman and her friend) a little too much. It could be my imagination, and I'm sure it is, but he still doesn't get it, that she is so hateful to me that I can't breathe when I look at her.

I still fear that I may find out one day I have some disease, that I don't deserve. That it gags me to think of what I've been exposed to. Yes, he did that to me/us, but he's sorry and she's arrogant. She wasn't blameless, and now I feel dirty from the filth of her life. Will he ever understand?

I told him he needed to go over the event in his mind and figure out for himself why I might be upset, because he knows very well what we need at this point and his actions are a choice, always have been.

First he said that I was over-reacting or imagining things. Then he talked awhile and said he supposed that it was an uncomfortable situation, sitting across the table from his assistant and her husband, who, by the way, kept trying to be nice to his wife and getting the cold shoulder.

Yes, I agreed with him that the seating arrangements sucked, except that it gave his assistant and him the chance to show all of us how well they communicate. There was inside work humor, gentle teasing, nothing bad, just too comfortable and familiar, for my taste.

He said, again, that he didn't do anything wrong. I agreed. But, he also didn't do anything to make sure I wasn't uncomfortable. I again asked him to turn it around as if we were seated at a table with a guy I'd snuck out of town with and have to listen to us banter like old buddies, would he be comfortable with that? He shrugged.

He denied the incident of joking with or taking pictures of her. I guess the pics will tell. I may be wrong, and she may have been away from the table at that moment. I hope so. I hope I'm wrong.

I have decided to see a counselor for myself again. I cannot handle the daily hyper-vigilance anymore. I try not to, but I get sucked in.

I told my husband that I am going and why, and asked him to join me or go for himself, because I can't stand the person I've become.

I asked him to explain why he thinks that I have to get help now, why he's not the one fixing everything, since he saw fit to destroy it in the first place. I am still so raw and angry. God help me.

He was really sad and seemed sincere in saying that he's so sorry he did this to us/me. And he said he will do whatever I need. But he doesn't understand why it can't be over and done with for both of us. It is for him. I believe that, but he seems to be oblivious to the fact that we cannot all just hang out and be buddies any more. It just doesn't work like that.

I truly think that if I hadn't gone ballistic on several occassions, stating exactly what the problem is he wouldn't remember that there ever was one.

Is that possible? Is it possible that they are so deep into the "fog," that it could stay suppressed if we betrayed spouses didn't dig it up? I believe that is the case with my husband.

I wouldn't have believed it if I hadn't lived it, but I think he "forgot" that he and she tried to have an affair, and that the little slut he did have one with means nothing to him, so it's a dead issue. If only I would drop it. The problem is, if I dropped it, we would be expected to socialize and laugh and joke like nothing happened.

I told him that I was tired of trying to figure out my insecuries and anxiety, that three sessions with a counselor who let me take the blame wasn't nearly enough to repair what he ripped apart, especially since we weren't allowed to bring the problem up.

That everything I believed to to true in my life had been shredded and in light of the fact that we stayed together, I was hurt, and baffled by his indifference to our wearing wedding rings. I am very strong on symbolism and he knows it.

I said nothing new, just repeat stuff from the beginning. It seems that each time maybe just one more sentence sinks in. Do you think so?

Will my mind just disintegrate and I won't know or care? It feels like it some days. I'm sick of calling it baby steps because it feels like stuggling in quicksand instead. Time to climb and run. Gosh this gets old. And maybe I am just too far gone to ever think rationally again. Would I know it or care?

Angela:

It sounds like he is compartmentalizing. You know, where you put the feelings, memories, whatever in a compartment, shut the door and ignore it. Some people can even pretend it isn't there. Men tend to be really good at this.

If you are still in the hyper vigilance mode I would agree that you need to get some help. I did tell my husband I would not be able to live like that myself and if I couldn't get past that then we might not make it and that reason would be on my shoulders.

Have you been able to get him to some couples counselling? I would encourage it. The third party can help him see the entire picture from your perspective, too. Sometimes there are things we know that our loved ones won't listen to us about, a lot of things. They need to hear it from someone else. Think about how many times your kids didn't listen or you didn't listen to your parents.

The other thing about public situations is that it looks really bad if the boss slights other people regardless of the reasons behind it. It reflects poorly on the boss. So you use the public face.

I think most of us don't even remember what we do with the public face. We put it on, then dump it. I suspect that may have happened at the luncheon. He put his public face on and then dropped it. It didn't mean anything.

Georgette:

Of course, if we had been the perfect mate, this wouldn't have happened to us. But, how often have we been unhappy with them and not turned it into an affair? You're right, there is no excuse for their behavior. I am convinced that open, honest, communication is the only way to survive this. The problem is that men are not great communicators.

My husband has said he's sorry more times and in more ways than I could ask for, but it stops there, and I need more now. I suggested the other day that he needs to focus on helping me get past this, not just through it.

He needs to deal now with anticipating and avoiding things that will set us back and not leave it to me to figure out. I expect him to keep me on the inside. This is the relationship he created.

It is very clear that in our marriage he had me and the children at home, and the girls at work. He lived two lives. I did not belong there and they did not belong here. He very much kept his office life private. I heard it in his comments that he felt very responsible for their happiness and security, much as a husband should. With him it went too far.

These women have their own families and husbands to cry and whine to when life gets difficult or work gets hard. He forgot that. However, when you work with and socialize with each other for 9-10 hours every day, building relationships with and having empathy for these co-workers, the family at home gets the worn-out, napping-on-the-couch, needs-time-to-unwind, don't-bother-me now leftovers — maybe 3 hours in the evening, it's no wonder they (the co-workers) come first.

He finally told me that at the time of the affair, he was sick of my whining about my job and my boss and it got to the point that he hated to come home. In those days they had some very difficult work situations to deal with and he had a lot of female workers with personal problems.

He told me about them, but hated any suggestion that it wasn't his problem. They were his priority, and he had enough on his plate keeping them happy, without me whining about my day. Anyway, that's when he started hanging out after work with the "girls." Dealing with an unhappy, lonely, complaining wife was overload for him. I now understand it, but it makes me angry that it ever happened.

We both blew up recently over something very trivial and I was taking it very personal. I don't know how to just be myself anymore. Out of the blue I asked him, "What is this really about?" He just crumbled. He said, "What did I ever do to make you feel you aren't okay just the way you are?" Then he stopped and just stared at me. It's like a light went on.

He scares me. He just wants it to disappear. He wants us to all just get along, and he doesn't know how to fix it. He's avoiding self-help of any kind and hoping it will just fade away and things will be okay. But, he does listen and talk when I confront him. In the meantime, he's exhausted again and has a "beaten" attitude.

I don't want this, but I cannot control what's spilling out of me these days. I was locked inside and living like a martyr to sustain a loving couple facade. I was not happy and didn't have a clue how to fix it. I was as frustated as he was.

I'm now being honest with him about all of that, and expecting the same from him. The trouble is, I'm pushing him in a couseling role, and it seems like we should be seeing someone with training.

The monster (me) has now been released, and really, she's not that bad, but she's not going to be locked up anymore. So we have to learn how to get along with her. At times it comes out too forceful, and I know it.

I feel like I want it all my way and on my terms and I can't stop the need to direct and control. I scare myself. But, I am hoping my emotions will swing back to somewhere more in the center and I will be able to relax and enjoy a simple moment without over-analyzing and the hyper-vigilance.

I just started counseling for myself and the counselor said we could bring hubby in at some point if he was willing. This may be what we need. This guy seems very open and caring.

I hope it works out. I am desperate for assurance and guidance. I don't want to end my marriage or start a new life with this monkey on my back. It's time to let go.

Miriam:

Yes, yes, and yes! It's never easy. Not if it's worth fighting for. The years my husband and I were separated was a nightmare time in my life. The first year I don't even really remember much, except for the tears and the anger and the pain. It's a blur. Thank God.

The second year settled down somewhat into a dull ache most of the time, interspersed with tears, rages at each other, and months when we didn't speak to each other, over the phone or in person. Every now and then we would talk to one another, but we hadn't learned how yet, and oftentimes, those conversations would end with one of us getting mad.

The third year was the one with the most clarity. I knew I loved him. I knew he loved me. It was quite a revelation to both of us, let me tell you. Especially in light of the hell we'd put each other through. I'd even filed for divorce, only to stop it later, because I thought it would ease the pain some. Didn't work. Nothing did, but talking to each other. So we did.

We're now in our second year back together. The first year, I was very antsy. Fight or flight mode. Ready to run at the drop of a hat some days. And I still wonder now and again if I haven't just lost my senses entirely.

I thought still a lot about "the betrayal" then. Even more so when we got back together, because then, you see, he was *right there*. There was no way to avoid it.

When I looked at him, I remembered. When he said something innocent, like "remember when we did this or that" I would respond with "yeah, I remember" and all the while I was thinking "yeah, that was when you were cheating on me, you sob." I was waiting for him to screw up. And if he did, I was going to be out of there so fast!

That first year I was the one who needed healing. So we talked. We cried. Or sometimes I cried and he held me. We yelled. We stomped off and came back. I obsessed sometimes. I doubted him, I trusted him, and I swore I'd kill him. Sometimes all in the same breath.

This second year, all that has gotten better. I don't think about it nearly as much as I did. Although I suspect it will always be a part of me, something that changed me in ways I don't even fully understand yet, and may never. I don't ask as many questions, I don't doubt as much, and don't get into fight or flight mode nearly as often.

But the point is, it just takes time to heal. Everyone is different. Someone who is doing their healing with their husband there with them has it in their face every day. I couldn't do that, I would have indeed killed him. I admire those who can do that.

Those who can repair their marriage and themselves while living with the person who helped tear that apart, it's got to be hard, and I think the trick may be in not expecting too much too soon. Let it come when it comes. It will.

But you have got to be *you*, who you are, and feel what you feel, at any cost. Anything less is not being true to yourself, or to what you expect from yourself. Or him, either for that matter.

One thing I did learn the hard way, lying to myself was the hardest mess to fix of all. The rest just came when it was time.

Georgette:

It feels good to have someone truly understand the "craziness" of the healing process. I love, I hate, I want, I don't want. Thank you for acknowledging that I am not wrong for feeling that way, and that I am not heading for disaster by being up front honest.

I feel that I am ripping apart what's left of *us* and I almost don't care. I am putting all of the burden on him to adjust and I can't help it anymore. It's just bursting out of me. Funny thing is, he's hanging in there and trying to figure it out. Poor guy, I know how hard it is to be blindsided. I didn't mean for this to happen, it just is.

I felt I was really letting everyone down by not just moving forward in peace and harmony, and by sharing the nasty feelings I've developed and can't seem to squelch. I felt badly that anyone looked to me for example when I still feel such rage. On the other hand, most days are really good. He's a reformed man, but nothing he does is quite good enough for me.

I find myself pushing him to the limits. I will deal with this in counseling and hope things go well. I am pretty sure that I still love him, but it's not a desperate "have to have him" feeling anymore and we're busy trying to define our new relationship. It may be less sensual and more affectionate. Maybe we're growing up? Can't know yet. And it will never be the "old" relationship. Too many changes for that. It's new and new takes time.

Some of us have to get the ball back into our court in order to move forward. I could not have walked away at the beginning. I don't do too many things half way. I would have turned away completely and done something I would live to regret, like get even. Instead, I decided I could look at him every day and know he was working with the other woman and somehow get beyond and/or above it. It has not been a picnic.

Adrenalin and starry-eyed were the only tools I knew how to use at the time, and the only focus I had was for him to want me again, any way I could manage it. I'm sure it was obvious that was *all* that mattered. And I hear that message in a lot of posts.

Some of us just need to stabilize things when possible, whatever that takes. Then, when life is a little more in our control and we can shift the focus a bit, that's where the honesty begins. You can't get there until you're there either. That's where the real pain lies and the anger, and where the ultimate confusion set in for me. Things were actually stabilizing, and it was hard to explain why I was so easily upset and anxious when things were actually very good at home!

I felt like I was/am constantly sabatoging my own success. When in fact, I was/am just getting to the root of my real feelings, which have been stifled for way too long.

The focus is now off of him and onto me and us. Whether that's the right way or the wrong way to deal with things, I don't know. But, for me, it was the only way I knew how, and I wouldn't want to discourage anyone from getting their feet on solid ground before diving into the mess of self-exploration.

I admire anyone who has clear boundaries, who is able to say, "That's it, I'm done," and make the other person do the needed work before they let them back into their life.

I did not have the strength or the self-esteem. Up to that point, I had depended on my roles in life to define me. I say had, because I now at least have a concept of self-respect and self-esteem and know what I will or will not allow. I'm growing a backbone and putting up boundaries.

My husband got off easy at first, but he's paying the price now. So, maybe it's just the old "pay now, play later" or "play now, pay later" concept. I let him off easy at first and just when he thought it was over, BAM! Some people hit it at first and then lay off. I'd like to think the healing just takes this long for some of us and I may someday get beyond it.

The other day I really looked at him and I startled myself. He's just a middle-aged, average looking man, not a god. He's a little overweight and has a paunch. Why all the panic? He's pessimistic, likes to be by himself and usually has to force himself to get out and socialize. Why am I so anxious over him? Who in their right mind would want to be married to that? This is the part that makes me think I do truly love him, faults and all.

Miriam:

You know, I was shaking my head in agreement when I read the part about where you just love him, warts and all, and then I realized, *we all* feel this way. Whether or not our marriages survived this storm, we all loved our partners enough to fight for that love in the only ways we knew how, no matter what it was at the time.

There are no right or wrong paths, no formulas to follow. And that's the hardest part for a person just starting out on this path to come to terms with.

We all wanted, at the beginning, a magic potion, the right words, anything at all, to just make it all go away and be the way we thought it was. But it never is, is it? Even for those who reconcile.

Those who move on to different challenges and joys in their lives know they are different now, know they have changed, but those of us who have stayed in our marriages also have changed. It's just that we have different challenges. And who's to say which is the hardest to do?

···+··+··+

Was it *your* fault your spouse cheated?

It's fairly unusual for a husband or wife to take the blame for their infidelity. They will blame their cheating on their spouse's deficiency or other circumstances they couldn't control. Did your spouse accept responsibility, or were you to blame for his or her adultery?

Raquel:

My husband didn't exactly blame me for his cheating although he suggested that a certain sameness in our sex life was a contributing factor. Unfortunately, I did believe this and, as a result, my self-esteem plummeted. If fact, I still worry about whether he is happy with our sex life now that we are back together. This is a real problem for me!

What he actually *did* blame me for was finding out. He contended (and perhaps still contends) that the only real problem with regards to his having had an affair was me having found out. He suggested on many occasions that he believed the affair would have run its course and we would have continued on with our marriage, me none the wiser, and him, well, you get the picture!

Miriam:

It took me a long time to realize that, no matter what our problems had been, or were, for that matter, there was no excuse for crossing a boundary that could prove to be an unforgivable hurt. In my case, adultery.

It took even longer to refuse to carry the blame. It took him awhile to "own" that. When he did, I think it almost destroyed him.

Emily:

Immediately following each of the times cheating, he blamed it on being *drunk*. Yes, he was -- but that doesn't excuse anything. But while in counseling, he said it had a lot to do with me not wanting him in bed any more and not wanting him to touch me.

I didn't mind the touching, but I didn't like the fact that he poked and prodded at me. I always felt like he was grabbing at me, never nice and gentle. There never was much foreplay. When he would start prodding at me, it could never be just for fun, it always meant we *had* to have *sex*.

Dana:

It didn't matter that we had a very good sex life, I enjoyed it as much as he did. I just didn't give him what "he needed," and he didn't really elaborate on it. He told me he'd "tried to talk to me about it" (what he "needed from me") while I was recovering from a serious illness and I was drugged out on painkillers. Of course, I don't remember, and I asked him why he picked that particular time to talk. He couldn't remember.

But, yes, because I didn't give him what he needed, he turned to another. And, yes, it was my fault. It wasn't for sex, that I know, but for some emotional intimacy he was unable to share with me, maybe?

Another thing that I can think of is he was "tired of me being sick all the time" and he wanted someone to take care of *him*. That's understandable, but if I rightly remember, the wedding vows did say "in sickness and in health." I also had the feeling he thought I made myself sick on purpose.

It took me awhile to get it that it wasn't my fault, I cannot control what my body does, but I still don't understand what he wanted. Superwife, maybe?

Teresa:

Whose fault is the adultery? Well, on one level there is no problem. It was his choice. He could have chosen to tell me he was unhappy. He could have chosen to try to work on our marriage but he didn't.

However, life is never really as simple as that is it? In his mind everything is quite clear. It is all my fault. I drove him to it. He simply isn't that sort of man (and, strangely, wasn't that sort of man on the previous occasion either).

On another level it's really no one's fault in the sense that I think we may both have married the wrong person. We rushed into marriage before really getting to know one another.

I can't tell you what my husband feels as he has never revealed his feelings to me during our entire marriage and my counsellor suggested that perhaps he simply isn't capable of talking about his feelings. Maybe I was wrong all these years to expect it?

I made the mistake of marrying a man exactly like my dad (Freud would have a field day). I chose someone I thought was the strong, silent, confident type. What I actually chose was someone who cannot express his feelings apart from anger and not even that very well. Someone who was extremely quick to criticize but never seemed to be able to say anything positive. Someone who is a doer rather than a thinker.

I, on the other hand, am the exact opposite. I am the talker, the thinker, the emotional one. However, we did have one thing in common, neither of us was good at giving praise. I've been told that it's partly because I did not receive any myself as a child that it makes me feel very uncomfortable, and partly a fear of making myself vulnerable to anyone. I need to be secure about someone else's feelings before I can reveal mine.

Anyway, our marriage initially was very tempestuous. He would criticize me or do something extremely insensitive and I would wildly overreact, shout, scream, and throw things. We would then calm down. I would get what was bothering me off my chest. He would listen but not tell me what he thought. We would make up. Have sex. Things would be fine for a while until the next blow-up. We seemed to thrive on the drama.

My temper tantrums were borne of insecurity and over the years I became less and less insecure. I developed a strong network of friends I could talk to, and, as talking to him never seemed to get me anywhere, I stopped even trying.

The emotional attachment between us seemed to break down completely. I seemed to be his emotional crutch and I simply didn't want the job any more. I got more and more resentful that he shut me out of his feelings and never seemed to understand mine. Without the emotional attachment, I no longer wanted sex with him. It was like sleeping with a stranger. Someone doing things to you rather than a union of two people.

I realize now that he wasn't being difficult. He really can't express his feelings. I think I made the mistake of believing if he didn't talk about his feelings he didn't have any and at times I think I was incredibly cruel as a result of this.

As I said, he is a doer, a practical man. He lives in the concrete world. For him, therefore, I think he expresses his love through physical acts, sex, buying gifts, etc. Therefore, when he feels he is lacking love, he seeks sex with someone else.

I, on the other hand, am an emotional person. I'm a talker. I want to know what is going on in someone's head. I want to be told I'm wanted. I want someone to be sensitive to my feelings. I feel certain if I had continued to have sex with my husband we would still be together.

He measured the success of our marriage purely by the amount of sex we were having. But I was starving emotionally and in that state, I couldn't give him what he wanted. I resented his ability to ignore everything else.

He thought my problem with sex was my fault. I needed to go and get my head sorted out. I needed professional help. I resented that and the anger grew and grew. I withdrew into my world with my friends and moved further and further away from him.

So, in the end, whose fault is it?

Angela:

He never blamed me. However, in working towards a better relationship I can see where I have some responsibility for not being there for him quite as much as he needed.

Does that mean I'm responsible? No! But I see where some of my behaviors toward him got him looking elsewhere.

The other side of the coin is that he could have communicated his needs to me. However, he came from a very non-communicative family and never learned any of that stuff.

It was still his decision to step outside of our marriage for intimacy and sex.

Candace:

I am writing as the other woman now. It was him that cheated on his wife. I was not married at the time. I expected him to separate from his wife before we got intimate but it didn't happen.

We're not a number now although we still talk. I am curious as to what made him step out on his wife. He is a nice man. I don't think he cheats as a hobby. I think he really cares for me.

Two things have occurred to me. First, he and his wife aren't on the same page of the book when it comes to sex. I am not excusing him for cheating, just explaining his behavior. The other thing is religion. He's Catholic. He will commit adultery before he divorces. Not being Catholic I don't get it.

He loves/respects his wife. He fell in love twice. True, he shouldn't have gotten here, but he did.

Whose fault is it? It isn't black and white. Life isn't simple.

Ashleigh:

Yep, initially I was to blame for his foray. You see, he traveled quite a bit for work and stated "had I traveled with him, this never would have happened." Apparently my flying once a month, for 3 - 5 days, to the state he was in for the last year didn't count.

Then, because I only open my mouth when I am right, he came up with a litany of other reasons. But, I asked three important questions prior to unearthing the truth about the other woman:

1. Is our sex life not satisfying? "No, it is awesome!"
2. Have I held you back from realizing or working towards any personal goals? "No, you are the best friend I've got!"

3. Is there someone else that has grabbed your attention? "No, I just don't want to responsible for all the stuff anymore!"

But once I unearthed the actual truth (I am a skilled sleuth) he hollered and screamed at me every time I confronted him. He attempted to turn it around and continue to blame me. Fortunately I am also skilled in arguing rationally.

Today, he no longer accuses me or blames me. Perhaps because I became deathly ill and self-destructive. Funny thing though, that cuts through my heart, is that his new other woman had to have surgery a few times over the past year and he actually took off from work to be there for her. He never ever did that for me. Ever.

Also, they are remodeling their new home and he seems to rush home to haul things out for her. But, I did all of the hauling myself for our home!

Misty:

Yes, I was the blame for my husband finding someone else. It was all me, I wasn't making him happy. I didn't know that I was supposed to, figured you had to do that yourself, how silly of me!

He was jealous of time I spent with our children and with volunteer work. It was my fault that I didn't want to give him that time I gave others.

He now has a girlfriend without children or outside interests that can make him her number one priority. So in this case, he may have been right.

···+··+··→

Which came first, the adultery, or marital problems that ended with adultery?

Did your husband or wife cheat because there was something wrong with your marriage, or, was there something wrong with your marriage because your spouse was cheating? Or, was it a mixture of the two?

Teresa:
Personally I believe it was a mixture of the two. Looking back over our marriage I found that the two worst times were when my husband was having an affair.

He seemed to be more confident to be nasty and offhand to me because he was comfortable in the knowledge that he had a back-up plan if I suddenly decided that I didn't like it and left. Any thoughts?

Miriam:
Well, I think for some of us at least, it would depend on which partner you ask. From my point of view, it was his cheating that made things so bad. If you ask him, he would probably say that it was problems in our marriage that drew him to an affair.

I can relate to how your husband was so much worse to get along with when he was cheating. A smug, superior, I-don't-care-how-you-feel-or-what-you-think attitude.

I just didn't realize why he was so cocky at the time. And I blamed myself for not being able to fix it, whatever it was. Trust me, if it ever happened to me again, I would have some ideas.

Teresa:
The more I think about it, yes, there were problems with our marriage but nothing that major. The real problems came when he decided to turn to someone else rather than me.

All I ever wanted was for some sort of sign that he loved me. I didn't get anything. Perhaps the other women did.

Dana:
My marriage "seemed" to be fine until I started to suspect the affair, and went downhill after my suspicions were confirmed. My husband told me "he didn't get what he needed," there were problems "we" (I wasn't consulted about this, understand) couldn't solve, "we" were unhappy, "we" this and "we" that.

As for his attitude, he was a verifiable Jekyll and Hyde. He would be so nice and gentle, and the next moment, blow his temper over something like if I accidentally (he was positive I did it on purpose) bumped his arm and he spilled his drink. He had more nasty and patronizing moments than his nicer ones.

I really thought I was "mentally unstable" (his words), because what did I do that "all of a sudden" I was a witch? Couldn't do anything right as far as I was concerned. Damned if I did, damned if I didn't.

I really do think it depends on which partner you ask. Our main problem was his non-communication (and truthfully, my subsequent withdrawal in the wake of the discovery), which can be worked on if both partners are truly committed. But he didn't want to make the committment, at least not with me.

Debbie:

In regards to this question, I am not to sure how to answer that from the betrayer's point of view. I think the reason I am involved with the other man is because he fulfills the need in me to be desired, to be adored. He tells me how beautiful I am and complements me all the time. That is the reason I am involved, he makes me feel good about myself.

·⋯◆⋯◆⋯◆

How much damage has the affair done to you?

Learning of a spouse's betrayal can blindside you. You doubt yourself, your capabilities, your worth. I think "Miriam" sums everything up quite well in the following statements.

Miriam:
You are trying so hard to hang onto something that is hurting you that you don't realize the damage *he's* done to you. How do you feel about yourself? Do you like yourself? Do you respect yourself? Have confidence in who you are? Feel worthy of being liked and loved and cherished because you are you?

How do you really feel about your husband? Put aside the fact that you're married to this man for the moment. Take a good look at him.

If he were married to your best friend, your sister, your daughter, what would your opinion of him be? Would you like him? Would you have any respect for him? Would you put any faith in him as a man of worth, of decency, of being the kind of man you could look up to and know he is what you thought he was?

Or would you tell your friend, your sister, your daughter, to run as far and as fast as she can to protect herself before he ruins the rest of her life? This is what you see in your life, too. Not anyone else's, but this is what *this* man has done to your life.

Give yourself a chance to be hurt, to cry, to be angry, to feel humiliated, to feel betrayed, to feel lied to, to feel second best. All those things that you are burying deep inside your soul because you are so afraid that if you let yourself know they are there you will die. You won't. Trust me. You may want to for a while. You may spend a lot of time in tears, and then being angry, but it is part of a process of healing from betrayal.

And before you can know if you want to keep this man in your life, you will have to acknowledge and get through this nightmare time. For *you*, not for him.

When the decision-making time comes, it will be up to you, not to him. You are not the one who betrayed your marriage vows, your trust, your faith. He is, and in doing so, he put that power of decision in your hands all by himself.

Make sure that you know what you are giving up if you decide to let him stay with you. Give yourself some time to think your life through, and that means looking deep inside, and realizing how you let your life get to this point.

And no, it's not your fault your husband betrayed you. It's his fault. It's your fault if you don't use this time to either make your life better and yourself stronger and wise from the hurt you feel, or if you stay on the merry-go-round for the rest of your life.

You need some backbone to get through the hard decisions, and quit allowing him to drag you hither and yon like some willow branch. You can do this. It's up to you. It always has been.

Joy:

Thank you, for saying what needed to be said so perfectly. What you speak of is so empowering, for *ourselves*, which is a new concept for so many of us who have literally given ourselves away trying to hold onto something (someone) who is often not at all good for us, especially not in their present state.

It is so difficult to find the difference between "real" love and simply wanting what you can't have, between "real" love and some variation on the "codependence" theme.

It is so difficult to love ourselves in this equation, too, and especially, and often for the first time ever. But until we do, like you say, we really have no basis for who we are, what we want, who we love, and why, and for what *we* would want *our* futures to hold.

What so many of us never understood is that loving ourselves and appreciating ourselves is not selfish or egotistical or arrogant. It is simply having self-respect and personal dignity. It is valuing ourselves and validating our own feelings and dreams and desires, rather than begging or trying to require someone else to do it.

Others can embellish our lives and add to our joy, but they cannot complete us. That is our task, and that is our own personal adventure.

···→·→·→

Dialogue with an Unfaithful Husband

As I was doing the final editing on this book, I received an e-mail from a man who calls himself "Ron De Vous." He is involved in a long term affair. We exchanged several e-mails and I think our dialogue is a good conclusion to this book. I have edited out some of his personal information but otherwise have kept his comments intact, including those that are fairly sexually explicit.

⸺➔

Hi Pat, I was reading your very interesting articles about cheating spouses and thought that I would share MY story with you. I am a mid-50s professional and I have been married to the same fantastic woman for 30 years. Our children are in college.

Ten years ago, I met a woman who is a few years younger than I am. She is in a long-term committed relationship with her husband and has children in high school. We live in the same neighborhood and wound up going to the same place at the same time and decided to "car pool". During the drives we began to talk quite a bit and we found that we did not have too much in common. However, somehow we ended up occasionally mentioning sex.

My wife and I have a passable sexual relationship and a great personal relationship. We both work long hours, bring work home and have busy lives. We probably don't have sex more than 8 to 10 times A YEAR. I masturbate every day, sometimes twice.

Early on in our marriage, I realized that my wife was not too sexual and tried to spice things up. She also does not need physical contact as much as I do. For example when we are in bed and I mention how nice a hug would be, she says that I can hug her, but she is "too tired" to hug me. I suggested that we have an "affair" to get a regular sex date with her many years ago, but she thought that I was weird.

Anyway, one night when leaving the meeting, my car pool buddy mentioned that she had not had sex with her husband since her youngest was about 3 years old. And she dared me to kiss her. I did and I have to tell you that it was like a whole fireworks display. She was so hot and sexy that it was freaky. I had never done anything like that in 20 years of marriage, but I had not experienced that kind of passion either.

Subsequent to that, on the drives home, we stopped to "make out" for a few minutes and it was wonderful. Just kissing and hugging. Then about a month later, she got more aggressive and started caressing my crotch. I didn't stop her. She got me very aroused and then asked if I wanted to come in her hand or her mouth. Well I was too embarrassed to tell her that I had never had oral sex and left the decision to her.

I won't go into detail, but suffice it to say that I was "hooked". That was 10 years ago and since then we have gotten together about every six weeks at a local motel for the most mindblowing experiences you can imagine. We have explored many facets of our sexuality including anal, light SM and bondage. By comparison, my "plain vanilla" infrequent sex life at home is not even worthy of comment.

Neither of us is interested in leaving our spouses and we recognize that we probably would not make a good couple, but the sex we have is incredible. It provides us with the sex lives we wish we had at home and don't, and certainly makes us way less frustrated than we were before we met that we do not have great sex lives at home.

It may be trite, but I truly believe that the "infidelity" has allowed each of us to remain in committed realtionships with our spouses since we do have to depend on them to provide the sexual gratification we need. We are discreet, unpredictable and unpatterned to reduce the risk of detection and I hope we can continue pleasing each other for many more years. We just celebrated our 10th anniversary (at the motel with sushi, vodka and love-making).

I can not see a victim here. I would appreciate your comments.

Ron de Vous

...→

Ron De,

If you have read my articles I don't see how you could think I wouldn't find your story of adultery any less victimless than others. Ten years of sex with a married woman in your neighborhood? You really don't think anyone knows?

What would happen if your wife decided she was tired of this game? What if your lover's husband decided he wanted a wife who wasn't putting out to her car pool buddy? Are either of you ready to be kicked to the curb for your "incredible sex" that leaves you so relaxed and satisfied?

I think your wife and your lover's husband deserve better than they're getting. They certainly deserve to meet someone who can fulfill their fantasies since they aren't getting them taken care of at home.

Pat G.

PS: Any problem with me including your story in a book I'm writing about adultery?

···→

Hi, Thanks very much for the reply. I had suspected that your reaction would be negative. The first point that you mentioned was whether "anyone knows" and I can absolutely tell you that beyond any shadow of doubt -- no one (except us) knows.

Yes, we are both married, but as I mentioned before, our relationship has helped our marriages rather than hindered them since we have been able to deal with the different sexual needs of our spouses. I play tennis and I love the release of endorphins from a strenuous game. And guess what, my wife doesn't play tennis and I have had to find other people to play with. I don't resent the fact that she doesn't enjoy tennis and I don't resent the fact that she doesn't want to have sex with me either.

My friend has been taking post-graduate courses since before I met her and she also exercises to keep in terrific physical shape. Her husband has a dead-end job and is a couch potato. She has friends who share her interests and leaves him at home with the kids and the TV. She is also not resentful that he doesn't share her passions.

We are not ready to be "kicked out to the curb" and I do not think that we deserve to be. Our relationship has protected our marriages.

About 5 years ago, my lover mentioned that she was thinking of leaving her marriage. I helped her work through it and advised her that if she did, then our relationship would have to end. I was not comfortable with having an "affair" with a single woman. Our "raison d'etre" was to provide each of us with that which was lacking in our marriages, and if she was not married, then the landscape would be different. And the affair -- over.

So, yeah, Mr. Potatohead can continue in blissful ignorance that all is OK at home. I am taking care of his wife for both of us. And I am taking care of my needs so that my wife doesn't have to say "no" as much as she did before.

My wife and my lover's husband do not need to meet people who can take care of their fantasies and sexual desires. They LIVE with them. All they have to do is ask or act like they have needs to be fulfilled and the affair would be OVER. But they don't and I am not ready to sit back and be frustrated like I was before.

Ten years is not a fling. It is a serious matter. Not all adultery is bad. Ours is very good and healthy -- for everybody. If you want to include this story in your book, feel free, but you have to include it in a positive light without your "home wrecker" pre-disposition.

Ron

PS -- I would like your comments on my dissertation above. Try to have an open mind and realize that maybe adultery=victim is not true for everyone.

···➔

Ron,

If this is working for all of you, that's great. I really don't know why you wrote to me, knowing in advance that I would have a negative reaction.

There are plenty of open marriages, swinging couples and polyamorous relationships that work. What is missing from the relationship you have is honesty. You and your lover hide what you're doing from your spouses. If it's the perfect solution to what's wrong in both marriages, why hide? You're doing your spouses a favor so why continue to live a lie?

If I include your story, it will be one of many that have been provided to me by people involved in various aspects of adultery and said in their own words, without my "home wrecker predisposition" to taint them.

Pat

···➔

Hi Pat,

Sorry to continue the dialogue. I know that you're right and I guess what I need is acceptance. I don't expect to get it from you. That's not a negative comment, just a factual one.

Society does not approve of what we are doing and I am quite sure that our spouses would not either, in spite of my protestations that we are doing them a "favor." The Bible, the Qur'an and the Torah all have commentary on adultery and as I recall the admonition is one of the "Top Ten."

I cannot honestly tell you that my lover and I do not feel guilt about what we're doing, but it's easier for us each to live with the guilt than the lack of passion which we were faced with before we met. It's definitely a dilemma.

I have tried to interest my wife in a physical relationship. I would gladly exchange the affair for an active sex-life at home. I guess after a while I gave up on trying. We have discussed it (many times) and she said that she would try, but it is not in her nature.

Your business is saving marriages and helping couples over the rough spots. If you have any advice I'd be happy to listen.

Regards and thanks,

Ron

⋯→

Ron,

The dilemma you're in is loving your wife but wanting more than she currently is able to provide. A sexually unbalanced relationship can't be pleasant and some marriages don't survive when partners are unable to compromise. You might say you are compromising with your affair, but your wife hasn't agreed to this arrangement so it is only a one-sided compromise designed to meet *your* needs.

I don't know what the answer is. Living in a sexually frustrating marriage isn't satisfactory. Neither is constantly living in guilt. Neither is gambling that your spouses will always be oblivious to what's going on.

Have you considered getting a divorce and then searching for someone who will meet all of your needs? Someone who isn't committed to someone else?

Don't you deserve more than what you have right now? Admittedly you have a wife who is a great friend and a friend who is a great lover. Maybe this quadrangle will last as long as you need it to and no one will be the wiser. What happens if it doesn't, and you lose your wife, your friend, and perhaps a lot of your financial security in a bitter divorce?

Again, I don't have any answers although I really can empathize with your situation. Unfortunately, I also see a future that might not be so rosy because of your current actions. You might want to consider marriage counseling or even therapy for yourself to figure out how to get your marriage back on course or to decide if it's even worth saving.

Pat

⋯→

Hi Pat,

I hope you don't mind that I am emailing you. You're a lot more convenient than a therapist and cheaper too!

You're right. I am conflicted about the affair. It's been 10 years and that's a lot of guilt and pleasure. I am a hard-driving professional without a lot of free time and my wife is a business executive who has managed to build a successful career and raise our children, and keep the household running like a Swiss clock, have a social life, etc. There's not a whole lot of time left over for passion and sex.

I do resent the lack of a physical relationship, but there is a lot of love between us and the time we can spend together is very good. Many nights we both bring work home and then fall into bed and lose consciousness until the morning. But I try to make time for intimacy and have not given up. She has though, and so far this YEAR we are up to 5 times.

A few years back, in an attempt to get something going, I suggested that WE have an "affair." She thought it was strange, but said that we'd try to be more intimate. I did - she didn't.

A couple years later, we were on vacation and we had a room with two queen-size beds. I was reading on one and she was reading on the other and we both fell asleep. Then, I slept apart from her for the remainder of the trip. She was really upset and when we were home, we "had it out." I told her that I was really comfortable sleeping apart since it was getting very difficult to sleep beside someone who rebuffed my physical advances.

During the heated discussion, she said she understood my feelings, was happy that I was still very attracted to her and would try to be more intimate. Lasted about a month.

I don't think counselling will help us and I am definitely not interested in a divorce. I guess I "want my cake and to eat it too" and that's why I have a lover. I love your description of a "wife who is a great friend and a friend who is a great lover."

I cannot get the marriage "back on track" myself. I am not sure how she would react to a counselling suggestion. She'd probably think I was a "sex maniac" (which I am!).

This will be my last email. I've gotten my feelings out. There is no really good solution and I am going to continue to pretend -- my life will never end, and flowers never bend with the rainfall (apologies to Paul Simon).

Thanks for listening. God bless us all.

Ron

...→

Ron,

No need to reply to this email but I need to get some thoughts out before we end this "cheap therapy."

I can guarantee that if your affair has been going on for the past 10 years, your wife knows. If your lover wears perfume or uses a different soap than you do, your wife has smelled the scent on you or on your clothes.

No matter how clever you have been, she is too intelligent not to know what's going on. Some time within this 10 year period she made a decision to stay in the marriage, maybe until the kids are grown and on their own, maybe as long as she isn't embarrassed by the affair, maybe as long as it takes to get the strength to walk away. Or maybe she has decided that not having the pressure of sex is a good trade-off for the security marriage provides her.

Whatever decision she has made, she made one years ago. You could probably pinpoint an approximate timeframe yourself, although when you're involved in an affair you spend a lot of time concentrating on your affair partner and not on your wife, so the clues may have passed without you seeing them.

She may have immersed herself even more into her work or into community involvement or some other activity to take her thoughts off of what was happening with you. She sublimated into her work; it made her better, may have gotten her advancements or otherwise more focused on her career. She might even have had an affair or two just to prove to herself that she is still desirable.

You made attempts at a more active sex life with her after your affair began, right? At that point she would have felt so hurt and betrayed that she could have cared less about being intimate with you.

I think the price you may pay for this affair could be enormous. I hope I'm wrong.

End of our session...

Pat

⇢

Pat, A brief epilogue to our discussions. I will check in with you periodically and let you know whether you're right -- or the jury is still out.

Thanks and best regards,

Ron

⇢⇢⇢

Final Thoughts

As I read through the various stories as I edited them, my thoughts kept changing to the point that I now believe all participants in adultery are victims— the betrayed may be the greatest victim but the betrayer and the other person are also victims.

If you are reading this, there is a high probability you fall into one of the three adultery categories: betrayed, betrayer or other person. You may have been in more than one role at some point in your life. I think it's the very rare person who has never been directly touched by adultery in some manner.

If you are the betrayer, you may fear the consequences of having your affair discovered or you may be cheating to exit your marriage and the affair is your method of leaving. Does your spouse suspect you're being unfaithful? Are you caught in an affair that has turned sour? Should you come clean or deny everything despite the evidence? Whatever your situation, your world is going to change, though perhaps not the way you expect or would like it to. The stories of betrayers are not included to make excuses for adultery. If you are a betrayer, perhaps you will see yourself in one or more of these stories and gain new insight.

If you are the other person in love with a married man or woman, and perhaps even married yourself, do you want your lover to disentangle from his or her spouse so the two of you can make a life together? Are you smothered with promises but seeing no action? Have you put your life on hold, taking sloppy seconds and living for stolen minutes? Is your spouse suspicious of your activities? Do you have the courage to walk away from your lover until the two of you are legally free to be together? If the two of you do "clear the way" to marry in the future, will you be able to trust that he or she won't cheat on you as well?

If you are the betrayed, you may only suspect your spouse of cheating or perhaps you have substantial proof and you're trying to figure out what to do next. You may be confused, depressed, angry, and/or distressed because the affair or its very real possibility is consuming your thoughts. For you, it's time to validate your feelings and take control of the situation.

Love and lust are powerful forces but with enough time and tears each of us comes to a point of decision making. Do you confront? Do you leave? Do you give ultimatums?

Perhaps once you have read the stories of others who have been where you are, you will be more focused as to the best path for your personal situation.

If your spouse is cheating, does he (or she) suspect that you suspect? If not, keep him in the dark as to your suspicions, let him believe you are blind to the cheating, and you'll gain the upper hand in this unwanted threesome in which you've found yourself. By not letting on until you're ready, you will move into a position of control. You will be the one who will be prepared to make the right move at the time that is right for you.

If you have been accusing your spouse of cheating, now is the time to stop the accusations. Your actions are harming you because you are focusing on something you have no control over and your actions are making your spouse even more secretive. To collect evidence, to gain the upper hand, and to make the best plan for yourself, a spouse must believe you have absolute trust in his (or her) innocence, that you suspect nothing.

It isn't easy shifting from betrayed spouse to "spouse with a purpose" but that's what you have to do. Your mission involves evidence gathering, financial planning, legal strategies, and personal damage repair. For the most part you'll want to do everything without enlisting the aid of family or friends. And, when it comes to making the major decisions regarding your marriage, whether to keep it or let it go, that must be *your* decision because only you will live 24/7 with the results of the choices you will make.

Adultery is a choice. Living with an adulterous spouse is a choice. Being intimately entangled with a married person is a choice. Divorce is a choice. Forgiveness is a choice. Each day is filled with choices, some better than others, some more painful than others.

Can *you* survive adultery? I don't know. Can you?

I hope my choice to write this book has helped to validate your situation as well as provide you with what you need in order to make the choices that are best for you.

Pat Gaudette

Recommended Reading

The following are a few of the excellent books I've found which deal specifically with various aspects of adultery.

Addicted to Adultery: How We Saved Our Marriage/How You Can Save Yours, Richard and Elizabeth Brzeczek and Sharon DeVita

Adultery: An Analysis of Love and Betrayal, Annette Lawson

Advice for an Imperfect Married World, Pat Gaudette

Advice for an Imperfect Single World, Pat Gaudette

Affairs: Emergency Tactics, Carol L. Rhodes, Ph.D.

Affairs of the Heart: Men & Women Reveal the Truth about Extramarital Affairs, interviews by Virginia Lee

After the Affair: Healing the Pain and Rebuilding Trust When a Partner Has Been Unfaithful, Janis A. Spring

The Anatomy of an Affair, Reena Sommer, Ph.D.

Avoiding the "Greener Grass" Syndrome: How to Grow Affair-Proof Hedges Around Your Marriage, Nancy C. Anderson

Beyond Affairs: The true story of James and Peggy Vaughan, James and Peggy Vaughan

Beyond the Wedding Vows: Circumstances, Choices and Consequences of an Extramarital Affair, Carmella Antonino

Boomer's Guide to Divorce (and a New Life), Marlene M. Browne, Esq.

Can Men and Women be Just Friends? Andy Bustanoby

The Casanova Complex: Compulsive Lovers & Their Women, Peter Trachtenberg

Caught in the NET: How to Recognize the Signs of Internet Addiction and a Winning Strategy for Recovery, Dr. Kimberly S. Young

Emotional Infidelity: How to Avoid It and 10 Other Secrets to a Great Marriage, M. Gary Neuman

Gotcha!!! How to Tell if Your Lover is Having an Affair, Alda Wirsche and Marnie Milot

How Could You Do This To Me? Learning to Trust After Betrayal, Dr. Jane Greer with Margery D. Rosen

How to Break Your Addiction to a Person: When and Why Love Doesn't Work and What to Do About It, Howard M. Halpern, Ph.D.

How to Keep Your Man Monogamous, Alexandra Penney

How to Survive Your Husband's Midlife Crisis: Strategies and Stories from The Midlife Wives Club, Gay Courter and Pat Gaudette

Husbands Wives & Lovers: The Emotional System of the Extramarital Affair, David J. Moultrup

Infidelity & You: A Recovery Guide for Anyone Caught in a Love Triangle, Elissa Gough

Infidelity on the Internet: Virtual Relationships and Real Betrayal, Marlene M. Maheu, Ph.D., and Rona B. Subotnik, M.A., MFT

More Than Just a Friend: The Joys and Disappointments of Extramarital Affairs, Dr. Tom McGinnis

The Myth of Monogamy: Fidelity and Infidelity in Animals and People, David P. Barash, Ph.D. and Judith Eve Lipton, M.D.

Never Satisfied: How & Why Men Cheat, Michael Baisden

NOT "Just Friends": Protect Your Relationship from Infidelity and Heal the Trauma of Betrayal, Shirley P. Glass, Ph.D. with Jean Coppock Staeheli

The Other Man - The Other Woman: Understanding and Coping with Extramarital Affairs, Joel D. Block, Ph.D.

Patterns of Infidelity and Their Treatment, Emily M. Brown

Private Lies: Infidelity and the Betrayal of Intimacy, Frank Pittman

Secret Lovers: Affairs Happen... How to Cope, Dr. Luann Linquist

The Sex-Starved Marriage: A Couple's Guide to Boosting Their Marriage Libido, Michelle Weiner-Davis

Spying on Your Spouse: A Guide for Anyone Who Suspects a Partner Is Cheating, Kelly Squires

Stalemates: The Truth About Extramarital Affairs, Marcella Bakur Weiner, Ed.D. and Bernard D. Starr, Ph.D.

Surviving Betrayal: Hope and Help for Women Whose Partners Have Been Unfaithful, Alice May

Surviving Infidelity: Making Decisions, Recovering from the Pain, Rona Subotnik, M.F.C.C. and Gloria G. Harris, Ph.D.

When Your Lover Is a Liar: Healing the Wounds of Deception and Betrayal, Susan Forward, Ph.D.

Why I Cheat On My Wife: Confessions of Anonymous Men, T.W. Binyan

Women Who Stay with Men Who Stray: What Every Woman Needs to Know About Men and Infidelity, Debbie Then, Ph.D.

Online Resources

Due to the everchanging aspect of the Internet, I am reluctant to list every site I've found which currently offers support and resources for adultery. Below is a short list of sites I believe will be available on a longterm basis:

Pat Gaudette's Divorce site with a 24/7 support forum: http://DivorceSupport.about.com
Peggy Vaughan's site: www.DearPeggy.com
Michele Weiner-Davis' site: www.DivorceBusting.com
Pat Gaudette's Midlife Club: www.MidlifeClub.com
John LaSage's wife left him for someone she met on the Internet which inspired him to create: wwwChatCheaters.com
Dr. Willard F. Harley, Jr's site: www.MarriageBuilders.com
Emily M. Brown, LCSW's site: www. Affairs-Help.com
Bob Huizenga, D.Min., LMFT, CSW's site: www.Break-Free-From-The-Affair.com

www.ingramcontent.com/pod-product-compliance
Lightning Source LLC
Chambersburg PA
CBHW031246090426

42742CB00007B/332

9 780976 121046